INDUSTRIAL HERITAGE PROTECTION AND REDEVELOPMENT

Edited by
Michael Louw

images
Publishing

Published in Australia in 2018 by
The Images Publishing Group Pty Ltd
Shanghai Office
ABN 89 059 734 431
6 Bastow Place, Mulgrave, Victoria 3170, Australia
Tel: +61 3 9561 5544 Fax: +61 3 9561 4860
books@imagespublishing.com
www.imagespublishing.com

The Images Publishing Group Reference Number: 1463

NATIONAL LIBRARY OF AUSTRALIA

A catalogue record for this book is available from the National Library of Australia

Title: Industrial Heritage Protection and Redevelopment
Author: Edited by Michael Louw
ISBN: 9781864707786

Production manager | Group art director: Nicole Boehringer
Senior editor: Gina Tsarouhas
Assisting editor: Bree DeRoche

Printed by Toppan Leefung Packaging & Printing, in Hong Kong/China

Contents

Preface

Michael Louw

Most countries are littered with what are perceived as the relics of previous industrial revolutions. Widespread de-industrialization and a move towards knowledge-economies, or re-industrialization due to the obsolescence of older industries, often results in these structures being abandoned to remain as monuments to former technologies, economies, and societies. While they are still perceived by some to be eyesores representative of urban decay and pollution, they are increasingly being regarded as valuable representations of tangible and intangible heritage, and as potentially valuable assets.

This publication showcases a selection of works completed since 2010, with a wide global distribution; the selection can easily be expanded on even further, and it highlights an encouraging increase in the practice of the transformation, redevelopment, and adaptive reuse of industrial structures. From underutilized, disused, or discarded reminders of times past, their latest metamorphoses have imbued them with new purpose in what could be regarded as one more stage in a continuous process of industrial evolution.

The essays in this book were written by authors from a variety of backgrounds and locations. They all highlight the importance of industrial heritage and a number of them describe the industrial buildings as being connected to wider industrial landscapes or post-industrial landscapes, which Luis Loures argues should be an expansion of the concept of cultural landscapes. While these connections extend beyond their immediate physical surroundings, most of these buildings and their new uses now have a global reach through digital technologies and they are often still underappreciated in their own environments. Some of the essays make a case for the proper assessment of these resources, while some provide design tools and principles for their reuse. Most of the authors lament the purely visual conception where only prominent visible landmarks like chimneys and towers are recognized as important markers in the landscape, while the buildings' spatial aspects, their connections to the landscape and wider systems, their internal industrial processes, and their intangible heritage are often dismissed. The essays provide a rich addition to the selection of built works and they offer potential avenues for further research.

Figure 1 | Casa Mediterraneo headquarters (designed by Manuel Ocaña del Valle, photo by David Fruto)

Adaptively reused industrial buildings are layered texts that were authored by many hands over time, resulting in numerous overlapping narratives. At times, they may resemble something akin to the practices of collage or palimpsest, while at others there can be a clear juxtaposition of old and new. In all cases, however, they are richly imbued with meaning, as the built and written works in this publication demonstrate so admirably. It is hoped that they create awareness of the inherent potential of former industrial buildings and that the book may serve as a record of contemporary adaptive reuse practice, while providing some motivation for similarly creative transformations. The built works are all essays that show how the tangible and intangible heritage of past industry can be retained through imaginative redevelopment and adaptive reuse.

Figure 2 | OostCampus (designed by Carlos Arroyo Architects, photo by Miguel de Guzmán)

What is industrial heritage?

Michael Louw

The International Committee for the Conservation of Industrial Heritage (TICCIH) jointly published *Principles for the Conservation of Industrial Heritage Sites, Structures, Areas and Landscapes* in 2011, which followed TICCIH's adoption of the *Nizhny Tagil Charter for the Industrial Heritage* in 2003. ICOMOS and TICCIH define industrial heritage as consisting of

> sites, structures, complexes, areas and landscapes as well as the related machinery, objects or documents that provide evidence of past or ongoing industrial processes of production, the extraction of raw materials, their transformation into goods, and the related energy and transport infrastructures. Industrial heritage reflects the profound connection between the cultural and natural environment, as industrial processes—whether ancient or modern—depend on natural sources of raw materials, energy and transportation networks to produce and distribute products to broader markets. It includes both material assets—immovable and movable, and intangible dimensions such as technical know-how, the organization of work and workers, and the complex social and cultural legacy that shaped the life of communities and brought major organizational changes to entire societies and the world in general[1].

TICCIH[2] argues that the inherent value of the industrial heritage lies in the evidence of activities that have historical significance. This evidence can be found in landscapes, structures, the technology itself, written or drawn documentation, and in local memories or traditions[3]. It serves as a societal and technological record and its structures may also have exemplary aesthetic qualities, while rare or pioneering examples of industrial processes or structures are of particular interest.

Industrial buildings often become obsolete because they were designed and constructed for a very specific purpose, technology, or technological process, which means that it can be difficult to adjust them or re-tool them as technologies evolve. The 19th and 20th centuries have witnessed a series of industrial revolutions,[4] with each revolution often leading to the obsolescence of technologies that developed during the preceding one in a process that is sometimes referred to as 'creative destruction.' Industrial buildings can also become unsustainable as economies, laws and regulations, politics, societies, or their physical environment changes; they were (and still are) often the cause of environmental pollution, and some were dependent on the excessive or exploitative use of physical and societal resources. In light of the need for sustainable development and the aim of decoupling development from the excessive consumption of resources, the adaptive reuse of these buildings, which may initially seem fraught with problems, presents opportunities for development that could be environmentally, economically, and socially advantageous.

Opportunities and challenges

It will become clear that in most cases related to the adaptive reuse of industrial structures, opportunities and challenges are one and the same thing. These structures, as found objects, each have unique characteristics that require creative solutions and attempting to fit new uses into purpose-made industrial artifacts can often be similar to fitting the proverbial 'square peg in a round hole.' Their transformation may involve certain challenges, but most of these can be regarded as opportunities. The uniqueness of found conditions usually necessitates innovation and the development of one-of-a-kind solutions, which can result in unique forms of architectural expression.

One of the most important factors in the adaptive reuse of industrial structures is the somewhat rare breed of a visionary, brave, and often foolhardy client with a strong business sense. The client, especially with these types of projects, requires the support of a range of specialists, which provides an opportunity to form collaborative partnerships with a variety of professionals. In addition to project managers, engineers, quantity surveyors, surveyors, landscape architects, interior architects, and urban designers, the list often includes other professionals whom architects do not often get to work with, which may include, among others, heritage practitioners, industrial archaeologists, restoration experts, sociologists, anthropologists, environmental practitioners, and decontamination specialists.

The buildings are often found in environments that have deteriorated environmentally, socially, and economically, and they are sometimes in need of decontamination. Because of this, they can sometimes be acquired at relatively low cost, but their redevelopment can act as an economic stimulus that could lead to the regeneration of their context. This is often supported by financial institutions and local governments that offer incentives as part of their regeneration and development strategies—their construction cost and overall construction time is often less than that of new buildings, which results in a faster return on investment. Former industrial buildings are usually well-placed in terms of transportation and services networks, while they also tend to be close to potential markets, and they are usually of a much larger scale than other buildings in their surroundings, which means that they can offer developmental capacity that exceeds the regulatory constraints for new buildings. While they are often subject to numerous planning constraints, their very nature can be used to motivate for unique solutions to standard approval requirements and regulations that deal with health and safety in particular.

The integrity and design of their structure, envelope, services, circulation, and internal volumes can simultaneously present both opportunities and constraints. In some cases, they may exceed the requirements of the new uses, while in others they may require innovative solutions that can often be used as drivers of the overall design. One of the biggest factors to consider in terms of adaptive reuse (and the harvesting and reuse of materials onsite) is the saving of embodied energy that is inherent in the building fabric being retained; the resultant savings in terms of extraction, processing, transport, and waste, significantly reduce the impact on the environment.

The size and architectural features of former industrial buildings regularly make them prominent features or landmarks in the surrounding landscape, and combined with their unique appearance and atmosphere, it gives them the potential to act as touristic drawcards. The buildings can act as repositories of social and technological memory and meaning, which gives them value in terms of both tangible and intangible heritage. Their adaptive reuse can provide opportunities for skills building in the community, and according to a number of studies, adaptive reuse projects typically provide a higher percentage of employment than new construction.

The projects that are featured in this book engaged admirably with the above-mentioned issues and each one had to deal with its own unique opportunities and challenges. They include former factories, power stations, pumping stations, warehouses, silos and storage facilities, production facilities for beer and wine, a mill, a coal mine, and a railway station. They range in size from 4844 square feet (450 square meters) to over 91,493 square feet (8500 square meters) and some form part of former industrial precincts of more than 17 acres (7 hectares). They have been adapted to house multiple uses, which include offices, commercial space, manufacturing facilities, galleries and exhibition areas, museums, schools and educational facilities, community centers, hotels, residential developments, and sports facilities. While both their original functions and their new uses are wide-ranging, a few dominant trends do present themselves, and these merit further discussion.

Establishment of a suitable brief

Industrial buildings do not always lend themselves to standard commercial uses, and because of their complex spatial configuration, architects are often called on to assist with the development of a suitable brief and mix of uses, as is the case with a number of the projects featured in this book. Architectural teams are also often commissioned to perform additional duties, which might include the preparation of Heritage Impact Assessments, archival research, the preparation of Conservation Management Plans, urban frameworks or precinct plans, building surveys and documentation, the management of restoration work to buildings and machinery, and the supervision of contamination removal and environmental rehabilitation, among others. Because of all their intricacies, industrial buildings often require significantly more input from professional teams than would be the case with new buildings. This usually involves additional time and costs during the planning and design phases, but as will be discussed further, these costs could be offset through savings made by adaptively reusing the buildings.

Context

Industrial buildings often find themselves in radically transformed environments with different uses to their original industrial nature—these areas may have been gentrified or transformed, but are generally well positioned with good access to transport networks. While their environments may have changed, the buildings themselves usually remained as disproportionately large spaces full of latent potential waiting for the right client and program. They have the ability to link dislocated environments, contributing to urban regeneration and transformation, and they can form key parts of governmental planning frameworks and so-called smart growth plans. They can also form part of a regional industrial context, the Ruhr in Germany being a well-known example.

Some may find themselves in a post-industrial landscape that requires extensive decontamination and rehabilitation. This will require the careful consideration of natural systems, ecosystem services, and biodiversity during the urban and landscape design of its surroundings; however, this is also a remarkable opportunity for urban regeneration and the design of meaningful public space when a large adaptive reuse project brings with it the possibility of a substantial capital injection.

Scale and spatial variety

Industrial buildings in a changed landscape are usually much larger than the newer buildings that surround them[5]. This offers many opportunities in terms of inserting a new function, which requires more floor area than might typically be available elsewhere, and which can act as an anchor or drawcard for a specific area. Large, former industrial spaces with long-span roofs, which are rare in dense urban environments, could lend themselves easily to adaptation into galleries, exhibition spaces, performance spaces, or museums and this, combined with their industrial aesthetic (and often a reasonable acquisition cost), could be why these buildings often attract creative industries. The large spaces are often supported by smaller ancillary spaces, which can prove difficult to work with, but they can often retain their role as servant spaces to the larger volume, and it means that these buildings lend themselves to adaptation into a variety of functional uses. Depending on the nature of the building, which could either consist mostly of a single, large volume, or a series of smaller cellular spaces, or a combination of both, they generally tend to require a more innovative approach to the planning and arrangement of spaces; this generally enriches the design and it can allow for visual connectivity between spaces and uses that would otherwise have remained disconnected.

While it can be difficult to achieve sufficient levels of natural lighting and ventilation in very large or very small interconnected spaces, this presents the opportunity for innovation both spatially and in terms of a building's skin. This is reflected in many of the projects in this publication, where the initial challenges were turned into opportunities for architectural expression.

Circulation and connectivity

Incorporating new circulation into an existing structure, especially one that was designed specifically for productive flows, can be a challenge. Industrial buildings have overlapping movement routes or circulation systems for people and products. These naturally conflict where they need to cross one another, and the circulation systems for products are taken up mostly by machinery that is often automated. They are not designed ergonomically for human movement, but are tailored to the dimensions of the raw material or product, which means that one cannot simply reuse them for circulation by people, especially if the intention is to retain a substantial proportion of the existing machinery. Incorporating new routes into these systems, especially for members of the public, may also raise health and safety concerns since the walking surfaces, handrails, stairs, ramps, and protruding machinery do not necessarily comply with the latest building regulations. Inserting elevators or escalators, allowing for disabled access, and establishing the required fire escape routes and smoke separation envelopes can also prove difficult; some of the proposed solutions will most probably not be up to standard specifications and will require special approvals or regulatory departures.

Despite these challenges, however, these buildings usually provide the opportunity to create an architectural promenade that gradually reveals the narrative of the existing building. Their circulation routes can either follow the route of the new (mostly human) productive flows or societal flows and offer glimpses into certain portions of the building—almost like windows into the past—or they can follow the logic of the original productive flow of the building, which means that visitors would be able to develop an understanding of the original production process that took place in the building. They can also both be retained, in which case the points where former productive flows and new social flows overlap can generate key moments of interest in the circulation system. In most cases, the circulation route becomes more experiential than expedient, which enhances the idea of these buildings as living museums. This often succeeds in slowing people's rate of movement down to make them more aware of their surroundings. Different to the ocular-centric nature of many contemporary new buildings, these experiential routes enable the buildings to be experienced on a multi-sensory level, where visitors can become more aware of their spatial qualities, the tactility of their surfaces and well-used equipment, the smell of the machinery, or the sound generated while moving through their echo-filled volumes.

Structure

Industrial buildings require careful structural analysis to make sure that their existing shells and features like towers or chimneys are sufficiently stable. An advantage of many industrial buildings is that they were designed to accommodate high stresses, excessive heat, or heavy machinery, but they also faced extensive wear-and-tear, or may have been exposed to the elements for some time, which could have impacted the structure negatively, especially if it was made from iron, steel, or timber. This could have cost and time implications where extensive remedial work is required. Existing structural systems may not have sufficient bearing capacity to accommodate new additional loads, especially where additional floors are inserted into existing volumes, and it can also be a challenge to insert new structural members where the removal of an existing shell is not possible. This insertion of new structural members into the existing building fabric often requires structural separation between new and old, and new interventions might require an entirely different structural approach to the existing one. Once again, this is an opportunity for tectonic innovation and architectural expression.

Atmosphere

A theme in most of the projects was to preserve a sense of the original atmosphere of the buildings. This is often combined with the preservation of as much of the original machinery and industrial equipment as possible, while still accommodating all of the necessary new functions. Achieving a balance between the original 'mood' of the building and new requirements in terms of lighting levels and spatial separation can be challenging, especially where the new functions involve office space or laboratories. These challenges can, however, usually be solved fairly easily through functional separation of productive and experiential spaces.

The building fabric of these structures and the presence of existing machinery can sometimes be a challenge for residential or hospitality design, where clients may require a certain level of internal finishing that could potentially lead to over-sanitizing, and hence a loss of character. By functionally differentiating between the more experiential public spaces and circulation routes and the more cellular domestic spaces, one can achieve a balance that satisfies both the need for the retention of an original atmosphere, and for the creation of different atmospheres that allow for a specific level of finishing and natural lighting.

The industrial aesthetic is regularly contrasted with modern, often minimalist interventions, which help to accentuate the rough industrial finishes, the sense of weathering and patina on the old structures and equipment. This is in line with good heritage practice, which enables one to clearly differentiate between the new and the old, and it allows for a more nuanced, layered reading of a building. While it preserves certain memories from the past, it also allows a current generation to add its own contribution, while allowing future generations to understand the changing conditions over time.

Building skin

With rare exceptions, most of the projects in this book grappled with the generally enclosed and introverted nature of industrial buildings and with the need to provide larger openings for commercial exposure, natural light, and natural ventilation; a more open inside-outside spatial relationship is often required now that these buildings house more publically-oriented functions. The admission of light into the buildings is a prominent theme throughout, and a common trend that supports this is the provision of perforated metal panels or brick skins that create a more homogenous textured surface to either generate interesting light patterns on the inside, or to conceal portions of the existing structure. In a few cases, the existing buildings had openings that were too big and had to be reduced to accommodate specific functions. One either needs to find functions that suit the building's current levels of enclosure, or one needs to accept that the building will have to be adjusted. There will rarely be a perfect fit, but either way this design problem can generate significant richness in terms of the façade design.

Industrial buildings are often subjected to ad-hoc additions over time as production processes change, and aesthetic considerations are not necessarily high on the agenda when these changes occur. This means that the massing of these buildings is often of a random and additive nature, while the openings in their façade were usually not the subject of careful, compositional design, but were inserted based purely on functional requirements. Hence, the reason for a second skin, which provides a more presentable public face that still retains the original fabric behind.

Original building skins often do not conform to new insulation requirements, especially since thermal comfort was usually not of primary importance in industrial buildings and many tenants nowadays require environmental certification. The old buildings may also not be entirely waterproof and need to be augmented by additional climatic layers, which naturally affect their appearance. In some cases, this can be achieved by an outer climatic skin, but it may also require additional layering internally, depending on which side one would like to retain the original appearance of the building. Alternatively, the existing façade can be dismantled, properly weatherproofed, and reassembled.

Materiality

In support of the savings in embodied energy through adaptive reuse, most architects actively considered more sustainable material choices for the building fabric. These include the use of sustainably harvested timber, materials with a low embodied energy, materials that are easy to recycle, or materials that have been recycled themselves. A number of the included projects made use of recycled materials, or industrial materials like weathering steel, which are contrasted with smooth modern finishes to highlight the differences between new and old. Where recycled materials were used, they were often harvested from within the existing building, which can be regarded as a source for building material or 'urban ore.'[6] This, together with the practice of leaving existing building finishes exposed and unfinished, can result in cost savings or for finishing budgets to be allocated for use elsewhere in the building.

The environment, energy efficiency, and building services

The most obvious advantage of the adaptive reuse or transformation is the most difficult one to measure. The embodied energy of the retained building fabric generally results in a marked saving of resource consumption, energy usage, additional emissions due to production processes, transport, and waste generation.[7] Through a detailed life-cycle analysis (LCA), the embodied energy of the industrial building and its contents can be measured, but this involves additional specialists, costs, and time, which may not necessarily be of much interest to governments with

Figure 3 | Ding Hui Yuan Zen and Tea Chamber (designed by He Wei Studio/3andwich design, photo by Zou Bin)

specific political aims, or private developers who are usually motivated by potential financial gain or simply by a passion for old industrial buildings.

Besides the significant energy saving and reduction in waste achieved through the reuse of a building and through making more sustainable material choices, the reused structures in this book are further augmented with strategies that promote energy-efficiency, a reduction of waste, and a reduction in water use. Water heating and electricity production in a number of the featured projects is achieved through solar power, heat pumps, or geothermal heating, while new building services and fittings are usually of an energy-efficient nature. Research has shown that improvements to existing buildings can reduce their energy consumption by up to 20 percent[8] and, while certain functions like hotels and offices require mechanical heating and cooling, some portions of industrial buildings are regularly allowed to not be subjected to artificial climate control. Water is regularly harvested or recycled, and this is usually combined with the specification and installation of water-saving devices.

Old redundant or unsafe building services like electrical reticulation and plumbing often need to be removed in order to be replaced with new upgraded services, but fortunately industrial buildings can be quite forgiving when new services need to be installed, so new piping runs or conduits are often surface-mounted. However, where these fittings do require concealing, doing this without impacting existing surfaces and navigating complex structural systems and spaces often requires a high level of precision during design and construction. The new service runs might follow the circulation routes through the building, in which case consideration should be given as to whether they can be installed without compromising the clarity of the traces of former processes and services.

Economics

In economic terms, a number of case studies and surveys have shown that the adaptive reuse of industrial buildings can result in a significant cost-saving when compared to new constructions of a similar size.[9] Unfortunately, some buildings may need extensive structural stabilization, material replacement, the remediation of contamination, or they may require the removal of harmful materials like asbestos roofing, which could all result in their reuse being more expensive than a newly-built structure. However, even studies that mention this still indicate that the reuse of heritage structures results in a higher return on investment.[10] While this is encouraging, it is still advisable to allocate a substantial contingency amount in a project's cost estimates that can help to accommodate unforeseen expenditure during construction. A key factor to consider in terms of a return on investment is the overall construction time of a project: a number of results have shown that adaptive reuse projects can be completed 20 to 50 percent faster than newly-built structures,[11] which generally helps to reduce construction costs and it means that owners can begin to recoup their initial financial investment sooner. Old buildings were often constructed by skilled craftspeople, indicating that much of their built fabric could be of a superior quality; this can increase their lifespan and result in a reduction in maintenance costs, which could sometimes be prohibitive in heritage buildings.

Because of their unique appeal (sometimes referred to as their 'gimmick factor'), reused industrial structures can become landmarks and drawcards for tourism. These buildings, and the land that they are situated on, are located in post-industrial landscapes that are well-located but have not been subjected to development, which means they can be purchased at prices that are comparatively

Figure 4 | The Turbine Boutique Hotel and Spa (designed by CMAI Architects, photo by Ian Flemingia)

lower than those in surrounding areas. Since the reuse of industrial buildings can contribute to urban regeneration, tourism, and the local economy, local authorities sometimes offer rebates on municipal rates and taxes, a reduced parking requirement, or lower augmentation fees in order to make the option to reuse more viable, while some financial institutions offer heritage bonds or loans that can assist developers. These buildings are usually fairly large and visually dominating in urban and rural landscapes, which means that once redeveloped, they can often spur a flurry of redevelopment in their surrounding context. While this type of regeneration holds many advantages, developers need to be cognizant of the potentially negative aspects of gentrification and these structures, which were often important social spaces in a community, should be designed to make allowance for public accessibility and for inclusive residential accommodation if their new use permits it.

Society, memory, and sense of place

Many of the buildings in this book, and in some cases their machinery or evidence of their industrial process, are protected by heritage legislation; the buildings also sometimes form part of heritage areas. However, it is on a social level that these structures often embody the collective memory of a community, and they often accommodated the biggest employer in a specific region. They may have been the places where a large proportion of a community spent most of their working lives, which gives these buildings a sense of gravitas as the embodiment of many lifetimes' labor. An important socioeconomic consideration of adaptive reuse, especially in so-called developing countries, is that it generally results in a higher percentage of the construction cost being spent on labor.[12] While material savings usually comfortably offset this additional labor cost, the additional labor requirement does offer many potential advantages in terms of job creation, skills building, and a renewed sense of ownership of an old industrial structure.

Spatially and technologically, industrial buildings tend to have a strong genius loci or sense of place. This can be attributed to a variety of reasons, which may include the vastness of their spaces, the massiveness of construction, the presence of large machinery, their connectedness to their surroundings, the weathering of the buildings and their contents, or the signs of human interaction with the buildings and their machinery over many years. It is often the evidence of peoples' interaction with industry that is the most poignant reminder of a building's previous life, and in a number of case studies in this book, the architects have managed to interact with the former occupants of the buildings in order to capture their stories and to find ways to include them through narration or in the form of skills transfer to current generations. The embedded stories and histories make most of these buildings living museums that play an educational role, and they act as repositories for societal memory.

This requires careful recording and documentation by capturing the structures, processes, and narratives through various means. These documents can play an educational role and can be used to raise awareness of the importance of the industrial heritage, but it does require that these materials are readily available to facilitate further research or dissemination.

Past, present, and future

Technology and industry are subject to continuous change and the oppositional nature of industrialization and de-industrialization often results in the prompt demolition of disused industrial buildings. There is, however, substantial merit in their reuse, which allows for a sense of intergenerational continuity where both a new generation of makers and a new generation of technologies are employed to regenerate the former sites of social and technological production. While the use of modern industrial technologies to rejuvenate older industrial buildings presents some ironies, it does offer the opportunity to reflect on the socio-technological nature of making and inhabitation.

In some cases, the detailed documentation and demolition of a building, or parts of a building, might be considered to be justified and more appropriate than adaptive reuse or regeneration, while in other cases preservation or conservation might be required. It is about discovering, or uncovering, the building as a found object, and about critically deciding which aspects of it to value and amplify. Some buildings, or parts of buildings, require delicate insertions, while others demand more drastic interventions. Adaptive reuse or transformation requires an inclusive and holistic approach, where the need for restoration and preservation in some instances has to be balanced with demolition, addition, and adaptation in others.

New digital surveying tools, three-dimensional scanners, and the use of photogrammetry can all be employed to assist design teams to gain a better understanding of the complex interiors of these buildings when they intend to reuse them. When these tools are combined with more advanced documentation tools like Building Information Modeling (BIM) and thermal modeling software, they can help to maximize the potential of industrial buildings by providing greater clarity for designers and easier visualization for clients and developers. These tools can also help to simplify the coordination of services, and they can help to minimize unnecessary spatial or climatic intrusions. Coupled with construction techniques that involve pre-manufacturing and digital fabrication techniques, they can also contribute to the mitigation of negative structural or visual impacts.

Any changes made to these buildings should be distinguishable from the existing building fabric and they should be done with future adaptability in mind. Allowance has to be made for flexibility in terms of their planning and use (contrary to their original purpose-made nature), and new interventions should be reversible so as not to prevent the possibility of preservation, restoration, or further adaptive reuse in the future. This also requires a certain level of commitment from clients and users of the building, who often continue the process of adaptation on their own during use. Conservation management plans are usually required to prevent long-term deterioration of the original built fabric, but also to prevent unconsidered changes to the building.

Adaptive reuse is different to restoration or conservation—it is about imbuing buildings with new life and while it is important to preserve their inherent memories and meanings, it is not about the resistance to change. Many of these buildings may have been adaptively reused a number of times before, and this round of adaptive reuse may only be one stage within a longer life cycle of continuous change and evolution, which means that a balance needs to be achieved between the preservation of memory while allowing for the imagining of future possibilities. Industrial buildings were often catalysts for the economic and social development of their particular contexts and regularly formed part of a wider industrial landscape; their adaptive reuse or transformation should be a mechanism that is used with the explicit aim of reactivating this catalytic potential.

1 The International Council on Monuments and Sites (ICOMOS) and The International Committee for the Conservation of Industrial Heritage (TICCIH), *Principles for the Conservation of Industrial Heritage Sites, Structures, Areas and Landscapes, XVII General Assembly,* ICOMOS, Paris, 2011, p. 2.

2 The International Committee for the Conservation of Industrial Heritage (TICCIH), *Nizhny Tagil Charter for the Industrial Heritage,* TICCIH, Moscow, 2003, p. 1.

3 Zhang, Song, 'Conservation and Adaptive Reuse of Industrial Heritage in Shanghai', *Frontiers of Architecture and Civil Engineering in China,* 2007, 1(4), 481–490, accessed 9 July 2015, https://link.springer.com/article/10.1007/s11709-007-0065-4.

4 Perez, Carlota, *Technological Revolutions and Financial Capital: The Dynamics of Bubbles and Golden Ages,* Edward Elgar Publishing Ltd., Cheltenham, 2002. According to Perez there have already been five technological revolutions, which include the original Industrial Revolution, the Age of Steam and Railways, the Age of Steel, Electricity and Heavy Engineering, the Age of Oil, the Automobile and Mass Production, and the Age of Information and Telecommunications.

5 Stratton, Michael (ed.), *Industrial Buildings: Conservation and Regeneration,* E & FN Spon, New York (2000), p. 83.

6 Chusid, M., 'Once is never enough', *Building Renovation,* Mar–Apr, 1993, p. 17–20.

7 Conejos, Sheila, Langston, Craig and Smith, Jim, 'Improving the Implementation of Adaptive Reuse Strategies for Historic Buildings', *Le Vie dei Mercanti S.A.V.E. HERITAGE: Safeguard of Architectural, Visual, Environmental Heritage,* 2011, 1–10, accessed 9 July 2015, http://epublications.bond.edu.au/cgi/viewcontent.cgi?article=1051&context=sustainable_development.

8 Bullen, P. and Love, P., 'Adaptive Reuse of Heritage Buildings', *Structural Survey*, Vol. 29, Issue 5, 2011, 411–421, accessed 9 July 2015, http://www.emeraldinsight.com/doi/pdfplus/10.1108/02630801111182439; Bullen, P. and Love, P., 'Factors Influencing the Adaptive Re-use of Buildings', *Journal of Engineering, Design and Technology,* Vol. 9, No. 1, 2011, 32–46, accessed 9 July 2015, http://www.researchgate.net/publication/235307181_Factors_influencing_the_adaptive_re-use_of_buildings; Bullen, P. and Love, P., 'The Rhetoric of Adaptive Reuse or Reality of Demolition: Views from the Field', *Cities*, 27, 2010, 215–224, accessed 9 July 2015, doi: 10.1016/j.cities.2009.12.005.

9 Ball, R., 'Developers, Regeneration and Sustainability Issues in the Reuse of Vacant Industrial Buildings', *Building Research and Information,* 27:3, 1999, 140–148, accessed 29 January 2014, http://www.tandfonline.com/doi/abs/10.1080/096132199369480, 143; Bullen and Love, 2009, Op. cit., p. 34; Eley, P. and Worthington J., *Industrial Rehabilitation: The Use of Redundant Buildings for Small Enterprises,* The Architectural Press, London, 1984., p. 79; Langston, C., 2008, 'The Sustainability Implications of Building Adaptive Reuse', *CRIOCM 2008 International Research Symposium on Advancement of Construction Management and Real Estate,* Beijing, China, 2008, pp. 1–11, 9; and Louw, M.P., 2016, 'The Adaptive Reuse of Industrial Structures: Revisiting the Thesen Islands Power Station Project in South Africa', *The Journal of Engineering, Design and Technology,* Volume 14:4, 2016, pp. 920–940, accessed 21 September 2017, http://www.emeraldinsight.com/doi/abs/10.1108/JEDT-04-2015-0024., 933.

10 Shipley Robert, Utz Steve, Parsons Michael, 'Does Adaptive Reuse Pay? A Study of the Business of Building Renovation in Ontario, Canada', *International Journal of Heritage Studies,* 12:6, 2006, 505, accessed 29 January 2014, doi: 10.1080/13527250600940181.

11 Langston, 2008, op. cit. p. 9; and Louw, 2016, op. cit. p. 935.

12 Langston, ibid., p. 10; and Louw, ibid., p. 933.

22@Barcelona: Creative economy and industrial heritage—a critical perspective

Fábio Duarte, Pontifical Catholic University of Paraná (Pontifícia Universidade Católica do Paraná), and Joaquín Sabaté of Polytechnic University of Cataluña

Introduction

In the latter half of the 20th century, many cities in developed countries saw their industrial areas become obsolete. Once the main economic engines of these countries, these areas became obstacles to much-needed economic and urban transformation. At first, the companies in these areas moved to the outskirts of the cities, only to see their activities outsourced later to developing countries because of the lower labor and business costs there. What were once lively industrial districts became extensive obsolete areas (indeed, sometimes completely abandoned and empty, almost falling into the category of brownfields). While their historical importance has been recognized recently, when such industrial districts occupy vast areas inside a city, they are more commonly seen as a hindrance to urban expansion.

Cataluña, the most industrialized region in Spain, experienced all of these processes.[1] When heavy industry moved to the outskirts of Barcelona during the 1980s and 1990s, 494 acres (200 hectares) of former industrial land in the core of the city began a slow but undeniable decline into economic obsolescence.

This situation has been compounded by the need for cities, as part of the paradigm of urban development since the end of the 20th century, to become competitive in a global economy and has led several cities to make desperate attempts to position themselves in a knowledge-based economy, where it is essential that there are adequate facilities for scientific and technological development.

The emergence of information and communication technologies (ICTs) represents a crucial change in today's economy and makes their incorporation in any strategic regional and urban development plan essential. However, concepts and models of territorial development change just as fast as ICTs do. Instead of science or technology parks (consolidated as part of strategic development policies in the mid-20th century), local authorities now want to promote the knowledge city, encouraging the creative economy, where cultural and social assets are the basis of new businesses.

In 2000, the municipality of Barcelona launched an ambitious project called 22@Barcelona. This had two main goals: to make the city a leading center of scientific and technological production in the knowledge economy; and to promote the integration and functional reconversion of a traditional industrial neighborhood located near the downtown area. Efforts such as this to shape an innovative district within an urban region with a strong industrial character seek to avoid one of the dangers of technological enclaves: as Richard Sennett observed,[2] 'the policy of global enclaves cultivates a kind of indifference in relation to the city (...) it does not share the responsibilities of the city where it is located.'

Figure 1 | The extension of the intervention

The first 10 years of the development of 22@Barcelona saw considerable social resistance and ideological, political, and technical disagreements between residents, scholars, and municipal advisors. Hence, 22@Barcelona during this period constitutes an interesting case study of the creation of a knowledge-based district within a complex industrial area.

From technology parks to the knowledge city

Since the emergence of information and communication technologies (ICTs) as one of the most important drivers of the global economy, different authors and regional planners worldwide have drawn up models for the transformation of territories based on these new technologies. At first, isolated technology parks were the main model. Their shape was inspired by Silicon Valley, in California: far from the main urban centers, dependent on big corporations, universities and research centers and reliant on significant public investment.

This model spread worldwide in the 1980s,[3] and in some cases particular regions were even strengthened as a result of the model rather than of national plans.[4] Technology parks usually appear in suburban areas and have the characteristics of a university campus,[5] where the production of knowledge is concentrated but the complexity of urban life is absent.

ICTs have gradually become an inherent component of the economic, social, and cultural dimensions of our society. While in the past the information economy was based essentially on hardware, it is now predominantly centered on the software and multimedia industry. In this context, some cities have been trying to attract ICT companies to inner urban areas, even using them to stimulate the recovery of central or former industrial districts, such as the Multimedia City, in Montreal.[6]

For some authors, industry in the emerging knowledge economy is independent of specific locations,[7] while others argue that this may be true when knowledge is coded but that when knowledge is tacit, location still matters.[8] A region dense in tacit knowledge represents an asset to innovative industries in a competitive market. This principle underlies the 'knowledge city' project launched by the municipality of Barcelona.[9]

This change in the ICT industry, where the production of knowledge instead of devices predominates, has led to a new kind of territorial development strategy called knowledge-based urban development (KBUD). The basic features of this strategy involve:

- creating mixed-use environments where business and housing complement each other
- providing a focal area in an urban context, with privileged access to communication and transportation infrastructure together with high-quality public spaces and facilities
- establishing a symbol, a hallmark of an innovative region
- ensuring a mix of learning and fun, where the area's qualities are attractive both for work and living

- encouraging social 'connectivity,' with an urban design that favors personal contacts and social networking.[10]

Although these features seem desirable for any neighborhood, according to Yigitcanlar and Velibeyoglu,[11] KBUD is a selective planning process that does not consider the whole city but tries to enhance the competitive advantages of specific areas, implying, consequently, that priority is given to particular social groups and districts over others. Some critics argue that 'knowledge' is just another denomination for science and technology and that it does not fully embrace any other kind of knowledge.[12] Ludovic Halbert[13] states that even allegedly culture-friendly economic development programs are actually only a 'neoliberal agenda' for stimulating competitiveness among cities.

The European Commission declared 2009 the Year of Creativity and Innovation, promoting 'creative' industries as a factor for economic development. This echoes Richard Florida's statement that in contemporary society, creativity and economic growth are bound together. People involved with art, design, entertainment and communication, law, finance, management, health, education, and, certainly, science and technology form what he calls the creative class.

There is a growing interest on researches correlating the so-called creative activities and the actual economic growth—with the emergence of a creative class.[14] Creative activities represented 10 percent of jobs in the United States in 1950 and 30 percent in 2005.[15] Florida[16] argues that regions and cities should therefore work hard to attract and retain creative industries, as they generate a virtuous circle of economic development. Creative cities are dependent on and stimulate three important characteristics of the knowledge economy: technology, talent, and tolerance. Vergara Gómez[17] even suggests that the convergence of these three characteristics is one of the most important challenges contemporary cities face.

Nevertheless, Florida points out that there are only a few places in the world 'where significant innovations are generated' and that the tendency is for the global economy to make them increasingly stronger, leading to growing economic and social disparity between cities.[18] In that sense, it is clear that the creative, or knowledge, economy tends to create gaps or deepen existing gaps despite a discourse of social integration and economic diversity.

The great urban transformation of Barcelona

Many observers of the European urban scene regard Barcelona as a contemporary success story. Indeed, Barcelona's transformation from a city with huge service and infrastructure deficits in the midst of a deep economic crisis in the 1980s to a restructured, dynamic, outward-looking metropolis in the mid-1990s shows that the city was able to change its own history based on its own resources.

In the last quarter of the 20th century, Barcelona developed increasingly sophisticated urban and metropolitan plans, all derived in one way or another from the 1976 General Metropolitan Plan.[19] This period had three phases: preservation and modernization (until 1986); innovation (1986 to 1992); and consolidation and efficiency (from 1992 to date). The first phase started in the midst of a profound economic crisis, when former local authorities were suffering a loss of moral authority and there was a serious deficit in infrastructure and services. In this critical environment, the majority of citizens, civic organizations, and trade unions jointly supported major administrative and financial reform under strong municipal leadership.

A comprehensive policy of land acquisition helped to promote some urgent projects needed to meet the considerable demand for housing, schools, and open spaces. The result was a patchwork of projects that, although dispersed, were of outstanding quality.

Even before Barcelona was nominated in 1986 to host the 1992 Olympics, the city already had a mature, original urban policy. This was the beginning of one of the most fertile and innovative periods in the city's very rich planning history. However, although the Olympics had fostered innovative projects as the games approached and many projects had to be completed urgently, it soon became apparent that traditional management instruments were inadequate for the task.

In 1989, the consequences of the pressure imposed by the Olympic Games were evident: the resignation of some local authorities and technical staff; difficulties in keeping to the objectives of the previous master plan; and the lack of a comprehensive urban strategy. Customized institutions were set up to coordinate the Olympic projects, and public participation declined dramatically. A management policy driven by efficiency was put in place but was limited to a shrinking circle of decision-makers.

In March 1989, Vittorio Gregotti, a privileged spectator of the urban transformation of Barcelona, praised the efforts made and results achieved during the 1980s. Nevertheless, he also expressed his fears that the extraordinary drive to renew the city was disappearing in the face of a 'succession of complexities, obstacles, contradictions, favoritism and political and administrative bureaucracy, and administrative decisions that have a certain tendency towards the showbiz and towards politics understood as a simple matter of consensus.'[20]

In the 1990s, the population of Barcelona decreased, but the number of consumers, workers, and visitors increased considerably. The decade inaugurated the internationalization of Barcelona, and many foreign investors flocked to the city. Large international real estate groups became important and constant partners of the municipality and started playing a leading role in the reshaping of some neighborhoods.

A walk along the last section of Diagonal Avenue[21] shows the recent urban policy of Barcelona as a story of lights and shadows. The city finally extended its main avenue to the seafront, as Cerdà had originally intended. The renewal of a degraded area was also part of this project, including an incipient social housing program in a traditional industrial neighborhood. However, the project was clearly driven by private interests and did not allow for public participation in the decision-making process.

Therefore, while urban planning in Barcelona in the 1980s had as its general framework the General Metropolitan Plan of 1976 and was characterized by clear rules and a constant call for public participation after decades of a brutal dictatorship, in the last quarter of the 20th century and early 21st century, urban strategies in Barcelona were marked by an attempt to transform the city into a global city without a general planning framework but rather through fragmented urban interventions marked by iconic buildings designed by architects belonging to the star system. As Joaquin Sabaté[22] stated, this is opaque urbanism, not openly discussed or negotiated.

22@Barcelona: The genesis of an urban project

In 1999, the Barcelona City Council created the Knowledge City Department. The 22@Barcelona plan was the urban manifestation of an overall strategy to consolidate Barcelona as a knowledge city and a reference in technology innovation in Europe. The intention of the Barcelona City Council was to make 22@Barcelona 'the main economic and technological platform in Barcelona, Cataluña and Spain, in the perspective of the 21st century.'[23]

In line with this objective, the General Metropolitan Plan was amended to adapt land zoning in the industrial neighborhood of Poblenou to cater for a wide range of ICT industries, media companies, and housing. In 2000, the Barcelona City Council set up a municipally owned company to administer 22@Barcelona, with responsibility for assessing the plans and projects proposed by private companies and implementing the required infrastructure and urban facilities. Since 2010 its duties have also included the management of other rehabilitation projects in the Poblenou area.

22@Barcelona intended to recover 494 acres (200 hectares) of industrial land in the Poblenou district, where there are more than 247 acres (100 hectares) of mainly obsolete industrial plants in the very center of the city less than 3 miles (5 kilometers) from the Ramblas.

Poblenou was the most vigorous industrial region in Cataluña and Spain in the 19th century, but, like other industrial areas in the developed world, its activities shrank during the last quarter of the 20th century. Indeed, between 1970 and 1986, Barcelona lost 250,000 industrial jobs, and 92,000 more in the following 10 years. Nonetheless, during the same period, 240,000 jobs were created in the tertiary sector, and the city entered the 21st century with 80 percent of its jobs in services and retailing,[24] indicating a shift in its economic profile.

The 22@Barcelona plan had at least three aims. The first was to attract high-tech industries in five well-defined areas: media, information and communication technologies (ICTs), medical technologies, energy, and design. The second was the large-scale recovery of industrial heritage, to be integrated into a renewed urban environment, improved with transportation, parks, leisure amenities, and public equipment.

Broadband telecommunications is universally available; renewable energy is used in all new buildings, and a green energy plant was built at the southern extremity of the Diagonal Avenue; garbage is collected in a pneumatic system and rainwater is recycled and reused; a bus service has been extended to the area, which is also served by the metro; two tram lines link the area with Barcelona and the neighboring cities; and, finally, dozens of public bicycle-sharing stations have been installed all over the district.[25]

New squares and parks will provide an additional 18.5 acres (7.5 hectares) of green area in the region. To boost the housing industry, approximately 4000 new housing units for a range of social classes are under construction.

To achieve 865 acres (350 hectares) of built area, 790 acres (320 hectares) of which are intended for economic activities, 18.5 acres (7.5 hectares) of new green areas and 35.8 acres (14.5 hectares) of urban facilities, the zoning of the district is more flexible than elsewhere. This third aim is thus intended to boost social housing and the so-called @ activities companies, offices and training facilities related to ICTs, media, medical technologies, energy and design.

The current construction potential in other industrial areas of Barcelona is 21.5 square feet for every 10.7 square feet (2 square meters for each square meter—2 m^2/m^2) of land. To promote the intended transformation and offset higher development costs, the construction potential was increased to 23.6 square feet (2.2 square meters) inside the 22@Barcelona perimeter and to 29 square feet (2.7 square meters) for specific activities related to the knowledge economy. Additionally, a further 3.2 square feet per 10.7 feet (0.3 square meter per 1 square meter) was allowed for subsidized social housing, and another 2.1 square feet per 10.7 feet (0.2 square meter per 1 square meter) for the so-called @ facilities. Therefore, the construction potential can vary between 23.7 square feet (2.2 square meters) and 34.4 square feet (3.2 square meters) depending on the use to which the land is being put.

Most of the land in the 22@Barcelona area is private. A transfer to the municipality of 334 square feet (31 square meters) for every 1076 square feet (100 square meters) of construction is mandatory, allowing more green areas and public equipment to be provided.

A good city, however, is created slowly and gradually adjusts to meet the needs of the different actors. According to Miquel Barceló,[26] director of the 22@Barcelona plan until 2008, the infrastructure is funded almost entirely by private property owners, but for Jose Maria and Sen Tato,[27] the costs of the intended transformation far exceed the local investment capacity. Consequently, foreign investors interested in the project have been imposing their own values on the neighborhood, bringing an alien volumetry to the traditional image of the Barcelona district of Eixample.

Industrial heritage and urban planning in Poblenou

The social interest in industrial heritage in Spain stems from the deindustrialization that affected Europe in the 1980s. The importance of industrial areas as cultural heritage was first stressed by academics and professionals from a variety of fields, such as geography, architecture, and economics. In the 1990s, when it was clear that the industrial activities in these areas would no longer recover, their testimonial value for urban history was recognized. The areas where these industrial activities took place could not only help revitalize the economy and reinforce the identity of territories in cultural and social crisis, but also become a tourism product.

As an example, in the 1980s the Mel Clot Special Plan was developed. Mel Clot is a suburban area located next to the former garrison of Barcelona, in the San Martin de Provençals neighborhood, near Poblenou. During the 20th century, the eastern metropolitan region of Barcelona underwent constant transformation from a patchwork of agricultural land crossed by streams to a site crossed by radial roads and railway facilities that imposed a limit on urban growth, and from a landscape of fields and mills to another of industrial sheds and chimneys. This burgeoning industrial growth made San Martin de Provençals Barcelona's economic engine, in blatant disregard for the urban fabric guidelines proposed by Cerdá.

At the end of the 20th century, abandoned industrial sheds gave way to housing. The street pattern proposed by Cerdá was resumed, along with the regeneration of the neighborhood and the setting up of new public spaces. These were some of the main objectives of the Mel Clot Special Plan, which also stressed the extent of the industrial heritage in the region, emphasizing the importance of keeping a mix of uses and a balance of different urban patterns characteristic of the diverse urban occupation that could still be found in the area.

Even greater emphasis was placed on the preservation of Poblenou's industrial heritage in the proposal to open Diagonal Avenue. As a team of experts had compiled the cadastral history of the area from 1891 to 1929, safeguards for a considerable number of industrial buildings could be proposed.

Nevertheless, when the works to open the avenue started, part of the plan had been abandoned by the municipality. As a result, some industrial buildings and small factories were knocked down, causing a drastic change in the socioeconomic characteristics of the neighborhood.

A more recent recovery plan for the Diagonal-Poblenou Avenue was expected to be a key opportunity to implement some land-purchase mechanisms in the public interest in order to support a strong social housing policy and retain the neighborhood's social mix.

Such expectations, however, turned out to be exaggerated, or the mechanisms were not well designed. Indeed, in most cases it was medium-sized or large real estate companies that bought (probably at good prices) vacant sites and huge historical buildings, speculating over zoning reclassification, which would eventually allow these to be used for new purposes. Thus, it was these private real estate companies that ultimately effected the transformation of this area. While this process has accelerated the opening of some sections of Diagonal Avenue and fostered the creation of some public areas, the hard tasks remained. Unfinished social housing projects, for instance, have virtually disappeared from this transformation.

Some of the perverse effects (radical changes in existing uses, gentrification) were already present in other areas of the district, like the Olympic Village and the Maritime Front. Indeed, in all these plans the expected effects should be exactly the opposite. This would suggest that the mechanisms put in place were not sufficiently clear to avoid such perverse results.

Possibly because of such setbacks, the development of the 22@Barcelona plan was always accompanied by intense local debate over the eventual expulsion of residents and the disregard for industrial heritage.

Until the 1990s, this area of Poblenou was occupied by large building ensembles that did not fully respect the urban and architectural guidelines proposed by Cerdà. These ensembles stood out in the midst of industrial sheds and agricultural fields because of their remarkable size and height, and could only be accessed over bumpy dirt roads. Small houses were irregularly distributed in agricultural parcels or along traditional axes, and most were of substandard quality. Many of the factories had already shut down. While some of these were beautifully crafted and had significant historical value, there were also many industrial sheds that were of little historical value and were generally used as warehouses because of Poblenou's strategic location in the heart of the metropolitan area.

Large companies have long since closed their facilities or moved out, speculating over the announced transformation of the area. Meanwhile, many of the sheds occupied by these companies have been subdivided and sublet and are occupied by other companies carrying out a range of minor, barely legal activities with a lifespan of only two or three years.

Areas reserved for the opening of avenues or the construction of public parks, as planned by Cerdá, were occupied by buildings, soccer fields or orchards.

At the time the 22@Barcelona plan was approved, in 2000, 46 industrial buildings were listed as industrial heritage, although in the case of 18, only the chimneys were intended to be preserved.[28] There was a strong critical reaction from residents, professionals and scholars, who pushed for a major review of the plan.

This resulted in the creation of the Industrial Heritage Plan, under which the original industrial heritage list was recompiled to include 114 items of architectural interest.

Four interventions in the industrial heritage of Poblenou

The transformation of this district is analyzed here with reference to four projects: Poblenou Central Park, a public space that was planned long ago but until recently occupied by a variety of activities and buildings; Can Aranyò, which represents the desire to attract universities to the region by granting them use of historic buildings; Can Framis, a private museum of contemporary art; and Can Ricart, an industrial complex that will combine different uses and epitomizes what can be achieved by public mobilization of residents, scholars, and professionals advocating the preservation of industrial heritage.

One of the most symbolic projects in this district is Poblenou Central Park. In the mid-1980s, the Diagonal-Poblenou Special Plan proposed this site as the main open space for the district.

The proposed space would have had an area twice that available today but was occupied by companies and workers' housing until the early 21st century, when a project was commissioned from Jean Nouvel, the architect who designed the Torre Agbar, Barcelona's new global icon.

Although the project was an opportunity to reintegrate the rich but fragmented complexity of industrial ruins and a unique urban fabric, the walled park shows a startling autism, ignoring the potential permeability it could have represented between the new Diagonal Avenue and remaining industrial areas.

In the first inventory of the industrial heritage of Poblenou, only one of the chimneys in the Can Ricart industrial complex, the largest industrial complex in the neighborhood,[29] was listed. Following protests by local citizens, the Industrial Heritage Group[30] presented a more thorough and better-documented report attesting the historical value of the Can Ricart ensemble. The original design of the Can Ricart complex is attributed to Josep Oriol I Bernadet, one of the first architects to design a mechanized factory. The complex occupies the equivalent of four blocks of Cerdá's Eixample and, as usually occurs with manufacturing plants, is the result of several parts that were combined over more than 150 years, each reflecting the prevailing industrial architectural design of a particular period. As the Grup de Patrimoni Industrial[31] stated, the result is a 'kaleidoscope of companies

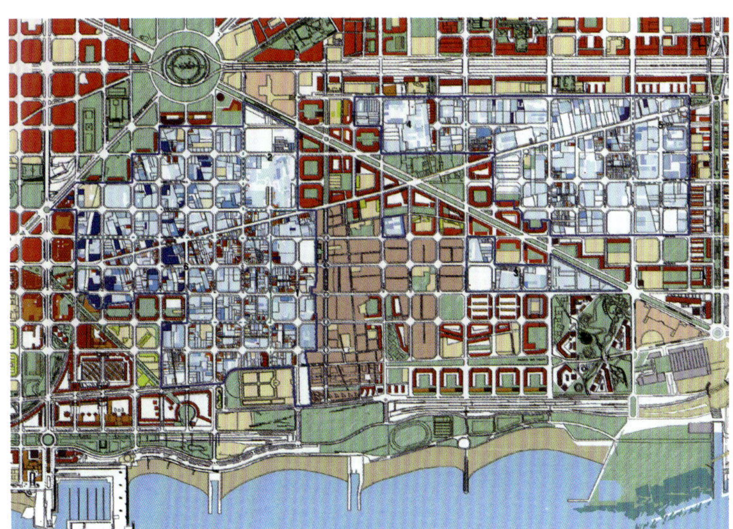

Figure 2 | The previous uses of the area (blue: industrial; red to orange: residential)

in a variety of situations and diverse potential.' Despite the historical value of Can Ricart, the first design for this industrial complex proposed that many of the existing buildings be demolished. The Grup de Patrimoni Industrial advocated careful intervention restricted to the elimination of a few recent additions; that is, step-by-step intervention to retain the ensemble.

As a result of pressure from local residents, media, and scholars, the municipality abandoned the first design. Following this, in 2006, the architectural office EMBT won an international competition to design the House of Languages in the main building. The design is intended to recognize and value the architectural differences between the different buildings in Can Ricart.[32]

Can Aranyò is a former flour mill designed by a British firm in the mid-19th century and adapted to Catalan construction techniques by a local master builder, Josep Marimon. Today it is occupied by a department of Pompeu Fabra University, dedicated to audiovisual activities. The design by Josep Benedito and Ramon Valls shows a refined balance of industrial heritage and contemporary interferences.

Can Framis is another example of the successful functional and architectural conversion of industrial heritage by the architectural office BAAS. It occupies four blocks in Eixample, but the urban fabric is dismantled into smaller pieces. The businessman and art collector Antonio Vila Casas transformed it into a contemporary art museum. The design is a reinterpretation, rather than simply a mimetic recovery, of the industrial heritage and has received several awards. Two original sheds have been maintained, and a contemporary but discrete building was built in exactly the same place as one that was demolished. Cristina Arribas[33] noted that although the remaining buildings do not have a special value from an architectural point of view, they have been kept as testimony to the urban fabric typical of this industrial neighborhood, which does not follow the urban fabric proposed by Cerdà.

Final remarks

The 22@Barcelona project is one element in the City of Barcelona's strategy for positioning the city in the knowledge economy. While this aim may be similar to that of other countries and even other cities in Spain, the chosen area Poblenou is unique, having once been known as the 'Spanish Manchester' for its industrial activities. However, these industrial activities and their unique urban fabric, which disregarded the guidelines of the Cerdá plan, fell into decay in the 1980s, when part of the neighborhood was in an unequivocal state of abandonment.

Poblenou is strategically located in the core of the Eixample plan proposed by Cerdà, with logistical facilities and a road system linking the city to France. Several interventions have been proposed for the area in different urban projects, including the 1992 Olympic Games and Forum 2004 (also known as the Universal Forum of Cultures).

Therefore, 22@Barcelona would seem to demonstrate Barcelona's ability to reinvent itself based on a comprehensive urban plan.[34]

In part, this is a feature of what Jordi Borja[35] calls a method of urban planning typical of Barcelona or, as Busquets[36] put it, a method that highlights the urban project as the 'overcoming of the sterile debate between urban planning and architectural design, which had reduced the first to a zoning and the second to an isolated proposal.Additionally, Oriol Bohigas[37] notes that the continuity of Barcelona's urban development depends on a series of coordinated projects, rather than a uniform general plan. Although very critical of the so-called 'Barcelona model,' Horacio Capel[38] recognizes the positive changes in the city under a 'legal framework that allows public action over land use (...) with compensation rights, and social appropriation of the values induced by municipal plans.'

In the case of 22@Barcelona, the approach adopted to construct a knowledge-based urban environment was quite unusual, as the project occupies part of a decaying industrial neighborhood. Despite the municipal discourse recognizing the importance of industrial heritage, when the first plans were revealed, it became clear that the municipality did not appreciate its importance both for residents and for scholars.

In the first industrial heritage inventory, only 46 elements were listed. Of these, 18 were isolated chimneys, which would have made the 22@Barcelona an immense De Chirico tableau. The political pressure generated by residents in protest against some measures proposed by the municipality also exceeded government expectations. Residents were stunned by the demolition of some of the industrial heritage, which seemed to indicate a deep disregard for the community. In a document published with the support of the City Council, David Marín[39] described how numerous social conflicts arose when 22@Barcelona began, mainly because it was likely that residents would be relocated and small industrial workshops would disappear as they were forced to move out because of the expected increase in real estate prices. Supported by professionals and scholars, the City Council reviewed the industrial heritage inventory and classified 114 industrial items including parts of the urban fabric because of their historical importance.

Nevertheless, the relationship between the knowledge economy and urban planning instruments in Poblenou continues to be a cause for considerable concern and the subject of criticism. Peter Rowe[40] questions the capacity of Barcelona to become a reference in the knowledge economy, and, in particular, the usefulness of the 22@Barcelona project. For Rowe, it is simply an urban project with all the risks of gentrification that accompany the conversion of industrial areas. Horacio Capel[41] raises a similar criticism of the 'expropriation of cheap public housing and a significant public investment' with no mechanisms to prevent land speculation.

In response to such criticisms, the City Council argues that 22@Barcelona will result in more than 90,000 jobs being created in the area, half of them for university graduates.[42] Almost half of the companies already in place are start-ups, illustrating the vitality of the knowledge economy.[43] More than 70 percent of the approved projects are funded by the private sector, and over two thirds of these are related to the key areas of 22@Barcelona: media, ICT, medical technologies, energy, and design.

All of these controversies reinforce the idea that 22@Barcelona is a knowledge-based urban development project that deserves close attention because it represents an important economic transformation in a former industrial area, which has been accompanied at all stages by an extensive debate involving residents, scholars and the local authorities and echoed by the media. Finally, 22@Barcelona shows how vibrant city life continues to be even in the information society.

(The article has been published in *Theoretical and Empirical Researches in Urban Management* in May, 2013, Volume 8 Issue 2.)

1 Garcia-López; M. Á. and Muñiz, I., 'Employment Decentralisation: Polycentricity or Scatteration? The Case of Barcelona,' *Urban Studies*, 2010, vol. 47, n. 14, pp. 3035–3056.

2 Sennet, R., 'Le Nouveau capitalisme, le nouvel isolement (New capitalism, the new isolation),' *Quaderns* (*Notebooks*) no 239, 2003, pp. 63–67.

3 Castells, M., Hall, P., *Technopoles of the World. The making of 21st century industrial complexes*, New York, Routledge, 1994.

4 Aydalot, P., *Économie regionale et urbaine* (*Regional and urban economy*), Paris, Economica, 1985.

5 Yigitcanlar, T., Velibeyoglu, K., Martinez-Fernandez, C., 'Rising knowledge cities: the role of urban knowledge precincts,' *Journal of Knowledge Management*, Vol. 12 No. 5, 2008, pp. 8–20.

6 Duarte, F., 'Cidades inteligentes. Inovação tecnológica no meio urbano (Smart cities. Technological innovation in the urban environment),' *São Paulo em Perspectiva* (*São Paulo in Perspective*), 2005, Vol. 19, no. 1, pp. 122–131; Tremblay, D-G. Rousseau, S., 'The Montreal multimedia sector: a cluster, a new mode of governance or a simple co-location?' *Canadian Journal of Regional Science/ Revue canadienne des sciences régionales*, XXVIII: 2, 2005, pp. 299–328.

7 Aurigi, A. and De Cindio, F., *Augmented Urban Spaces. Articulating the Physical and Electronic City*, London, Ashgate, 2008.

8 Viladecans-Marsal, E. and Arauzo-Carod, J-M., *Can a knowledge-based cluster be created? The case of the Barcelona 22@Barcelonadistrict*, Document de treball de l'IEB 38. Institut d'Economia de Barcelona Facultat d'Economia i Empresa Universitat de Barcelona (Barcelona Institute of Economics, Faculty of Economics and Business University of Barcelona), 2009.

9 Trullén, J., El proyecto Barcelona (the Project of Barcelona), 'Ciudad del Conocimiento desde la economía (City of Knowledge from the economy),' Barcelona, Ciudad del conocimiento (City of knowledge), Los monográficos de Barcelona (The Monographs of Barcelona), *Metrópolis mediterránea* (*Mediterranean Metropolis*), no. 1. Barcelona, Ayuntamiento de Barcelona (Town Hall of Barcelona), 2002.

10 Yigitcanlar, et al., 2008, op. cit.

11 Yigitcanlar, T. and Velibeyoglu, K., 'Knowledge-based strategic planning: harnessing (in) tangible assets of city-regions,' in: *International Forum on Knowledge Asset Dynmics*, 26–27 June, Italy, Matera, 2008.

12 Collinge, C. and Staines, A., 'Rethinking the knowledge based economy,' *Built Environment*, special issue: Can we plan the creative knowledge city?, 2009, Vol. 35, no. 2, pp. 166–172.

13 Halbert, L., 'La ville creative pour qui? (The creative city for whom),' *Urbanisme* (*Urban Planning*) no. 373, 2009, pp. 43–45.

14 Reese, L., 'Creative class or procreative class: implications for local economic development policy,' *Theoretical and Empirical Researches in Urban Management*, vol. 7, issue 1, 2012, pp. 5–26.

15 Florida, R., *Who's your city for?*, New York, Basic Books, 2008.

16 Florida, R., *La clase creative. La transformación de la cultura del trabajo y el ocio en el siglo XXI* (*The Creative Class, the Transformation of the Culture of Work and Leisure in the 21st Century*), Barcelona, Paidós (© 2002 en Inglés), 2010.

17 Vegara Gómez, A., 'Territorios inteligentes' ('Smart territories'), in Rodríguez González, Román (ed.), *Território: ordenar para competir* (*Territory: Order to Compete*), Oleiros, Netbiblio, 2010, pp. 1–17.

18 Florida, 2008, op. cit.

19 Winn, M., 'Barcelona: Planning and Change 1854–1977,' *Town Planning Review*, Vol. 50, no 2, 2010, pp. 185–202.

20 Gregotti, V., 'Introducción,' *Rassegna* (*Review*) no. 37, 1989, pp. 5–7.

21 Sabaté, J., *Luces y sombras en el proyecto urbanístico reciente de Barcelona en Globalización y grandes proyectos urbanos* (*Lights and Shadows in the Recent Urban Project of Barcelona in Globalization and Large Urban Projects*), Ediciones Infinito (Infinity Editions), Buenos Aires, 2006.

22 Ibid.

23 City of Barcelona, *Modificación del PGM para la renovación de las zonas industriales del Poblenou—Districte d'Activitats 22@Barcelona* (*Modification of the PGM for the Renovation of the Industrial Zones of the Poblenou-District of Activities 22@Barcelona*), Barcelona, Ayuntamiento de Barcelona (Town Hall of Barcelona), 2000.

24 Marrero, I., 'Del Manchester catalán al Soho Barcelonés? La renovación del barrio del Poblenou en Barcelona y la cuestión de la vivienda (From Catalan Manchester to Soho Barcelonés? The renovation of the Poblenou neighborhood in Barcelona and the question of housing),' *Scripta Nova* (*New Writings*), Barcelona, vol. VII, núm. 146(137), 2003.

25 City of Barcelona, *22@Barcelona. El districte de la innovación* (*The District of Innovation*), (Map and current situation) Barcelona, Ayuntamiento de Barcelona (Town Hall of Barcelona), Julio, 2010a; City of Barcelona, *El plan 22@Barcelona* (*The Plan of 22@Barcelona*), Un programa de transformación urbana, económica y social (A program of urban, economic and social transformation), Barcelona, Ayuntamiento de Barcelona (Town Hall of Barcelona), 2010b.

26 Barceló, M., 'Faire entrer Barcelone Dans le réseau mondial des villes creatives (Bring Barcelona into the global network of creative cities),' in Masboungi, A. (ed.). Barcelona, *La ville innovante* (*Barcelona, the Innovative City*), Paris, Moniteur, 2010.

27 Sen T. and José M., *Reflexión sobre el Ensanche Cerdà. Una propuesta para el siglo XXI* (*Reflection on the Ensanche Cerdà. A Proposal for the 21st Century*), Barcelona, Ed. Viena, 2019.

28 City of Barcelona, *Elements i edificis industrials inclosos al Pla especial de protecció del patrimony arquitectònic historicartístic de la ciutat de Barcelona* (*Elements and Industrial Buildings included in the Special Plan for the Protection of the Historic-artistic Architectural Heritage of the City of Barcelona*). *Districte de Sant Martí a l'àmbit de la modificació—vigent* (*District of Sant Martí in the Scope of the Modification-current*), Barcelona, Ayuntamiento de Barcelona (Town Hall of Barcelona), 1999.

29 Tatjer I M., Mercé; U. I, Domènech, M., Can Ricart Estudi Patrimonial (Síntesi) [Can Ricart Patrimonial Study (Synthesis)], *Biblio 3W* (a magazine on bibliography of geography and social sciences), vol. X, 2005, no 598.

30 Grup de Patrimoni Industrial (Industrial Heritage Group), Proposta de pla integral de patrimoni industrial de Barcelona (Proposal for a comprehensive industrial heritage plan of Barcelona), Nou Projecte (New Project), *Biblio 3W*, Vol. X, 2005b, no 581.

31 Grup de Patrimoni Industrial (Industrial Heritage Group), Un patrimoni únic, un futur brillant, un model de fer ciutat Can Ricart – parc central de Barcelona (A unique heritage, a bright future, a model to make the Can Ricart city – central park of Barcelona), Nou projecte (New Project), *Biblio 3W*, 2005a, Vol. X, no 580.

32 EMBT, *Projecte bàsic Casa de les Llengües al recinte industrial de Can Ricart* (*Basic project House of the Language at the Can Ricart industrial center*), Barcelona, 2009.

33 Arribas, C., 'El silenci com a contrapunt (Silence as a counterpoint),' *L'Informatiu* (*Informative*), 2010, no. 320, abril; pp. 58–62.

34 Clos, O., 'The transformation of Poblenou: the new 22@Barcelona district,' in Marshall, T. *Transforming Barcelona*, London and New York, Routledge, 2004, pp. 191–201; Masboungi, A., 'Comment rester la Mécque de l'urbanisme (How to remain the Mecca of urbanism),' Masboungi, Ariella (ed.). *Barcelone. La ville innovante* (*The Innovative City*), Paris, Moniteur, 2010, pp. 10–21; Rowe, P., *Building Barcelona: a second reinaxença, Barcelona*, Actar, 2006.

35 Borja, J., *Llums I ombres de l'urbanisme de Barcelona* (*Lights and Shadows of the City Planning of Barcelona*), Barcelona, Empóries, 2010.

36 Busquets, J., *La construcción urbanística de una ciudad compacta* (*The Urban Construction of a Compact City*), Barcelona, Serbal, 2004.

37 Bohigas, O., 'Ten points for an urban methodology,' in Marshall, T. *Transforming Barcelona*, London and New York, Routledge, 2004, pp. 91–96.

38 Tremblay and Rousseau, 2005, op. cit.

39 Marín, D., *La Gran Via al districte de Sant Martí: História d'una gran transformació* (*The Gran Via in the Sant Martí District: History of a Great Transformation*), Barcelona, Ayuntament de Barcelona (Town Hall of Barcelona), 2007.

40 Rowe, 2006, op. cit.

41 Capel, H., 'El debate sobre la construcción de la ciudad y el llamado "modelo Barcelona," (The debate on the construction of the city and the so-called "model Barcelona")' *Scripta Nova* (*New Writings*), Universidad de Barcelona, Vol. XI, núm. 233, 2007.

42 City of Barcelona, *Estado de Ejecución* (*Execution Status*), Barcelona, Ayuntamiento de Barcelona (Town Hall Barcelona), diciembre, 2009.

43 City of Barcelona, 2010a, op. cit.; Barcelona, 2010b, op. cit.

Advanced assessment of industrial heritage buildings for sustainable cities' development

Milan Holický and Jana Marková of Czech Technical University in Prague, Klokner Institute

Figures 1 | Public library and music school in Almonte (designed by Donaire Arquiectos, photo by Fernando Alda)

Introduction

A number of factories, warehouses, power plants, and other industrial buildings, built since the beginning of the Industrial Revolution in the second half of the 18th century, have been registered as industrial cultural heritage in the Czech Republic and abroad. Such structures are mostly of significant architectural, historic, technological, or social value.[1]

They often form part of the urban landscape and provide the cityscape with visual historical landmarks. However, insufficient attention seems to be paid to systematic recognizing, declaring and protecting the industrial heritage in many countries including the Czech Republic. This is an alarming situation as the lack of attention and awareness of the industrial structures may gradually lead to their extinction.[2]

When out of use, industrial heritage buildings are degrading and often turn into ruins. Re-use and adaptation of such buildings allow for integration of the industrial heritage buildings into a modern urban lifestyle and help protect cities' cultural heritage.[3] These buildings are often adapted to become hotels, museums, residential parks, commercial centers, and so forth.

This section attempts to increase awareness of the high architectural and cultural significance of the industrial buildings and indicate the positive influence of their preservation on the sustainable development of cities. In addition, the section aims to promote discussion among experts on sustainable use of the industrial heritage structures, and a framework for complex, reliable assessment of such structures is provided.

Importance of protection of industrial heritage for sustainable development

Protection (including adaptations and re-use) of the industrial heritage structures is an important issue of the sustainable development of cities. More specifically, it has been recognized[4] that the protection and re-use may positively contribute to this sustainable development by allowing for:

- preservation of the cultural values
- recycling of all potential resources and avoiding wasting energy
- facilitating the economic regeneration of regions in decline that may provide psychological stability for communities facing a sudden high rate of unemployment.

It follows that the protection has considerable ecological and social contexts that are becoming even more important due to the global shortage of energy, economic crisis and environmental protection. The re-use of the industrial heritage is thus no longer an isolated issue, but is of general significance and may directly represent a city's policy of sustainable development. The protection of historical sites and the full use of limited resources deserve considerable public attention and participation.

Initiatives concerning industrial heritage

The protection of industrial heritage is a multidisciplinary topic including historical, architectonic, civil engineering, and ecological aspects. The first initiatives aimed at research and conservation of industrial buildings started in the 1950s on an amateur basis.[5] In 1973, the Society for Industrial Archeology was established and the First International Congress on the Conservation of Industrial Monuments took place. When the third congress was held in 1978, the International Committee on the Conservation of the Industrial Heritage (TICCIH) was founded to study, protect, conserve, and explain the remains of industrialization.

The recent cooperation of TICCIH and the International Council on Monuments and Sites (ICOMOS) has resulted in the registration of more than 40 industrial sites in the World Heritage List, such as Völklingen Ironworks in Germany.

In the Czech Republic, numerous industrial heritage structures including structures of railway infrastructures, breweries, sugar factories, and other industrial structures were built in the period from 1870 to 1930. Due to historical reasons, views of Czech architects and civil engineers on protection of the industrial heritage are often considerably different[6] and an important issue may then be to achieve consensus on significance of the heritage value to be preserved. To provide a desired coordinating platform for experts in the fields of historical-structural research, monument conservation, and the reconstruction of the industrial heritage buildings and sites, the Research Center for Industrial Heritage has been established as an independent research institution of the Czech Technical University in Prague. The Center—the Czech local representative in TICCIH—synthesizes findings from various research fields, maintains a database of the Czech industrial monuments (containing more than 10,000 monuments) and seeks for new uses of the industrial heritage buildings.

To promote discussions among experts from various fields, the international conference Vestiges of Industry is organized every two years.

On the occasion of the third biennial conference held in 2005, international cooperation relating to the conservation, documentation, promotion, and interpretation of a common European industrial heritage was declared. The activities that deserve special attention include:

- the promotion of education, knowledge, and a deeper understanding of the industrial heritage by conferences, seminars, and educational programs
- the evaluation and conservation of industrial heritage
- the conversion of industrial heritage to new uses as a positive form of cultural potential with the objective of revitalizing industrial regions, towns, and brownfields in decline.

In 2009, the Czech Technical University in Prague and the University of Applied Sciences in Ås (Norway) launched the research project 'Assessment of Historical Immovables,' mainly focused on assessment of the industrial heritage structures. The project is aimed at developing the general methodology for the complex assessment of the industrial heritage structures that is an inevitable part of their preservation. The innovative methods based on probabilistic approaches and optimization techniques are being developed to provide operational tools and background information for decision making concerning the protection, conservation, renewal, and extended use of the industrial heritage structures. The target group of the project includes researchers, designers, practicing engineers, cultural heritage management and local authorities involved in preservation of cultural heritage.

Principles of design of construction interventions

As a rule, re-use and adaptation of the industrial buildings require assessment of structural reliability. It has been recognized that many heritage structures do not fulfill requirements of present codes of practice. Minimization of construction interventions is required in rehabilitation and upgrades, but sufficient reliability should also be guaranteed. When dealing with the preservation of heritage buildings, it may be difficult to propose construction interventions that respect all requirements for preservation of the heritage value. According to Lourenco,[7] modern principles, interventions seem to include the following aspects:

- removability
- unobtrusiveness and respect of the original conception
- safety of the construction
- durability and compatibility of materials
- balance between cost and available financial resources.

Differences between assessment of heritage structures and design of new structures

Decisions about adequate construction interventions should be based on the complex assessment of a structure considering actual material properties, use, and environmental conditions. However, it appears that insufficient attention has been paid by experts to specific issues of reliability assessment of such structures so far. Only a few scientific publications seem to be available.[8] The following differences between assessment of heritage structures and design of new structures should be carefully considered:

- social and cultural aspects—loss of cultural and heritage values, in some cases also restrictions or relocation of users and performance (these aspects do not influence design of new structures)
- economic aspects—additional costs of measures to increase reliability of a heritage structure in comparison with a new structure (at a design stage cost of such measures is normally minor while cost of strengthening and in some cases also costs related to unavailability of a structure are much higher)
- principles of sustainable development—waste reduction and recycling of materials (these aspects may be more significant in case of the assessment of heritage structures)
- lack of information for the assessment of the heritage structures—commonly, characterization of the mechanical properties of materials is difficult, expensive, but also very important due to variability of mechanical properties and changes that may have occurred during the working life of a structure (influence of deterioration and damage).

Probabilistic assessments of the industrial heritage structures

Significant uncertainties related to actual material properties and structural conditions usually need to be considered in the reliability assessment of the industrial heritage structures. Application of simplified procedures used for the design of new structures may lead to expensive repairs and losses of the cultural and heritage value.

Figures 2 | Yingliang Stone Archive (designed by Atelier Alter, photo by Atelier Alter)

In accordance with EN 1990[9] and ISO 13822,[10] a general probabilistic procedure is thus proposed to improve the reliability assessment of the industrial heritage buildings. The procedure allows for inclusion of results of inspections, testing, and consideration of successful past performance of a structure.

Specification of models for basic variables

Models for basic variables should be adjusted to the actual situation and state of the structure and verified by inspection and testing. Design documentation and original standards should be used as a guidance material only. The following principles should be taken into account:

- Material properties should be considered according to the actual state of a structure verified by destructive or non-destructive testing. It may often be appropriate to combine limited new information with prior information. Bayesian techniques, described (e.g. in ISO 1249111 or the Joint Committee on Structural Safety (JCSS) publications,[12]) provide a consistent basis for this updating.
- When significant deterioration is observed, an appropriate deterioration model should be used to predict changes in structural parameters due to foreseen environmental conditions, structural loading, maintenance practices and past exposures, based on theoretical or experimental investigation, inspection and experience.
- Dimensions of structural members should be determined by measurements. When the original design documentation is available and no changes in dimensions exist, nominal dimensions given in the documentation may be used.
- Load characteristics should be introduced considering the values corresponding to the actual situation verified. For structures with significant permanent actions, the actual geometry should be verified by measurements and weight densities should be obtained from tests.
- Model uncertainties should be considered in the same way as at a design stage unless previous structural behavior (especially damage) indicates otherwise. In some cases, model factors, coefficients, and other design assumptions may be established from measurements.

It follows that reliability verification of a heritage structure should be backed up by inspection including collection of appropriate data. Evaluation of prior information and its updating using newly obtained measurements may be one of the most important steps of the assessment.

Figures 3 | Wine Experience Hotel (designed by FCC Arquitectura, photo by Fernando Guerra)

Failure probability

The failure probability related to a working life t_D can be obtained from a general probabilistic relationship:

$$p_f(t_D) = p\{z[x(t_D)]<0\} \qquad (1)$$

where, $z(\cdot)$ = limit state function; and $x(t_D)$ = vector of basic variables including resistance, permanent, and variable actions and model uncertainties. Models of basic variables may be updated considering results of inspections and tests.

It may be reasonable to consider satisfactory past performance of a structure during a period to the time of assessment t_A in the reliability assessment of a heritage structure. This may be taken into account in the reliability analysis by considering the conditional failure probability that a structure will fail during a working life t_D given that it has survived the period t_A. This probability may be estimated by several ways. When the load to which the structure has been exposed during the period t_A is known, the resistance or a joint distribution of time-invariant variables may be truncated (a lower bound is set to the value of load). Using the bounded distribution, the conditional (updated) probability $p_{f,upd}(t_D \mid t_A)$ can be estimated. This approach, similar to the updating for proof load testing, is described in Lourenco's 'Computations on historic masonry structures,'.[13]

Alternatively, the updated failure probability may be determined as:

$$p_{f,upd}(t_D \mid t_A) = [p_f(t_D+t_A)-p_f(t_A)]/[1-p_f(t_A)] \qquad (2)$$

where, $p_f(t_D+t_A)$ = failure probability related to the period $t_A + t_D$.

Reliability verification

Reliability verification may be based on the following relationship:

$$p_{f,upd}(t_D \mid t_A) < p_t \qquad (3)$$

where, p_t = target failure probability. The reliability level is commonly expressed in terms of the reliability index β_t. Equation 3 can be rewritten as:

$$\beta_{upd}(t_D \mid t_A) = -\Phi^{-1}[p_{f,upd}(t_D \mid t_A)] \geq \beta_t \qquad (4)$$

Where, Φ^{-1} = inverse cumulative distribution function of the standardized normal variable. The target reliability level can be taken as the level of reliability implied by acceptance criteria defined in proved and accepted design codes. The target level should be stated together with clearly defined limit state functions and specific models of basic variables. For the industrial heritage buildings, moderate consequences of failure and moderate costs of safety measures may often be assumed. In this case, ISO 2394[14] indicates $\beta_t = 3.1$.

The target reliability level can also be established taking into account the required performance level of the structure, reference period, cost of upgrades (including potential losses of the cultural and heritage value), and possible consequences of failure or malfunction. Lower target levels may be used if they are justified on the basis of social, cultural, economical, and sustainable considerations, ISO 13822.[15] A simple model for estimation of the target reliability level was proposed by Schueremans and Van Gemert:[16]

$$P_t = S_c\, t_D\, A_c\, C_f \,/\, (n_p\, W) \times 10^{-4} \qquad (5)$$

where, s_c = social criterion factor (recommended value for listed historical buildings 0.05); t_D =remaining working life (considered as 50 years); A_c=activity factor (recommended value for buildings 3); C_f =economical factor (5 for a moderate consequences, recommended values: 10—not serious, 1—serious consequences of failure); n_p=number of endangered persons (in accordance with Trbojevic,[17] the most favorable and unfavorable estimates $n_{p,min}$=1 and $n_{p,max}$=10, respectively, are considered for significant risk of injury or fatalities—a middle class of consequences); and W=warning factor (1—sudden failure without previous warning). Considering these indicative data, lower and upper estimates of the target reliability level are obtained from Equation 5 as follows:

$$P_{t,max} = 0.05 \times 50 \times 3 \times 5/(1 \times 0.3) \times 10^{-4} \approx 3.8 \times 10^{-3};$$
$$\beta_{t,min} = 2.7$$
$$P_{t,min} = 0.05 \times 50 \times 3 \times 5/(10 \times 0.3) \times 10^{-4} \approx 3.8 \times 10^{-4};$$
$$\beta_{t,max} = 3.4 \qquad (6)$$

It appears that the target reliability is within the broad range from 2.7 to 3.4. The value recommended in ISO 2394[18] is approximately in the middle of this range. If a structure does not satisfy the reliability requirements, construction interventions may become necessary. Decision-making concerning construction interventions may be based on a cost-benefit analysis. Application of the proposed methodology is numerically illustrated elsewhere.[19]

Discussion and conclusions

Protection of the industrial heritage structures may positively contribute to sustainable development by preservation of the cultural values, recycling of all potential resources, avoiding wasting energy, and facilitating the economic regeneration of regions in decline. It is recognized that most heritage structures do not fulfill the requirements of present codes of practice.

In many cases significant uncertainties related to actual structural conditions can hardly be realistically described by simplified procedures used for design of new structures that may lead to expensive repairs and losses of the cultural and heritage value.

Application of probabilistic methods is thus proposed to better describe the uncertainties and take into account results of inspections and tests and the satisfactory past performance. For moderate consequences of failure, the target reliability index might be selected from the broad range from 2.7 to 3.4.

The industrial heritage structures often form part of the urban landscape and provide the cityscape with visual historical landmarks. Present insufficient attention to systematic recognizing, declaring and protecting the industrial heritage may, however, lead to their extinction. The desired protection of the industrial heritage structures requires a public recognition of the industrial heritage to be of equal importance as other cultural heritage. The introduction of educational programs and relevant legislation is needed.

Acknowledgement

This study has been conducted at the Klokner Institute, Czech Technical University in Prague, within framework of the research project A/CZ0046/2/0013 Assessment of historical immovables (www.heritage.cvut.cz), supported by a grant from Iceland, Liechtenstein and Norway through the EEA Financial Mechanism and the Norwegian Financial Mechanism.

1 TICCIH, *The Nizhny Tagil Charter for the Industrial Heritage*, The International Committee for the Conservation of the Industrial Heritage, Nizhny Tagil, 2003, p. 6.

2 Läuferts, M. and Mavunganidze, J., 'Ruins of the past: industrial heritage in Johannesburg,' *Proc. STEMAH XI*, WIT Press, Ashurst Lodge, 2009, pp. 533–542.

3 Ibid.

4 TICCIH, 2003, op. cit.; Zhang, S., 'Conservation and adaptive reuse of industrial heritage in Shanghai,' *Frontiers of Architecture and Civil Engineering in China*, 1(4), 2007, pp. 481–490.

5 Zhang, 2007, ibid.

6 Fragner, B. Přístupy kzáchraně průmyslového dědictví v České republice (Approaches to protection of the industrial heritage in the Czech Republic – in Czech), *Stavebnictví*, IV(01/2010), 2010, pp. 16–18.

7 Lourenco, P.B., 'Computations on historic masonry structures,' *Progress in Structural Engineering and Materials*, 4(3), 2002, pp. 301–319.

8 de Bouw, M., Wouters, I. and Lauriks, L., 'Structural analysis of two metal de Dion roof trusses in Brussels model schools,' Proc. *STREMAH XI*, WIT Press, Ashurst Lodge, 2009, pp. 121–130; Läuferts and Mavunganidze, 2009, op. cit.; Zhang, 2007, op. cit.

9 EN 1990, *Eurocode – Basis of Structural Design*, CEN, Brussels, 2002, p. 87.

10 ISO 13822. *Bases for design of structures – Assessment of existing structures*, ISO TC98/SC2, Geneve, Switzerland, 2003, p. 35.

11 ISO 12491. ISO 12491:1997, *Statistical Methods for Quality Control of Building Materials and Components*, ISO (International Organization for Standardization), Geneve, Switzerland, 1997, p. 30.

12 Diamantidis, D., *Probabilistic Assessment of Existing Structures*, Joint Committee on Structural Safety, RILEM Publications S.A.R.L., 2001; JCSS. JCSS Probabilistic Model Code, Joint Committee on Structural Safety, Zurich, 2006.

13 Lourenco, 2002, op. cit.

14 ISO 2394, *General Principles on Reliability for Structures*, ISO, Geneve, Switzerland, 1998, p. 73.

15 ISO 13822, 2003, op. cit.

16 Schueremans, L. and Van Gemert, D., 'Assessing the safety of existing structures: reliability based assessment framework, examples and application,' *Journal of Civil Engineering and Management*, X(2), 2004, pp. 131–141.

17 Trbojevic, V.M., 'Another look at risk and structural reliability criteria,' *Structural Safety*, 31(3), 2009, pp. 245–250.

18 ISO 2394, 1998, op. cit.

19 Sýkora, M., Holický, M., Jung, K., Marková, J., Kvaal, K. and Thiis, T., 'Reliability Assessment of Industrial Heritage Structures and Application to a Light-Weight Steel Roof', *Proc. ICSA2010*, Balkema, Rotterdam, 2010, p. 10.

Industrial heritage: Merging past and future towards sustainable cities

Luis Loures of the Polytechnic Institute of Portalegre, Portugal

Introduction

'Cities are by far the largest creations of humanity,'[1] cultural entities that contain representations from the past, via the present, to the future, running through the entire cultural evolution of the 'city as object.'[2] In this way, intrinsic values need to be determined, meaning given to elements of the city, its importance identified, and exceptional sites highlighted.

The history behind the birth and development of a city should be traced and features revealed in order to retain, amend, and transform implicit values. This analysis of society and this understanding of an area lead to a social perception of the kind of place people wish to live in, and to the realization that the 'whole' city is our 'heritage,'[3] regardless of whether it is large, small, historic, industrial, old or new. Cultural landscapes give us a sense of place and reveal our relationship with the land over time.[4] They are special places that contain aspects of our origin and development through their forms, features, and history of use.

The concept of cultural heritage has clearly meant different things to different groups of scholars and the public interested in reclaiming traditions—and landscapes—presented as part of shared, remembered pasts.[5] In 1949, the Statute of the Council of Europe, adopted in London, quoted that: 'to achieve a greater unity it is imperious to safeguard cultural heritage and to facilitate economic and social progress.'[6] The years ahead proved that the conservation and safeguard of the natural and cultural environment (people's common heritage) was one of the major issues confronting society. Since then, several basic legal instruments were adopted in order to protect this heritage: the Bern, Granada, Valetta, Lugano, Strasbourg, and Florence conventions are good examples of this purpose.[7]

The fact that historic areas are progressively coming under threat of new development,[8] and that the impact of new construction is noticed not only at nationally important sites, but also in local areas—where small changes can be very significant, diminishing landscape character and local distinctiveness—increased the need to develop new strategies and frameworks to protect and highlight our cultural heritage, an idea directly connected with the necessity to enhance the sense of place.[9]

Considering that industrial heritage is an integral part of our culture, and that the member states of the Council of Europe, which have adhered to the European Cultural Convention on the 19th of December of 1954 committed themselves—under Article 1 of that Convention—to take appropriate measures to safeguard and to encourage the development of their national contributions to the common cultural heritage of Europe; they recognized that heritage, regardless of being architectural, vernacular, industrial, and so forth, is an irreplaceable expression of the wealth and diversity of common culture. It is an 'entity' shared by several people, which every country must show real solidarity in preserving.

This section presents a set of design principles that might be applied to post-industrial landscapes that possesses environmental, cultural, and social value. These principles describe in a general manner the reasons why relevant resources created and deposited by the industrial society should be identified and how they can best be reclaimed and used.

The industrial landscape

Industrialization promoted significant changes in the landscape: greater densities in urban areas and the urbanization of the natural and rural environment. The city acquired a new—industrial—face, and a new order.[10] This new landscape was defined by the concentration of industries and by the needs of a growing population, often new workers in a new society who demanded new public services and infrastructures, thus contributing to the image of the typical 20th century settlement.

However, over the past decades, globalization, deindustrialization, industrial relocation, and economic (re)conversion has had a profound effect on traditional industrial areas all over the world and produced a vast array of obsolete industrial facilities and the various impacts, which are generated from them.[11] The formal products of the modernist movement have become obsolete, forcing this generation to decide on the disposition of the last generation's industrial environment.[12]

In recent years, several researchers have contributed to evaluating, documenting, and developing remnants of the industrial society[13] in order to emphasize the necessity of taking post-industrial landscapes into consideration in the planning of the city, considering industrial heritage as a resource and as an integral part of collective identity. The classification of the landscape as industrial implied a qualitative perception in which territory and industrial infrastructures were analyzed from a functional, cultural, and historic perspective.[14] In this sense, and according to Borsi (1975), the industrial landscape may be defined as 'the landscape resultant from a thoughtful and systematic activity of man in the natural or agricultural landscape with the aim of developing industrial activities.' This definition enabled the recognition of an entire landscape as a single 'element,' as opposed to simply recognizing a building, or a group of buildings of an industrial site, allowing the expansion of the conception of industrial preservation to accommodate 'recognized patterns of activity in time and place.'[15]

The concept of industrial landscape is, in this logic, used to describe and classify the 'remnant' materials of the industrial culture in order to attribute them a new meaning,[16] with the objective of creating a theoretical basis and a practical methodology both for the study and for the intervention in these landscapes to adapt them to new production systems and new cultural uses.

Post-industrial landscapes: Heritage or dereliction

Few towns or cities escaped factory closing in recent decades. This economic upheaval has caused the industrial landscape to be re-envisioned as no-man's land between former industrial buildings and the ascendant post-industrial economy.[17] This reality added to the fact that several countries are now facing various problems produced by landscapes constructed during the modern period (e.g. industrial revolution), currently in complete physical and functional decadency, contributed to enlarge the negative public perception about these spaces.

Even so, the meaning and the relevance of industrial landscapes is now larger than ever, especially because of the creation of the Nizhny Tagil Charter for the Industrial Heritage in 2003. This charter specified clearly that the buildings and structures built for industrial activities, the processes and artifacts used within them and the towns and landscapes in which they are located, along with all their other tangible and intangible manifestations are of fundamental importance.[18] They should be studied, their history should be taught, their meaning and significance should be probed and made clear for everyone, and the most significant and characteristic examples should be identified, protected and maintained, in accordance with the spirit of the Venice Charter (1964),[19] for the use and benefit of today and of the future.[20]

However, the spaces that have been recognized and defined as industrial heritage still face inappropriate appraisal of material and cultural resources and stereotyped ideas of industry, once the way in which they were designed do not satisfy the aesthetic, ecological, and functional requirements and standards.[21] Appearance was and continues to be almost everything, given that the assessment of the industrial heritage is often anchored to visual values rather than to any other consideration of function or history.[22] Additionally, the interventions developed to post-industrial landscapes are frequently reprehensible, contributing to the disappearance of various buildings with significant meaning (e.g. Figure 1 and 2); besides that, they are often realized to isolated buildings, which is a mistake,[23] as the analysis and intervention in these landscapes should never be directed to a single building, but to the entire industrial landscape.

When analyzing and re-developing these landscapes, landscape architects, architects, designers, and other planning professionals need to realize that post-industrial, typically part of ordinary or vernacular landscapes, incorporate the passage of time,[24] representing multiple layers of time and cultural activity, therefore, being part of the identity of a people and a place.

In this sense, these landscapes should be seen as assets, once as historic sites they enhance the possibilities of creative practice in preservation, design, and planning, given that they are by definition unique, resulting from the combination of natural landforms and buildings defining a particular place or region. These changes in perception contributed to increase the relevance of industrial landscapes and to highlight the need to study and protect the material and immaterial remains of our industry from a different perspective.[25]

What future for the industrial heritage?

The concept of industrial heritage was only introduced in England in the middle of the 20th century, during a period when several industrial buildings and landscapes were destroyed.[26] By this time the concept of heritage crossed the boundaries of the industrial era, moving to a past much closer to the present.[27] Since then, several efforts have been made in order to define what should and should not be considered as industrial heritage. According to the Nizhny Tagil Charter the 'industrial heritage consists of the remains of industrial culture which are of historical, technological, social, architectural or scientific value' and 'the historical period of principal interest extends forward from the beginning of the Industrial Revolution up to and including the present day, also examining its earlier pre-industrial and proto-industrial roots.'[28]

Figures 1 and 2 | These photos represent good examples of several interventions that have been realized in post-industrial buildings in the Algarve during the last decades. The designers chose to destroy the buildings completely, leaving the chimneys as if they represented the entire value of the building.

Figures 3 and 4 | Before and after images of the Arraial Ferreira Neto, a post-industrial landscape located in the Natural Reserve of Ria Formosa, Tavira.

In this sense, it is mandatory to recognize that landscape and architectural heritage are a capital of unique spiritual, cultural, social, and economic value.[29] Each generation places a different interpretation on the past and derives new inspiration from it, contributing to the creation of a capital built up over the centuries; the destruction of any part of it leaves us poorer, since nothing new that we create will substitute that loss.[30] The cultural heritage is not renewable, because it cannot be rebuilt once it has been destroyed.[31]

Given that, it is important to note that landscape has tended to change incrementally, with occasional major interventions that have been more frequently resultant of economic or technical factors than political ones—note, for example, the case of the Algarve's region, where the change from an economy based on agriculture and industrial activities to an economy based on tourism has changed the landscape completely, posing serious problems to its management and safeguarding. The Arraial Ferreira Neto (Figures 3 and 4) is an example of a conversion of a cultural landscape associated with fishing activities in which the spirit of the place was not totally maintained, once the new use (a five-star hotel) introduced considerable changes in the original structure of the building. Nonetheless, this space is located in the Natural Reserve of Ria Formosa (a protected landscape), which is the reason why the impacts of this intervention were noticed not only in the former industrial landscape but also in the natural one).

Nowadays, it is common to hear such phrases as 'landscape architecture must be sensitive to its surroundings' or 'it is essential to develop a sustainable sensitive approach.' The problem is that many times, technicians or local authorities do not really understand what these phrases mean, allowing the use of some design techniques and strategies that modify the spirit of the place (Figure 5).

In this sense, before starting to develop a reclamation or rehabilitation project for a post-industrial landscape it is important to find the answer for two different questions—'why?' and 'how?'—to reclaim and protect the industrial landscape.

The answer to the 'why' is often very clear. Industrial landscapes describe an important part of the history of a place, thus, constituting a testimony of cultural, social and economic conception, and evolution, which documents and interprets considerable values for urban heritage. Furthermore, the analysis and

Figure 5 | Boca do Rio Hotel Resort is a good example of where the use of some design techniques and strategies modify the spirit of the place, representing the conversion of a former industrial building into a hotel located right in the margin of the Arade River, where the chimney was the only element that lasts from the former structure.

recovery of these landscapes constitute an opportunity that tends to be lost in time, considering the growing urban pressure that, especially in pleasant and valuable landscapes, had several times led to the disappearance of various industrial infrastructures, some with high heritage value and significant relevance.

The answer to the 'how' is relatively more complex, even if there are several possible answers to this question; each one includes generally several restrictions enabled by the search for profit maximization by private and public sectors. Although it is recognized that the economic and social dimensions of the rehabilitation process cannot be dissociated from the environmental and cultural dimensions, and that the cultural heritage has become a key factor in improving people's surroundings, addressing issues of social cohesion and encouraging economic development, little has been done in order to rehabilitate the industrial buildings and its surrounding landscapes which were often the catalysis to the creation of the urban settlement. In addition to that, design professionals tend to highlight 'how' to manage cultural landscapes (redevelopment proposals, analysis, cultural landscape reports, heritage management plans, and so forth) but not 'why' should we be concerned with historic sites and places or 'what' are the expectations and 'which' are the objectives we seek to accomplish by working with them.

Now that the post-industrial landscape is (more than ever) considered an asset and as a catalyst for urban redevelopment by being a relevant element of the genetic code of the city, according to which rebuilding from degradation should be performed,[32] the answers to these questions should be formulated in order to maximize the benefits that may arise from its (re)development.

Fortunately, the changes introduced in the last years and the creation of normative documents related with the need to protect and rehabilitate the post-industrial heritage contributed to improve design's quality during the past years (Figure 6).

The post-industrial landscape of the left margin to the Arade River

The post-industrial landscape to the left margin of the Arade River is located in the municipality of Lagoa, Algarve, which is characterized by the presence of Mediterranean landscapes. The relevance of the Arade River and its surroundings in the local, regional and national context is attested by numerous archaeological evidences found submerged and around it.[33] In the beginning of the 20th century the implantation of an industrial center in the river margins promoted a significant development of the area, which was enhanced during the First World War.

The whole process was one of great dynamism, which would completely transform the existing landscape. At this time, almost two-thirds of the population worked on industry.[34] Nonetheless, during the late 1960s, the industrial activity collapsed and numerous industrial structures were left abandoned. This post-industrial landscape represents nowadays an historic and cultural environment, in the sense of being a 'system,' which can tell the history of how people have interacted with the landscape that they inherited, during a period of massive socioeconomic change as it was the industrial era.

The land on the left margin to the Arade River is located right above a visible chimney from a former industrial building associated with the fish transformation industry. The unity evidenced by this landscape is notorious, as well as the impact that un-thoughtful de-characterizing interventions might have on it. For this reason, any design solution developed for this landscape should take into consideration the fact that:

- This landscape has to be analyzed as a whole and that there must be analysis of [at least] five principles: (1) the sources of raw materials; (2) the manufacturing facilities; (3) the power sources; (4) the services related with the industrial complex, and (5) the transport network.[35]
- To achieve the expected aims the leading idea has to be clear and precisely defined.
- Cultural landscapes are related with recognized patterns of activity in place and time. 'They are manifestations of human activity in space (...) the essence of what gives character to and defines place.'[36]
- These landscapes should be analyzed using a holistic approach,[37] which includes the ecological reality, as the physical and biologic part of the ecosystems; the historic-cultural reality, as the element that connects people with their place and history and enhances the possibilities of creative practice; and the socioeconomic reality, as the factor that contributes to enhance the community's life quality.

In addition, the design solutions proposed to this landscape should follow these design principles:

- make explicit provision for public participation to ensure that the community can play a role in shaping the (re-)development proposals
- ensure that development responds both to site and context, reinforcing the sense of place and local distinctiveness

Figure 6 | An old post-industrial building located in the city of Tavira, Algarve, which will be converted into a residential area in the next year (image © Luis Loures 2008).

- promote adaptability and diversity through development that can respond to changing social, technological, and economic conditions
- promote the continuity of multifunctional spaces associated with industrial buildings and street frontages, encouraging the utilization of reclaimed spaces and promoting accessibility and local permeability
- reuse previously developed sites or unused buildings and ensure compact development that enhances accessibility, affordability conviviality
- promote legibility through redevelopment that provides recognizable ways, intersections and landmarks to help people find their way around and through relevant vistas, well massed with a clear hierarchy of building scale and spaces
- ensure that design creates places that have variety and choice through a mixture of different uses, functions, and activities
- ensure that all redevelopment of industrial buildings and spaces is of a human scale, well detailed and landscaped
- locate development to protect environmental quality by avoiding areas of ecological and cultural value, ensuring that new development enhances biodiversity and reduces pollution whenever possible.

A planning possibility results from the application of a normative theory based on the aforementioned principles, the reason being that several other planning options may be proposed. However, the main objectives of this study are to present a set of values and principles that should be used in order to reclaim this cultural landscape and to develop a specific plan where those values and principles are applicable.

The design analysis and the search for public consensus[38] related with the redevelopment plan of this landscape presents, at this point, a possible option for further research.

Discussion and conclusions

'The beauty that we see in the vernacular landscape is the image of our common humanity (…).'[39] This quote, by John Brinckerhoff Jackson, specifies perfectly the reason why certain industrial landscapes have an intrinsic value, that should be protected and highlighted in a similar manner as other cultural elements, and considered part of our heritage.

The essential notion behind the need to protect the industrial heritage is that those landmarks are not only connected with history, which is narratological, they are also connected with memory, which according to Moore and Whelan[40] is larger, or something more, than history. So, in order to maintain the uniqueness of a place, its memory must be protected, maintaining the 'genius loci' and the characteristics that bring the past into the present.[41]

In this sense, it is essential to continue studying the city as an evolutionary 'object,' by looking at culture and heritage, without forgetting that the values and the history of the city do not end in the 18th century,[42] they continue right to the 21st century. And, as Dolores Hayden[43] wrote: 'cultural landscapes (including industrial ones) tell us who we are, far more effectively than most architecture or exhibits in museums ever can.' For this reason, the recovery of post-industrial landscapes should be seen as part of larger, ongoing processes of architectural preservation and urban design; it is not confined to the most symbolic factories. It includes, also, all the additional elements and structures associated with the industrial activity.[44] It is imperative that politicians, developers, stakeholders, and planning professionals understand that the maintenance of the urban layout is one of the most important features for the cultural identity of a city, and that the industrial landscape is an important part of it. A place is only a fragment of a cultural space, which was given consciously or subconsciously certain meanings during the course of its creation.

In this way, industrial preservation and reclamation becomes more than the celebration of the past, as important as that is; it becomes part of reconstructing the future. Thus, industrial preservation that connects people, place, and history fosters a sense of place and the power for community renewal. As Stan Allen[45] said, we should realize that 'working with and not against the site, something new is produced by registering the complexity of the given.'

The last decades of the 20th century have been characterized by the protracted decline of industry and industrial landscapes coupled with an explosion of information technology. The progeny of the Industrial Revolution appear in the city as tangible and intangible, social and cultural heritage[46] represented by numerous industrial buildings, which are disappearing from our built environment.

Regarding the presented case study, we may conclude that industrial history has left deep marks on the Arade valley, which frequently provides an explanation for the current situation and points out references for understanding its complexity. The most obvious and urgent problem is certainly the inspection and recording of the state of industrial heritage in this landscape, where external assistance and involvement and the establishment of a formal program could probably facilitate major progress.

Furthermore, given the priceless historical and traditional heritage of the Arade valley and its surrounding landscapes, historical and cultural aspects may become a driving force in the development of the settlements enabling the creation of a cultural center with a very positive image that will attract investors as well as tourists. Nevertheless, caution is called for in this sphere; great care will have to be taken to ensure that the tourism that is developed is 'sustainable,' respecting landscape, environment, and heritage and producing fair benefits for the population.

Industrial reclamation proposals should therefore be a part of an overall urban project—a local development strategy—which requires a broad, integrated approach comprising all urban policy areas and promoting the reconciliation of heritage conservation with social progress and sustainable economic development.

Finally, the development of an increasingly multicultural urban society, emphasizes the need of rising the 'cultural dimension' of the city, where the rehabilitation of the industrial patrimony appears to be an essential contribution to the creation of a shared local identity and hence to the cohesion of the urban society. For this reason, post-industrial landscapes should be viewed as a resource and its recovery as an opportunity to develop new multi-functional landscapes.

[The essay has been published in *WSEAS Transactions on Environment and Development*, Volume 4(9), Page 784-793. (The original name was Industrial Heritage: the past in the future of the city)]

1 Register, R., *Ecocities – Rebuilding Cities in Balance with Nature*, Gabriola Island, New Society Publishers, 2006.

2 Loures, L., Industrial Heritage: a gear to redevelopment. Proceedings of the EURAU 08 – Cultural Landscape, 4th European Symposium on Research in Architecture and Urban Design, January 16–19, 2008, Madrid, Spain, 2008a, pp. 1–7.

3 Fadigas, L., *Fundamentos Ambientais do Ordenamento do Território e da Paisagem (Environmental Fundamentals of Spatial Planning and Landscape)*, Lisboa, Edições Sílabo, Lda, 2007; Storelli, C., 'The city as heritage,' in *Towns and Sustainable Development – Council of Europe, Naturopa*, Belgium, Bietlot – Gilly, 2003.

4 Cabral, F., *Fundamentos da Arquitectura Paisagista (Fundamentals of Landscape Architecture)*. Lisboa: Instituto da Conservação da Natureza (Lisbon: Institute of Nature Conservation), 1993; Carapinha, A., A escrita na Paisagem (Writing in the Landscape). In: *A escrita na paisagem* – Festival de performance e artes da terra (Writing in the landscape – Festival of performance and arts of the earth), Portugal, Colecção B – Mimesis, 1995; Drury, P., 'The historic and cultural dimensions of landscape,' in *Heritage and Sustainable Development – Council of Europe, Naturopa*. Belgium: Bietlot – Gilly, 2002; Magalhães, M., *A Arquitectura Paisagista: morfologia e complexidade (The Landscape Architecture: Morphology and Complexity)*, Lisboa, Editorial Estampa, 2001; Telles, G., O homem perante a paisagem (The man before the landscape), Portugal, Cidade Nova (New City), n°4, 1956, pp. 240–246; Telles, G., Um novo conceito de paisagem global: tradição, confrontos e future (A new concept of global landscape: tradition, confrontations and future) (Jubilação do Professor Ribeiro Telles) Évora: Portugal, Universidade de Évora, 1992.

5 Carr, E., Cultural Landscapes: Theory, Management, Design, Graduate Seminar, Department of Landscape Architecture and Regional Planning, University of Massachusetts, 2003, accessed January 3, 2009, http://www.umass.edu/history/ph/ph_word/Carrsyllabus.doc.

6 Statute of the Council of Europe, 1949, London, accessed September 9, 2007, http://cms.ifa.de/fileadmin/content/informationsforum/kulturabkommen/ec_ets001_en.pdf.

7 ICOMOS, accessed March 6, 2007, http://www.international.icomos.org /home.htm; O'Donnell, P., *The Evolving Concept of Cultural Landscapes as Settings: From the Athens & Venice Charters to the 2004 Combined World Heritage Criteria.* Xi'an, China, ICOMOS 15th General Assembly, 2004.

8 Strike, J., *Architecture in Conservation. Managing development at historic sites*, New York, Digital Printing, 2003.

9 Montaner, J., *A modernidade superada – arquitectura, arte e pensamento do século XX (The Modernity Overcome – Architecture, Art and Thought of the 20th Century)*, Barcelona, Editorial Gustavo Gili, SA, 2001.

10 Aguilar, I., *El orden industrial de la ciudad. Valencia en la segunda mitad del siglo XIX (The Industrial Order of the City. Valencia in the Second Half of the 19th Century)*, València: Diputació de València, 1990.

11 Loures, L. and Panagopoulos, T., Recovering Derelict Industrial Landscapes in Portugal: Past Interventions and Future Perspectives. Proceedings of the *Int. Conf. on Energy, Environment, Ecosystems & Sustainable Development*, July 24–26, 2007 Agios Nicolaos, Crete, Greece, 2007a, pp. 116–121.

12 Ibid.

13 Bergeron, G., *Le patrimoine industriel, un nouveau territoire (Industrial Heritage, a New Territory)*, Paris, Liris, 1996.

14 Tandy, C., *Industria y paisaje (Industry and Landscape)*, Madrid, Instituto de Estudios de Administración Local (Institute of Local Administration Studies), 1979.

15 Meinig, D., *The Interpretation of Ordinary Landscapes: Geographical Essays*, Oxford University Press, Oxford, 1979.

16 Hudson, K., *Industrial Archaelogy. An Introduction*, London, Historical Association, 1964; Hudson, K., *World Industrial Archaelogy*, Cambridge University Press, Cambridge,1979

17 High, S. and Lewis, D., *Corporate* Cornell University Press, Ithaca and London, 2007; Rose, M., *The Post-Modern and the Post-Industrial*, University Press, Cambridge, 1991; Stearns, P., *The Industrial Revolution in World History*, Westview Press, Cambridge, 3rd Ed., 2007.

18 Nizhny Tagil Charter for the Industrial Heritage, TICCIH (The International Committee for the Conservation of the Industrial Heritage), 2003.

19 Venice Charter for the Conservation and Restoration of Monuments and Sites, ICOMOS (Tourism at world heritage cultural sites), 1964.

20 Nizhny Tagil Charter for the Industrial Heritage, TICCIH (The International Committee for the Conservation of the Industrial Heritage), 2003.

21 Alanen, A. and Melnick, R., *Preserving Cultural Landscapes in America*, The Johns Hopkins University Press, Baltimore, 2000.

22 Smith, D., *Amenity and Urban Planning*, Crosby, Lockwood Staples, London, 1974.

23 Aguilar, I., *Arquitectura industrial (Industrial Architecture), Concepto, método y Fuente (Concept, Method and Source)*, Valencia, Diputación de València, 1998.

24 Loures, 2008a, op. cit.; Loures, L., 'Post-Industrial Landscapes as renaissance locus: the case study research methods,' in Brebbia, C., Gospodini, A. and Tiezzi, E. (eds.), 2008. *Sustainable City V*, Southampton, WIT Press, 2008b; Loures L. and Panagopoulos T., 'Sustainable Reclamation of Industrial Areas in Urban Landscapes,' in Kungolas, A, Brebbia, C.A. and Beriatos, E. (eds) *Sustainable Development and Planning III*, Southampton, WIT Press, 2007b, 791–800; Panagopoulos, T. and Loures, L., Reclamation of derelict industrial land in Portugal: greening is not enough. Book of Abstracts of the 10th European Forum on Urban Forestry, 16–19 May, Gelsenkirchen, Germany, 2007, pp. 71–72.

25 Casella, E. and Symonds, J., (eds.), *Industrial Archaeology: Future Directions*, Springer-Verlag, New York, 2005; Stratton, M. and Trinder, M., *Twentieth Century Industrial Archaeology*, London Spon Press, 2000.

26 Kuhl, B., 'Questões Teóricas Relativas à Preservação da Arquitectura Industrial (Theoretical Questions Concerning the Preservation of Industrial Architecture),' in *Revista Desígnio (Design Magazine)*, 1:101–102, 2004.

27 Choay, F., *L'allégorie du patrimoine (The Allegory of Heritage)*, Paris, Seuil, 1992.

28 Nizhny Tagil Charter for the Industrial Heritage, 2003, op. cit.

29 Burley, J. and Loures, L., Conceptual Landscape Design Precedent: Four Historic Sites Revisited, proceedings of the 1st WSEAS International Conference on Landscape Architecture, Algarve, Portugal, June 11–13, 2008, pp. 11–16.

30 European Carter of the Architectural Heritage, 1975, accessed May 16, 2007, http://www.unescobkk.org/fileadmin/user_upload/culture/cultureMain/Instruments/European_Charter.pdf.

31 Selfslagh, B., 'What future for our heritage?' in *Heritage and Sustainable Development – Council of Europe, Naturopa*, Belgium, Bietlot – Gilly, 2002.

32 Bielecki, C., *Gra w miasto (Playing in the City)*, Warszawa, Fundacja Dom Dostepny (Foundation House Available), 1996.

33 Loures, L. and Crawford, P., Finding Public Consensus: The Relevance of Public Participation in Post-industrial Landscape Reclamation, proceedings of the 1st WSEAS International Conference on Landscape Architecture, Algarve, Portugal, June 11–13, 2008, pp. 117–122.

34 Martins, J., *Estudo histórico-monográfico da freguesia de Ferragudo do concelho de Lagoa (Historical-monographic Study of the Parish of Ferragudo of the County of Lagoa)*, Faro, Algarve em Foco Editora, 1990.

35 Palmer, M. and Neaverson, P., *Industrial Archaeology*, in: Rutland Record, n° 11, 1991, pp. 44–45.

36 Francaviglia, R., 'Selling Heritage Landscapes,' in Alanen A. and Melnick, R., (eds.), 2000, *Preserving Cultural Landscapes*, Johns Hopkins University Press, Baltimore, 2000.

37 Cancela d'Abreu, A., Pinto-Correia, T. and Oliveira, R., *Contributos para Identificação e Caracterização da Paisagem em Portugal Continental (Contributions to the Identification and Characterization of the Landscape in Continental Portugal)*. Vol. I a V, Colecção Estudos 10, Lisboa, DGOT-DU, 2004.

38 Loures and Crawford, 2008, op. cit.

39 Jackson, J. B., *Discovering the Vernacular Landscape*, Yale University Press, New Haven and London, 1984.

40 Moore, N. and Whelan, Y., *Heritage, Memory and the Politics of Identity – New Perspectives on the Cultural Landscape*, Hampshire, Ashgate Publishing Limited, 2007.

41 Loures, L., 'A Paisagem Industrial da Foz do Arade (The Industrial Landscape of Foz do Arade),' 'in APAP – Lisboa (eds.) *Congresso 30 ANOS APAP – A Paisagem da Democracia (Congress 30 YEARS APAP – The Landscape of Democracy)*, Santa Maria da Feira: Rainho & Neves, Lda, 2006.

42 Custódio, J., *Cadernos de arqueologia industrial Série I (Industrial Archeology Notebooks Series I)*, Estudos, Lisboa, Associação Portuguesa de Arqueologia Industrial (Portuguese Association of Industrial Archeology), 1991.

43 Hayden, D., 'Forward: In Search of the American Cultural Landscape,' in Alanen A. and Melnick, R., (eds.), 2000. *Preserving Cultural Landscapes*, ohns Hopkins University Press, Baltimore, 2000.

44 Edelblutte, S., 'Industrial Landscapes Between Originality and Banality,' in *TICCIH 2006. XIII International Congress* (Terni / Roma 14–18 September 2006), accessed October 1, 2007, http://www.ticcihcongress2006. net/paper/Paper%20B/EdelblutteText.pdf.

45 Allen, S., *Points and Lines: Diagrams and Projects for the City*, New York, Princeton Architectural Press, 1999.

46 Loures, L., Heuer, T., Horta, D., Silva, S. and Santos, R., Reinventing the Post-industrial Landscape: A Multifunctional Cluster Approach as Redevelopment Strategy, proceedings of the 1st WSEAS International Conference on Landscape Architecture, Algarve, Portugal, June 11–13, 2008, pp. 123–129.

Postindustrial landscapes as locus of urban redevelopment

Luis Loures of the Polytechnic Institute of Portalegre, Portugal

Introduction

Even if the relationship between post-industrial land transformation and sustainable urban design is normally studied through empirical studies with a considerable number of cases due, in part, to the inherent and intangible character of design, in order to understand and evaluate the complex relationship between post-industrial landscape redevelopment and urban design, considering an effective analysis towards the identification of the effective impacts of post-industrial transformation is an urban redevelopment strategy.[1]

Given that, the present study focuses the profound analysis of a single post-industrial redevelopment project, developed 20 years ago, a period when the creation of new and more severe environmental legislation, and the public pressure related with the need to protect the environment, increased the necessity of converting post-industrial sites into multifunctional landscapes. Since the redevelopment project was developed almost two decades ago, it is now possible to ascertain the effective impacts of the project, not only in the site where it was developed, but also on its surroundings. Though it is generally recognized that landscape reclamation at large scale contributes to restore natural processes and functions, regenerating several areas of the city, while creating multifunctional landscapes and promoting sustainable growth,[2] the real impact of post-industrial land transformation approaches is not sufficiently studied in terms of reach, duration, and revenue.

The proposed approach intends to analyze Parque do Tejo e do Trancão, one of the most emblematic post-industrial redevelopment projects developed in Portugal, during the 20th century, the impact of which spanned far beyond the intervention site, reaching significance in terms of urban development that was surely unexpected.

From a derelict industrial site to a premium urban landscape

Contrariwise to the reform and redevelopment strategies that marked the central European countries since the 1990s (Figure 1), post-industrial landscape reclamation as an urban redevelopment strategy was not a common approach in Portugal. In this regard, even if Portugal was a member of the European Community, for more than three decades few landscape reclamation projects have been developed and implemented. This scenario is not difficult to understand since for a long period there was no governmental program for brownfield redevelopment in Portugal,[3] but also because Portugal had not followed the steps of several developed countries in which redevelopment of underused sites and landscapes have been used as a major urban sustainability approach, considering that it allows redevelopment, preventing the need for green space consumption.[4]

Figures 1 | An old post-industrial building located in the city of Duisburg, Germany, which was converted into park area (image © Luis Loures 2009)

However, even if there was only in recent years that part of the Portuguese stakeholders and decision makers that changed their view and attitudes toward older industrial infrastructures and sites—initially considered blighted elements in an urban area, derelict, undesirable or redundant—in 1998 Portugal implemented one of the most emblematic and holistic approaches towards post-industrial land transformation, the redevelopment project developed for the International Exhibition—Expo '98. As mentioned, the analysis of this project constitutes an interesting opportunity since the impact of the project, spanned far beyond the intervention area, reaching unprecedented levels in terms of urban growth and city development.

Brief description for Parque do Tejo e do Trancão

Located in the oriental part of Lisbon, in an area marked by abandonment and environmental degradation at the confluence of two rivers from which it takes its name, Parque do Tejo e do Trancão is one of the most emblematic examples of post-industrial landscape transformation projects realized in Portugal. The 222-acre (90-hectare) urban park was developed by PROAP Estudos e Projectos de Arquitectura Paisagista, Lda. together with Hargreaves Associates (consultant).

Before being a park, the site was composed by several industrial structures like a landfill, scraps, a sewage treatment plant, and many obsolete industrial buildings.[5] The construction of the railway line in the middle of the 19th century and the location of the port of Lisbon were determinant to the evolution of the study area as an industrial landscape. After the set-up of some lighter industries (a saw mill, a flourmill, a calico factory, and a pottery factory) the 1940s witnessed the establishment of the first oil companies and the construction of an abattoir and landfill.[6]

Together, these industrial facilities contributed in increasing the contamination levels of this landscape, which before the intervention was considered one of the most polluted areas of Lisbon.[7] This scenario—high indexes of contamination and visible degradation—coupled with the proximity of the Natural Reserve of the estuary of Tagus and the intention to develop the Expo '98 constituted decisive arguments for the intervention in this specific area. Still, as mentioned by Blokhuis and Schaefer,[8] the basis of this project was the long-existing need to redevelop the eastern part of Lisbon(Figure 2), an area that showed lack of occupancy and obsolescence for a long time.

However, even if, as mentioned by Castel-Branco,[9] 'those who visited the area at the time it was dominated by containers and giant oil tanks, and rubbish tips will never forget the anguish caused by feelings split between the quality of the views by the Tagus and the deterioration of the whole site,' the quality hidden by this scenario was evident and the potential of the area to be transformed into an urban/environmental park, combining human activity, technological infrastructures and environmental values and education[10] was undeniable.

In this regard, acknowledging the innumerous benefits that the project would bring not only for the area but to the city as a whole, the executive commission of Expo '98 proposed the development of the Parque do Tejo e do Trancão, launching and 'invited only' international call for tenders in 1994, considering that 'once the

Figures 2 | Aerial view of Parque do Tejo e do Trancão, Lisbon, Portugal (image © Luis Loures 2016)

concept and the purpose of the project had been developed, there was no problem of who would be given the responsibility for the design.'[11] Given the complexity of the task, the quality of the designers enrolled in the development of other major elements—for example, the Oriente Station by Santiago Calatrava's, the Portuguese Pavilion by Siza Vieira, among others—and the limitations set by schedule, the invited international competition was considered the best approach.[12]

In this regard, from a group of firms that had previously won similar competitions, seven candidates were invited (three Portuguese, two North Americans, a German, and a British one).[13] 'The program included a requirement for a local partner to facilitate implementation of the master plan. This requirement was also included with the intent of providing additional public stimulation as well as greater learning experience.'[14]

The invited firms were required to solve the general layout of the park with the existing infrastructures, such as the landfill, while refereeing to the overall theme of the Expo '98 (the oceans), responding to the treatment of the five elements of the program: areas for leisure sports; areas for competitive sports; areas for cultural activities; areas for passive activities and areas for environmental and artistic education).[15]

Considering the selection of the best proposal, the jury developed an evaluation method based on five criteria: creativity, layout of the park, integration of uses, feasibility of the solution and capacity of the team to complete the work.[16] In this regard, the jury selected the proposal submitted by the team formed between the North American firm Hargreaves Associates and the Portuguese firm PROAP,[17] represented namely by George Hargreaves and João Nunes.

After the competition, there was a period in which it was not clear if the promoters were willing to develop the project, however, by the end of 1995, the Expo '98 administration decided to attribute the develop of the first phase of the project to PROAP that required cooperation from Hargreaves Associates at the conceptual level.[18]

Considering the connectivity between the Park and Expo '98, the first phase corresponded to the construction of the south side of the park (24 hectares), which was accomplished during 1997. In fact, considering the framework under which the park was developed, the implementation had to be accomplished by phases (three), once the financing for its construction was sourced, which depended on the sales of the urban components of 'Vila Expo.' The other two development phases were planned to be implemented gradually after the exposition.

With approximated 222 acres (90 hectares), the park would be linked both physically and thematically with the park of Expo '98, which covering an area of 840 acres (340 hectares) was mentioned to be a self-contained urban center, with residences, stores, transportational infrastructure, parking facilities, and parks, able to re-establishing the link between the city and the river, while contributing to define the city as a whole.[19] 'The plan called for the creation of an attractive public green area, equipped for a new leisure culture that would create demand for the urban real-estate development.'[20] In this sense, while regenerating a disturbed environment, the proposed design would transform the site into a new attraction within the greater Lisbon area.[21]

Significance and uniqueness of the project

This land transformation project was very significant, not only because it promoted the redevelopment of a highly polluted post-industrial landscape, but also because it created a precedent for the transformation of similar areas around the country. In fact, the redevelopment of this area functioned as a catalyst for urban development, influencing directly the development of the surrounding landscapes, and contributing to increase the attractiveness, and consequently the land value of this part of the city.

Additionally, this redevelopment constituted an example of how municipalities can work together towards common goals, and how it is possible to transform derelict sites into attractive landscapes, filling them with a new spirit and a new vitality, while increasing accessibility, services and public infrastructures, and citizens' quality of life.

However, even if it was acknowledged that the project would bring many benefits to the city—once it implicated the decontamination of the site and the creation of attractive conditions, through the construction of high-quality multifunctional space where citizens could enjoy the riverfront area—not even the most optimistic previsions imagined the range of the impact this space would have in the city.

Twelve years after conclusion, this area is one of the most used public spaces of the metropolitan area of Lisbon. In fact, the achievements of this redevelopment project where far higher than expected, as it is possible to confirm in the idea expressed by Castel-Branco[22] according to which even if 'the potential of the river was exciting (...) the sight and smell of the areas further inland disheartened even the most optimistic spirit.' Conversely, the proposed design was not only able to create of a new public space[23] emphasizing the potential of the proximity to the river, but also to influence urban growth, redirecting the expansion of the city and re-establishing the relationship between city and river.

In this regard, Expo '98 and consequently Parque do Tejo e do Trancão have been considered best-practice examples towards environmental and urban renewal,[24] given that their construction highlighted the advantages of building a large public space respecting ecological principles that are socially responsible and feasible from the economic point of view. Additionally, the proposed design contributed to the 'public promotion of the field of landscape architecture, a fledgling profession in Portugal.'[25]

Redevelopment objectives

Following the main objectives defined in the urban development project established by Parque EXPO, SA (that is, environmental requalification and urban revitalization), the proposed project aimed to develop a new urban centrality with educational, cultural, and leisure activities capable of attracting millions of people yearly, while creating jobs, promoting wealth, and improving life's quality.[26]

In this regard, the introduction of citizens' needs, identified through extensive studies regarding potential commercial and residential occupants of this area, within the redevelopment strategy proposed for the area was a significant objective of the project.[27] Still, as stressed out by Vaccarino,[28] the proposed design did not mean to find a final form to the park to establish rigorous rules of composition, but to create a space that might function as a catalyst for redevelopment considering both economic, environmental, and social issues. Additionally, the envisioned project aimed to create a spatial organization that offered great scenic, visual, and sensorial diversity, sustained by a structure that reflects the coherence and formal unity in the perception of the broad intervention (PROAP, 2008).

Nevertheless, the objectives inherent to the park were somehow connected with solving the problems inherent to the site, identified by Walker and Castel-Branco,[29] which were:

- the creation of a vast green area adjoining the river
- increasing the value of the residential complexes proposed for the redevelopment area
- correcting existing drainage systems contaminating adjacent areas and challenging other parties responsible to stop pollution of the Trancão
- increasing public awareness through a precedent project for high-quality environmental rehabilitation that would serve the Lisbon metropolitan area
- to define the boundaries of the project and of the temporary and permanent building sites under way so as to minimize any negative impact on the park in the future
- creation of an experimental area to define the criteria for the selection of the vegetation for Expo '98, through determination of the resistance and adaptability of the various species to this environment.

Considering the aforementioned objectives and the proposed design strategy, the park results somehow formed a synthesis between traditional and recreational facilities for environmental education, considering the development of a multifunctional program.[30] In fact, the proposed design enabled the transformation of the former derelict site into a multifunctional landscape considering at the same level a place for leisure and recreation and environmental education.

Figure 3 | Parque do Tejo e do Trancão, circulation and vegetation diagram. Developed by author. Used sources: Google Maps (2010) and PROAP (2008).

Implemented program and design strategy

The conceptual solution proposed by PROAP and Hargreaves Associates analyzed the problems of the place, converting them into opportunities for artistic expression. Besides the ecological and functional sense of the proposed structure, the solution served the parallel intention of establishing a spatial organization to translate a coherence and formal unit reading the group. Following several land restoration measures applied in order to improve the environmental condition of the site, attention was given to shape the ecological and landscape structures considering wetland and habitat restoration and enlargement. Scenic values were also essential in the development of the concept of the park, supported by the creation of visual corridors and by the establishment of elevated platforms to observe the exceptional views on the river and the marsh.[31]

Though the proposed design would have to follow several recommendations regarding soil and water cleanup and remediation, the maintenance of the memory of the site was also considered a relevant aspect. In this regard, while some of the existing infrastructures were demolished (the storage tanks, the abattoir and the industrial front on the right margin of the Trancão River) others were recovered and transformed both for the Expo and for the city (the Olivais Dock, the Saponata jetty, the cracking plant tower, the rubbish tip, and the sewage farm).[32] Besides the aforementioned infrastructures, which somehow constituted the memory of the site, designers needed to also account for the integration of the existing landfill and of the largest of the three sewage treatment plants serving Lisbon in the proposed design.

Even if the inclusion of the landfill (which ended up being used by the designers as a way of telling the visitors a little about the history of the site) in the design did not require any special consideration besides the collection or elimination of the natural gas originated from the decomposition of the detritus of the caped landfill,[33] the sewage treatment plant, due to bad compatibility with some of the leisure and recreation activities programmed to the park, required a number of specific interventions regarding re-adaptation of the former plant to the new use of the surrounding landscape.[34]

After all the technical constraints of the site were resolved, the design team sought to develop the structure of the park through the creation of a unifying topography, which would be used as a significant factor in the differentiation of a series of spaces and functions.[35] In fact, the evident sculptural modeling of soil and the presence of abstract structures converted this project from a regular landscape architecture intervention to a land art one.[36] However, even if the proposed design seemed to be focused in land art considerations, it resulted from the combination between ecological, biophysical, and aesthetic considerations; that is, between the need to promote the rehabilitation of the site (considering both soil and water), the need to consider the characteristic of the site, and the will to develop a land art project.

In this scenario, revisiting the ideas put forward by Robert Smithson in his land art earthworks as the 'Spiral Jetty' or the 'Amarillo Ramp,' the design team envisioned a land model in which a new sequence of sharp aerodynamic ridges would emerge over the entire surface of the park, like dunes fashioned by the wind.[37] This proposal was both an attempt to symbolize the overall concept of the park (the oceans) and tackle the previous flat arrangement of the site, giving a recognizable aesthetic and symbolic quality to the new park, while creating a dynamic design with places to sit, rest, and play (sheltered from the wind) and places to enjoy the great vistas from the site to the river and to the city.

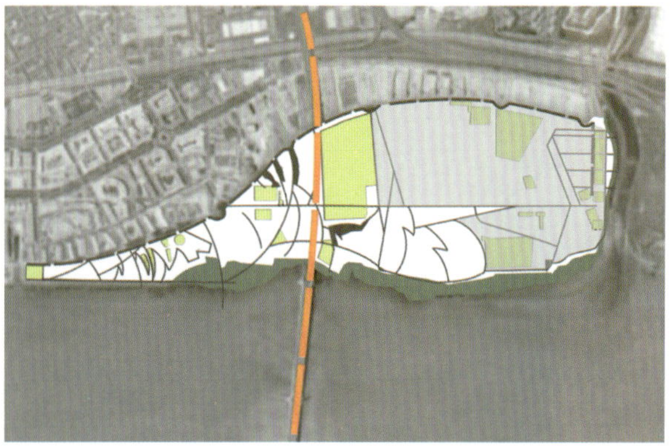

Figure 4 | Parque do Tejo e do Trancão, programmatic areas.
Developed by author. Used sources: Google Maps (2010); and PROAP (2008).

Still, the way in which the sequence of dunes evolves throughout the park (oriented according to sun exposure and dominant winds) revealed that the design was not simply an aesthetic composition.[38] Additionally, the proposed topography was accentuated both by the selected plant cover and the envisioned circulation system (Figure 3).

According to PROAP,[39] plantations were defined in order to match the envisioned ecological situations, anticipating, image wise, the results that would eventually be establish throughout time. Considering the proposed topography, different species were selected for the different biotopes. Similarly, the proposed path system, delineated according to a hierarchical network, defined a functional structure for the park, throughout which several uses, functions, and programmatic areas were located, assuring also that park visitors might usufruct from a close contact with one of the main assets of the site, the river.[40]

Another important component considered in the proposed design was the program. Bearing in mind the development of a multifunctional and flexible park, the design promoted a wide range of activities associated to numerous formal and informal spaces, organized throughout the park, which would provide varied social, cultural and physical activities,[41] namely: the environmental education center (which aims to help visitors to understand the various stages of recycling and how the systems work), the equestrian center, the arboretum, the park of the arts, the Trancão riverside area (with a plaza and a promenade with shops, cafés, and restaurants), the sport competition areas (including a golf center, several tennis courts, and informal lawns for active sports such as soccer and rugby), the sport recreation areas (including tracks for bicycles, docks for fishing, ramps for small boats, and so forth), the informal playing fields and event areas (considering the possibility of housing several cultural activities as exhibitions, theatre, and any other cultural event), the south square, the recreational meadows, the new marsh areas, the marginal footpaths and piers, and the parking area, among others (Figure 4).

As previously mentioned, the implementation of the park was planned to be accomplished in three different phases corresponding respectively to the south park, the central park, and the north park, the conclusion of which was foreseen for 2010.[42]

At the time of writing, the third phase was not implemented yet, due to several reasons, the developed proposal offered users the opportunity to witness the complex relationship between nature and technology, allowing them to get involved in issues related to pollution, recycling, sustainability and ecology, and to benefit from the amazing conjugation of land, water, and sky.

Lessons learned, project critics, and limitations

The presented project highlights the fact that by promoting changes in land-use patterns and land values and by developing territorial specialization and new infrastructure, it is possible to turn derelict landscapes (as the one in which the Parque do Tejo e do Trancão was created) into increasingly attractive sites.[43]

Moreover, the creation of the park was essential to convert one of the most polluted and repulsive areas of the city into one of the most attractive areas. This fact is even more relevant when analyzed under the lamps of the former characteristics of the site, which according to Andresen[44] was '(. . .) a place of chaos, a scary place.'

However, even if the Parque do Tejo e do Trancão project was considered a '(. . .) pilot project in Portugal, one in which the population was to witness the transformation of a run-down area of rubbish and urban waste into a living green area,'[45] it presented some limitations since the beginning.

One of the most evident ones is related to the fact that the international competition was an 'invited only competition.' In fact, this option, although anchored in the premise that the schedule was too tight, was somehow limitative, given that it did not offer equal opportunities for everybody. Actually, a well-structured selection method could have solved this issue, especially when, according to Walker and Castel-Branco,[46] the call for tenders for the Parque do Tejo e do Trancão used the international competition for Parc de la Villete (a totally opened competition in which 470 designers or design teams participated)[47] as a model.

The other is connected to the used approach, which, according to Andresen,[48] considering the localization of the site between the municipalities of Lisbon and Loures (an area characterized not only by environmental but also by social problems) was 'too much influenced by the arts, and too little by ecology.'[49]

Final considerations

The analyzed case study highlighted the fact that the incorporation of people's preferences and needs in post-industrial landscape redevelopment might constitute a safeguard to achieve success and to develop a sense of belonging, reinforcing project acceptability, especially by local citizens. This fact is particularly relevant in countries, as is the case of Portugal, in which post-industrial landscape are commonly experienced negatively as fragmented and incoherent because it is difficult to conceive a legible whole. The analyzed project constitutes a representative example of post-industrial landscape reclamation project that enables a sense of spatial enlargement, with high degree of complexity and with varied ecological, economical, social, and cultural benefits.

Moreover, the implementation of this redevelopment proposal had a positive cost-benefit relation, not only because it enabled the rehabilitation of a significant landscape with high environmental value, but also because it contributed to reduce urban sprawl, allowing urban development by reusing derelict spaces instead of consuming new ones.

This research highlighted that urban parks constitute a feasible use for large post-industrial sites, which contributes to strengthen the overall quality of the urban spaces in which they are inserted. Furthermore, it enabled us to conclude that the relevance and the social acceptability of a certain project should never be underestimated and that urban nature, especially urban parks, is extremely important for citizens' quality of life, contributing to increase land value and fostering sustainable city development.

Nevertheless, though fostering sustainable city development, there is still a long way to go for this type of intervention to achieve a significant impact on urban sustainability, as the private sector prefers the more cost-effective alternative of building new facilities than to renovate existing, abandoned, and degraded ones.[50] Unfortunately, reclamation projects, as the one presented in this section, continue to be associated with parallel goals that are not directly related with their positive impact on landscape and urban sustainability. Moreover, the current practice of post-industrial landscape transformation is mainly site-specific and driven by economic development motivations, not offering the full potential for sustainable reuse and revitalization beyond property lines.[51]

(The essay was presented on the International Congress on Interdisciplinarity in Social and Human Sciences at the University of Algarve.)

1 Loures, L. and Burley, J., 'Post-industrial Land Transformation – an approach to socio-cultural aspects as catalysts for urban redevelopment,' in *Urban Planning*, INTech, 2011, pp. 223–246.

2 Collins, T., 'Art and Ecological Restoration in Cities,' in Hall, T. and Miles, M. (eds.), *Urban Futures*, Routledge, London, 2001; Lootsma, B., Biomorphic Intelligence and Landscape Urbanism, *Topos*, 40, 2002, pp. 10–25.

3 CABERNET, 2003, State of the Art Portugal (1st edition), accessed February 18, 2016, http://www.cabernet.org.uk.

4 Loures and Burley, 2011, op. cit.

5 Craveiro, M., (Des)integração da EXPO '98 na Cidade (The Integration of EXPO '98 in the City), *Arquitectura e Vida* (*Architecture and Life*), 34: 16, 2003; PROAP – Estudos e Projectos de Arquitectura Paisagista (PROAP – Landscape Architecture Studies and Projects), 2008, *Parque do Tejo e do Trancão* (*Tagus and Trancão Park*), accessed May 18, 2008, http://www.proap.pt/site/L_por/projectos/parque_tejo_d.html.

6 Castel-Branco, C., 'The Land and the Vision,' in Commissariat of the 1998 Lisbon world Exposition (eds.), *The Green Book*, Fernandes e Terceiro, Lda., Lisboa, 1998b, pp. 31–41.

7 Castel-Branco, C., 'The Expo '98 Land in 1993,' in Commissariat of the 1998 Lisbon world Exposition (eds.), *The Green Book*, Fernandes e Terceiro, Lda., Lisboa, 1998a, pp. 15–30.

8 Blokhuis, E. and Schaefer, W., 'A sustainable approach for industrial area redevelopment in the Netherlands,' in Kungolas, A., Brebbia, C. and Beriatos, E. (eds.), *Sustainable Development and Planning III*, WIT Press, Southampton, 2007, pp. 81–94.

9 Castel-Branco, 1998b, op. cit.

10 Comeau, K, 2009, 'Expo '98 and Parc do Tejo e Trancao, Lisbon, Portugal (Expo '98 and Tagus and Trancão Park, Lisbon, Portugal),' accessed May 18, 2009, http://courses.umass.edu/latour/Spain/kcomeau/index.html.

11 Vaccarino, R., I Paesaggi ri-fatti / Lungo l'estuario, Lotus, 87: 100–101, 1995.

12 Ibid.

13 Ibid.

14 Ibid.

15 Ibid.

16 Ibid.

17 Mateus, A., *George Hargreaves e a Nova Arquitectura Paisagista Americana* (*George Hargreaves and the New American Landscape Architecture*). *Graduation Final Report*, Instituto Superior de Agronomia – Universidade Técnica de Lisboa (Higher Institute of Agronomy – Technical University of Lisbon), Lisboa, 1999.

18 Ibid.

19 Comeau, 2009, op. cit.

20 Vaccarino, 1995, op. cit.

21 Comeau, 2009, op. cit.

22 Castel-Branco, 1998b, op. cit.

23 Blokhuis and Schaefer, 2007, op. cit.

24 Ibid.

25 Castel-Branco, 1998a, op. cit.

26 Craveiro, 2003, op. cit.

27 Comeau, 2009, op. cit.

28 Spagna, R., 2002, *Parque do Tejo e Trancão* (*Tagus and Trancão Park*), accessed March 12, 2009, http://www.ocs.polito.it/biblioteca/giardini/tejo_s.htm.

29 Vaccarino, 1995, op. cit.

30 Lambertini, A., I Parchi-margine: Una Specie di Parco per i Paesaggi Urbani Contemporanei (The Parks-Margin: A Park Species for Contemporary Urban Landscapes), *Ri-Vista Ricerche per la progettazione del paesaggio* (*Re-Vista Landscape Design Research*), 6: 32–43, 2006.

31 Nunes, J. and Martins, R., *Parque do Tejo – PROAP/Hargreaves Associates* (*Tagus Park – PROAP/Hargreaves Associates*, Parque das Nações (Nations' park), Lisboa, 2000.

32 Castel-Branco, 1998b, op. cit.

33 PROAP, 2008, op. cit.

34 Comeau, 2009, op. cit.; PROAP, ibid.

35 PROAP, ibid.

36 Lambertini, 2006, op. cit.; PROAP, ibid.

37 PROAP, ibid.

38 Lambertini, 2006, op. cit.; PROAP, ibid.

39 Nunes and Martins, 2000, op. cit.

40 Comeau, 2009, op. cit.; Mateus, 1999, op. cit.

41 Loures, L., Planning and Design in Postinsdustrial Land Transformation: East bank Arade river, Lagoa – case study, Universidade do Algarve, Faro, Portugal – Ph.D Dissertation, 2011; Nunes and Martins, 2000, op. cit.; PROAP, 2008, op. cit.; Vaccarino, 1995, op. cit.

42 Vaccarino, 1995, ibid.

43 Ibid.

44 Andresen, T., in Commissariat of the 1998 Lisbon world Exposition (eds.), *The Green Book*, Fernandes e Terceiro, Lda, Lisboa, 1998a, pp. 15–30.

45 Vaccarino, 1995, op. cit.

46 Walker, V. and Castel-Branco, C. 'The International Call for Tenders for the Tagus and Trancão Park,' in Commissariat of the 1998 Lisbon world Exposition (eds.), *The Green Book*, Fernandes e Terceiro, Lda., Lisboa, 1998, pp. 45–69.

47 Chaslin, F., Bernard Tschumi: Parc de la Villette (Bernard Tschumi: The Villette Park), Paris, *Domus*, 1999, 817: 8–17.

48 Andresen, T., Prof.ª Teresa Andresen, in Castelo, S., 1998. *Arquitectura Paisagista e Land Art – Appendix* (Landscape Architecture and Land Art – Appendix), Graduation Final Report, Instituto Superior de Agronomia – Universidade Técnica de Lisboa, Lisboa, 1998b.

49 Ibid.

50 Blokhuis and Schaefer, 2007, op. cit.; Loures, L., A *Paisagem Industrial da Foz do Arade* (*The Industrial Landscape of Foz do Arade*), Congresso 30 ANOS APAP – A Paisagem da Democracia (Congress 30 Years APAP – The Landscape of Democracy), Outubro 12–14, 2006, Porto, Portugal. 2006, pp. 219–226.

51 Loures and Burley, 2011, op. cit.

Case studies

Rigot Stalars

Rehabilitation and extension of the old mill

Location-Dunkirk, France
Architect-Coldefy & Associates Architects Urban Planners
Area-9429 square feet (876 square meters)
Completion-2014
Photography-Julien LANOO
Client-Work & Co, Piet Colruyt (via SCI Social Square)

Site plan

01 Parking
02 Co-working offices
03 Nursery
04 Snack
05 Seminar room
06 Terrace
07 Parking entrance
08 Main entrance

The site is located in a historic industrial park along the railroad tracks at the entrance of the city of Dunkirk, just a stone's throw from the main railway station. It lies within the framework of a strategic urban zone in full transformation. Originally a cotton mill founded in 1928, the building itself had been abandoned and empty for years.

It was schemed to rehabilitate the building to house a contemporary co-working environment replete with workrooms, a conference space, a micro-nursery, and a cafeteria. The four functions needed to operate independently but enjoy a common entrance. The principal objective of the project was to preserve the major architectural qualities of the building and to transform this space to fulfil new functions while respecting the square opposite as a social hub for the neighborhood. The adjoining water-garden also had a similar impact on the design project because it was part of the visible panorama viewed from the bay windows of the cafeteria.

To give this symbolic building back its strength, the project fully preserved the existing as it was and implanted at its base two new ground-floor extensions that house the cafeteria and the nursery.

Grafting onto the existing, the extension opened the building up to the city through the large cafeteria windows and by extending the hardscape plaza to connect with the new urban park. These constructions on the ground level do not conceal the old mill overlooking them, but actually contribute to highlight the original structure.

In the original building, the contrast between the raw original materials and the new ones, which are fresher and more refined, creates rather a striking contrast. The original outlines were entirely preserved in order to obtain the same surface on the plateau as it was in the old times of its manufacturing days: the elevator took over the place once occupied by an industrial lift, while the staircase was conserved. To accommodate the entire program, two additional concrete slabs were delicately inserted within the existing structure, forming the first floor and third floor level. New openings in the thick brick walls were created within an existing regularity while the outside metal staircase brought out the singular façades.

Materials used in the building's conversion were carefully selected, and the glass and metal blend perfectly with the original red brick. A calming, peaceful ambiance was created, thanks to the clear tint of wood with which the extensions were built.

The furniture was designed and custom-tailored: office tables, the reception desk, and the cafeteria bar were made from materials recycled from the building's construction and several pieces of furniture were upholstered with jute fabric, thus reinforcing the continuity of the idea of renewal and heritage preservation.

01

01- The entrance

work&co
kids&co
coffee

02- Before the rehabilitation
03- The front façade
04- The common space
05- The offices
06- The entrance patio

02 | 04 05
03 | 06

Conceptual sketches

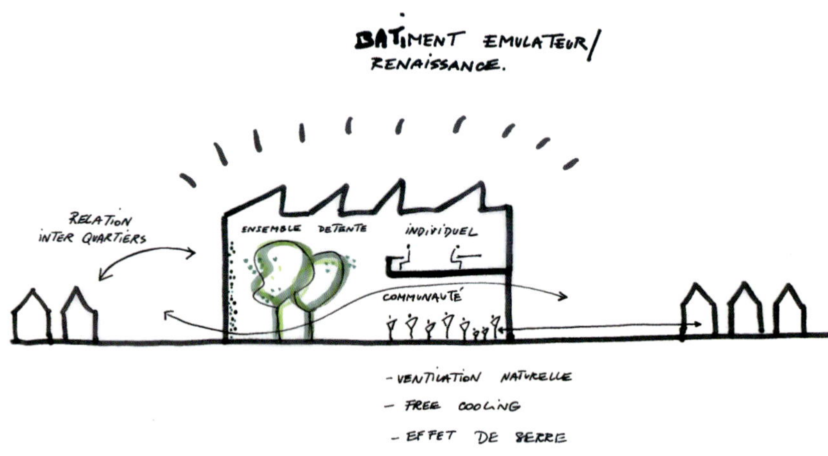

The provision of a generous new plaza, the addition of new elements and the careful insertion of new floors and openings allowed for a well-preserved mill to accommodate an interesting combination of new uses.

07, 08- Offices and meeting room
09- Micro-nursery
10- Caféteria

07|09
08|10

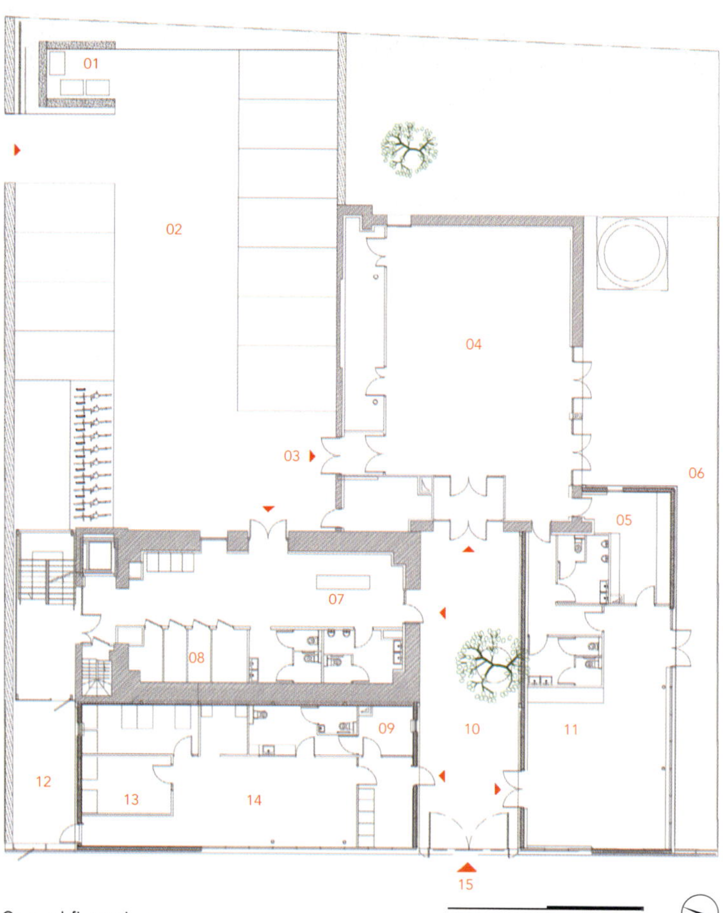

Ground floor plan

01 Garbage room
02 Parking
03 Access for deliveries
04 Community room
05 Kitchen
06 Terrace
07 Reception
08 Cellars to rent
09 Office
10 Patio
11 Caféteria
12 Children's garden
13 Dormitories
14 Playroom
15 Main entrance

Octapharma Brewery

Headquarter offices shining historic splendor

Location-Stockholm, Sweden
Architect-Joliark
Interior-White
Area-79,652 square feet (7400 square meters)
Completion-2015
Photography-Joliark
Client-Octapharma

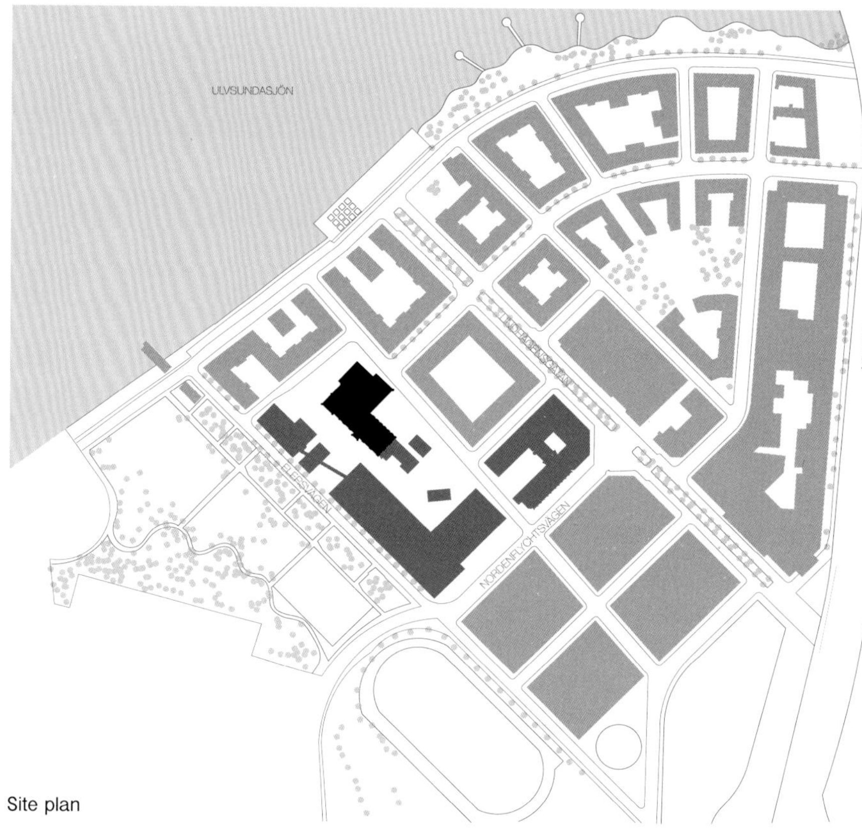

Site plan

The project was a result of Octapharma's rapid expansion and need for increased capacity, including office spaces, scientific laboratories, as well as factory and production spaces within its premises in western Kungsholmen. The former brewery, together with its surrounding facilities, was bought from Index Estate by Octapharma in 2009. Since then, the company strove to improve logistics onsite.

Built in the early 1890s, the brewery peaked during a 15-year period but soon faced economic difficulties and bankruptcy. The building was then used in various ways, slowly falling into disrepair due to neglect before, recently, being protected for its historic and cultural importance—it is currently a listed building. Octapharma made the decision to have the building transformed for administrative purposes, relocating its Nordic headquarters. In addition to offices, the transformed building now houses functions such as meeting spaces, conference rooms, changing rooms, storage, and a large canteen.

Together with experts in the field and in cooperation with Stockholm's planning authorities as well as the Stockholm City Museum, the architect carefully transformed the building for its new purposes. The façade went through a total renovation, assessing each brick, with a high level of precision.

The white interior design brings out the story from a time when beer was brewed in large copper vessels, and puts it in living contrast to the modern bright offices. New functions and needs were elegantly and tastefully incorporated into the old buildings' powerful volumes, with a system of exposed wooden beams and plastered stonewalls. Materials and furniture were carefully chosen to harmonize with the character of the building, as well as the core of Octapharma, which is Swedish, family-owned, and global.

Copper, limestone, and pine floors, combined with timeless furniture classics, created a calm and solid whole. Everything was thoroughly designed and elaborately selected, from the embossed leather desk pads to the copper-clad boxes that function as meeting rooms. In the Bistro, perhaps the brewery's most beautiful room, one sits down under the tree crowns of wooden beams to enjoy locally-produced and carefully-cooked meals. Octapharma's new Nordic headquarters in the brewery meet the global business standards, with a focus on life, people, and its Swedish roots.

Throughout the process, the project was gradually adapted and evolved as the understanding and knowledge of the building's cultural importance grew. With the former brewery now renovated and inhabited, the building has once again regained its original splendor.

01

01- Perhaps the most striking feature, seen from outside, is the glazed north-facing façade

02 | 03
04 05 06

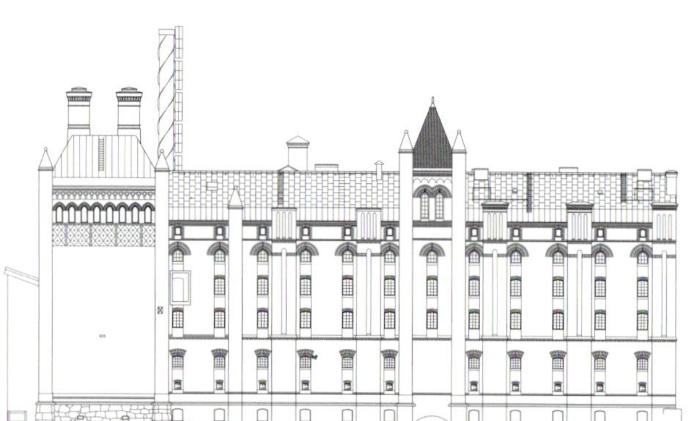

Western façade

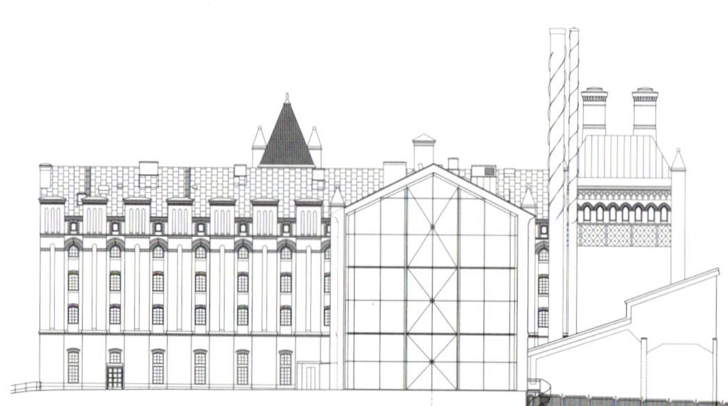

Northern façade

02- The building, with its chimney and glazed façade, marks the end of the street
03- Historic traces are kept within the building as a reminder of its original use
04, 05- Office spaces divided by central meeting rooms—some in white, some in shiny copper
06- Large numbers, made in copper, guide visitors throughout the building

Sleek new white interiors contrast beautifully with the richness of the thick wooden structure of this old brewery, which is admirably reinforced by careful detailing and precise workmanship.

07 09 10 11
08 12

07- Ongoing construction work in an interior space
08 Inside the north-facing office space—the original wood construction has been kept
09, 10, 11- Exposed original columns, in various shapes, are a key feature in the project , which contrast against the white, modern interior walls
12- An image from the cantina, where workers have their lunch

Reconstruction of the Shanghai Hobnail Factory

An architect's working studio

Location-Shanghai, China
Architect-Original Design Studio, Tongji Architectural Design (Group) Co., Ltd
Area-10,764 square feet (1000 square meters)
Completion-2013
Photography-GAO Wenzhong, Wang Yuan
Client-UNIECO SOC. COOP.

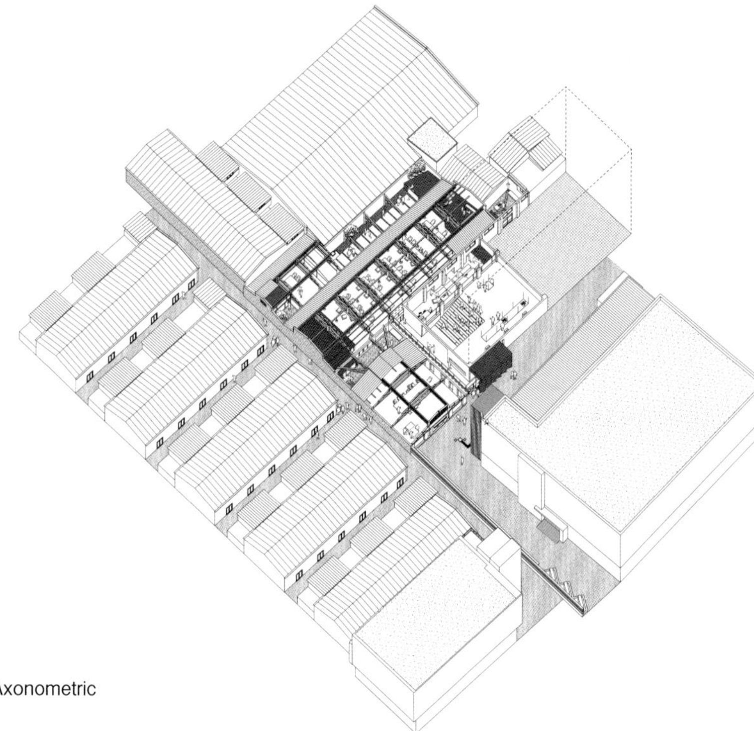

Axonometric

At No. 640 Kunming Road, the architects found the site for the Original Design Studio—an old factory built in 1937.

The lighting mode of high windows that the existing factory building used indicated that the scale of the original factory building may have been two-span larger than the existing one, created through the last expansion—part of the continuous brick-wood structure had been dismantled and replaced by a new three-story factory building. The original continuous-span building had no inner courtyard, but as some portions of its roof collapsed, three courtyards were formed. Additionally, the moss-covered black brick wall had been retained since it is also shared by factory buildings in nearby factory district.

The architects considered the transformation of these factory buildings as a process of exploring the site and separating the true from the false. Old factory buildings carry a historical memory of the industrial development of Shanghai; their unique urban fabrics and the industrial imprint reserved are of great value. Those three courtyards that formed during the development of history provided opportunities for people to get close to nature. Through opening to the courtyards, enclosed factory buildings were converted into bright and open office spaces, while through opening towards the black brick walls, hidden historical fractures in the site were revealed.

Moreover, seven trusses were unfolded continuously from the east to the west, giving this main ribbon-like space a sense of sequence and continuity. The architect restored a large space by removing the light partition wall added in the previous reconstructions, and inserted functional areas as partial elements, which not only have a close connection with the space and structure of the original factory buildings but create a sharp contrast by using materials that differ from that of the original buildings.

The reconstruction itself became a sort of archaeological excavation, which dug out the traces of the building's and city's growth, as well uncovering a sense of place and identity for the users. From the old factory building to the studio, the adaptive re-use avoided a series of modeled spaces, while the dissimilative spaces made it possible for people to gain a renewed awareness of the possibility of space. Functions are no longer the only criterion for defining a region; blurring boundaries and diffusing experiences promote the emergence of various activities. The reconstruction was also a process of organization and correction, which brought new possibilities. Unpredictable problems become a great source of inspirations, making design a system that allows correction and constant self-balance.

This building shows the imprinting of many years, and a continued sense of what happened in the past, what is happening, and what is about to happen, permeates this space.

01

01- The front façade

02 03 04 05

Sections

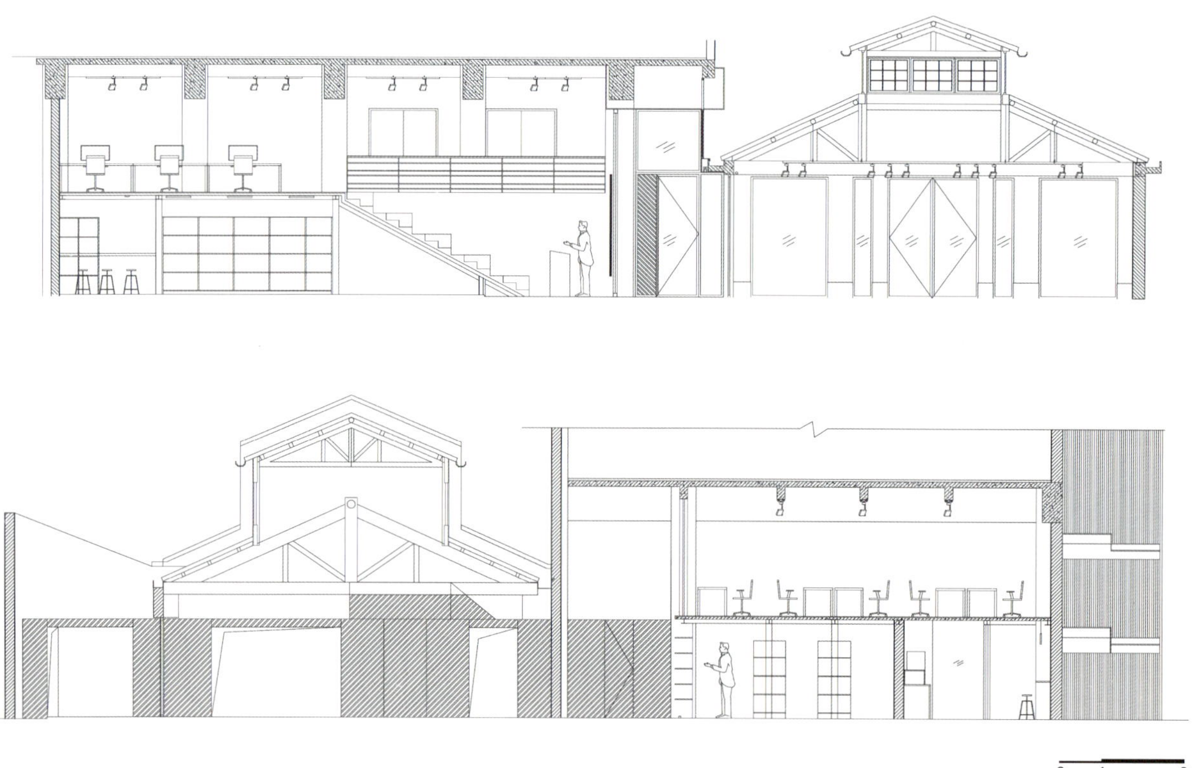

02- Before renovation
03- After renovation
04- Timber roof truss
05- View of rending yard from the timber roof truss

Axonometric function analysis

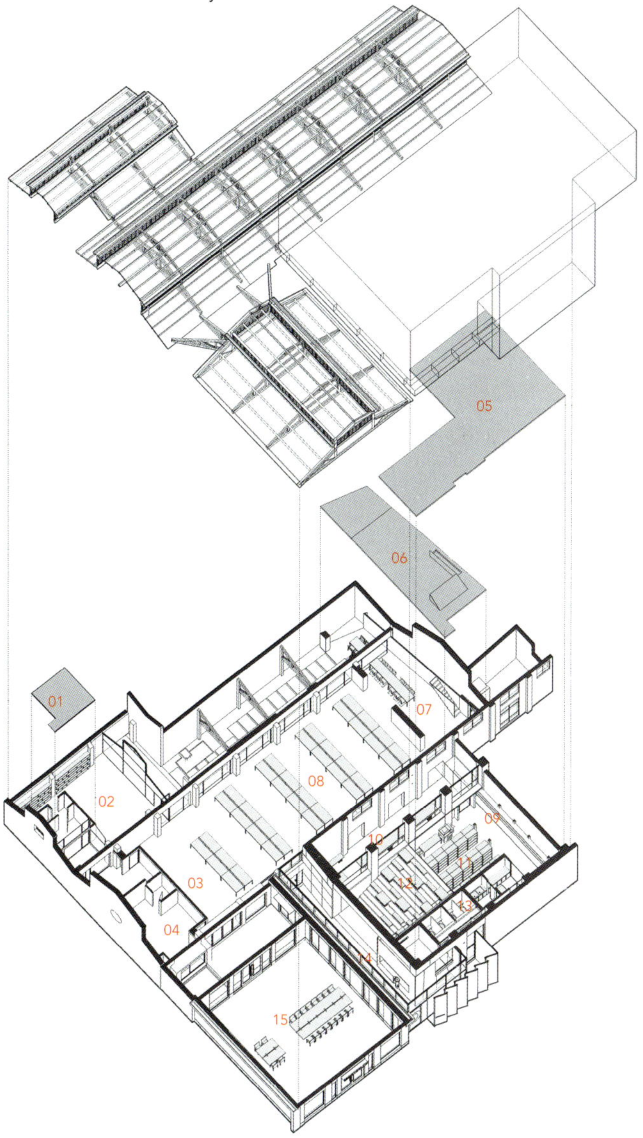

01 Temporary workshop
02 Independent workshop
03 Seminar/exhibition hall
04 Independent workshop
05 Exhibition hall
06 Seminar/rest area
07 Dining/rest/recreation
08 Group workshop
09 Liberary
10 Model-making/seminar/recreation
11 Storage
12 Seminar/exhibition
13 Service room
14 Reception/exhibition
15 Seminar/exhibition/reception

Elevations

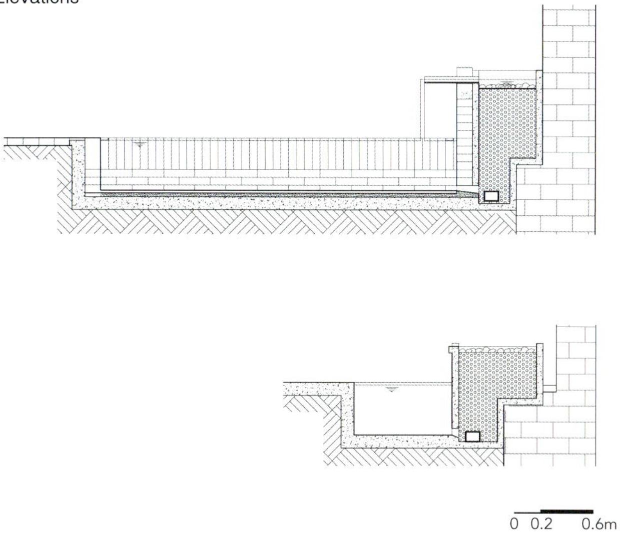

The retention of sections of this building that were left exposed, due to their roofs collapsing, allowed for an inversion of space where inside becomes outside; it also allowed the architects to create outdoor courtyards that flood the interiors with light, while celebrating the patina that has been built up due to their continued exposed condition.

06

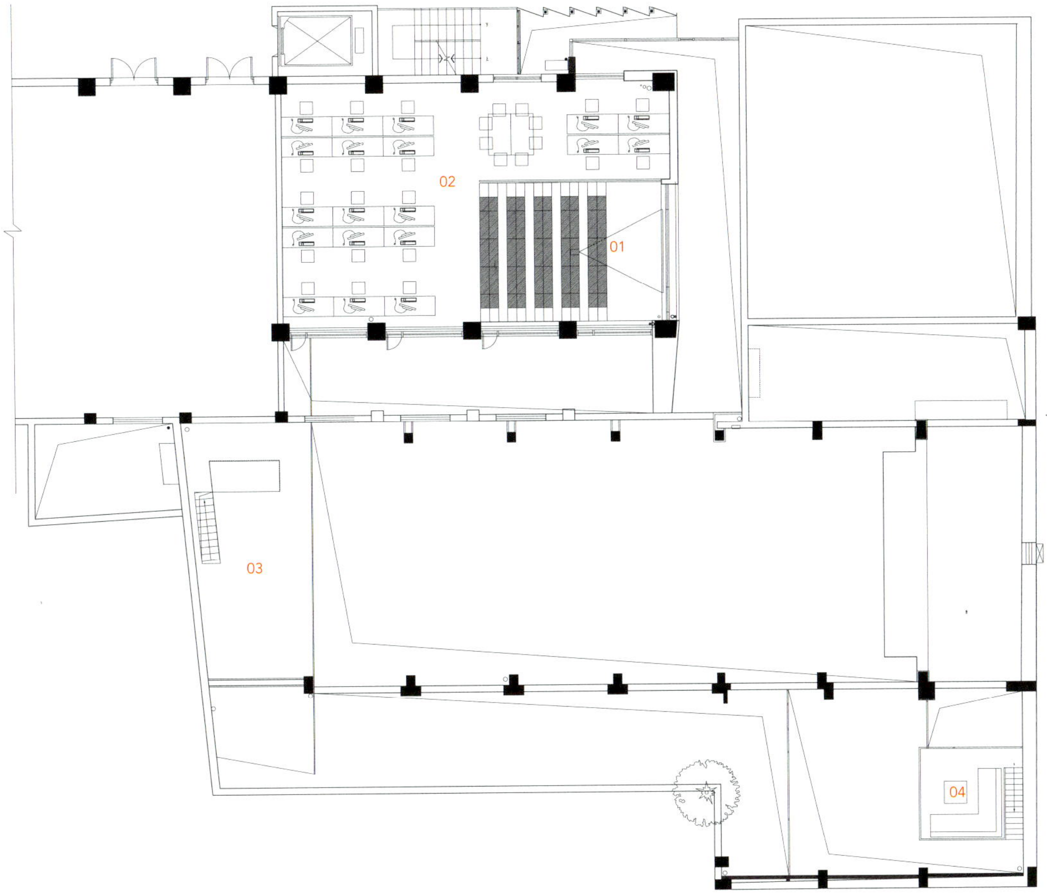

01 Large terrace
02 Exhibition hall/workshop
03 Rest area on the attic
04 Reception room on the attic

Second floor plan

01 Front desk
02 Corridor
03 Main meeting room
04 Yuzhong Yard
05 Workshop
06 Workshop
07 Ridie Yard
08 Workshop
09 Semi-outdoor reception
10 Rending Yard
11 Quejiao Pavilion
12 Tea break area
13 Riru Yard
14 Workshop
15 Model room
16 Small meeting room
17 Materials/information/storage
18 Kitchen
19 Lady's room
20 Men's room
21 Corridor
22 Pingdan Yard

First floor plan

07 08 | 10
09

07- Entrance hall
08- Workshop
09- Rending Yard
10- Yuzhong Yard

MixPace Mandela

Rehabilitation of a four-story factory

Location-Shanghai, China
Architect-RoarcRenew
Chief architectural designer-Robben Bai
Area-48,438 square feet (4500 square meters)
Completion-2016
Photography-OscarLok
Client-MixPace Coworking

Site plan

The four-story factory building in Shanghai was transformed into a new co-working space. Formerly a brick-concrete structured warehouse built in the 1980s, in 2014 it was renovated and reinforced with additional steel structures. The original concrete walls and its patched texture were well preserved and covered with clear glass. The four-story atrium epitomized the divinity of the holy space. The rising pathway of the arc stair points directly to the skylight opening, drawing outdoor light into the whole space and serving as an important place for traffic and social activities.

The inner space of the four-story warehouse is 131 feet (40 meters) long and 95 feet (29 meters) wide. The two fire escapes on the east and west side and the lift at the west part of the house form the vertical traffic flow. Through calculating the solar altitude angle in Shanghai, the designer concluded that direct sunshine couldn't reach the north or south area within 24.6 feet (7.5 meters) towards the center axis and the average daily sunlight received in this area was less than one hour. Considering these two factors, the designer inserted a vertical light shaft at the diameter of 11.8 feet (3.6 meters) all the way down from the fourth floor to the ground floor, which lights up the area that the sunshine could not reach before. Meanwhile, the curved staircase in the atrium supports the light shaft, dividing the interior into three major sections: the east, the central, and the west.

The design started from the concept of revering and respecting the history. An excellent building should not be pulled down but constantly renovated or developed with all new methods, while gaining 'new spirits' from the changing context. Thus, in this project, crumbling concrete walls were completely preserved. The designer fixed a piece of 1.47-inch (2-millimeter) laminated glass at a distance of 7.87 inches (20 centimeters) from the preserved walls, and posted texts that document the history on the glass. Like this, the past, the present, and the future of these walls coexist here.

Black was the color chosen for the working area, accompanied by the lights with a 3700 kilowatt color temperature, which creates a comparatively quiet and private working environment. In private offices, clear white walls, black strip lights, and authentic rubber wood seats leave the room for tenants to recreate and redesign. The collision between light and shadows, preserved walls, clear glasses, and old items, plus the methodology of the museum exhibition display design applied in Mandela's lighted co-working space, showed Roarchi's pursuit of spatial quality.

01

01- Spiral staircase in the atrium

02- Before condition
03- Construction status
04- A rendering of the new building
05- Resting area

Front elevation

Longtitudinal section

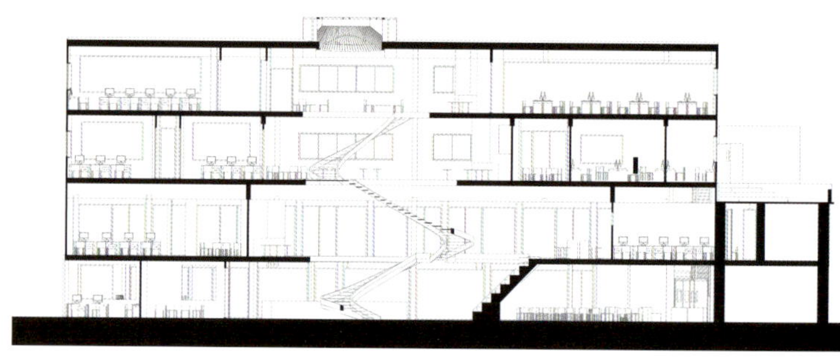

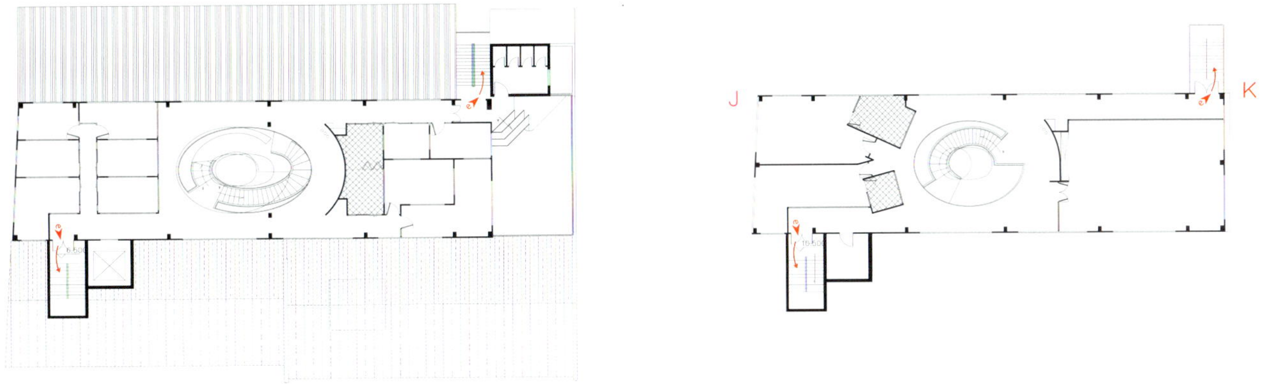

Second floor plan

Third floor plan

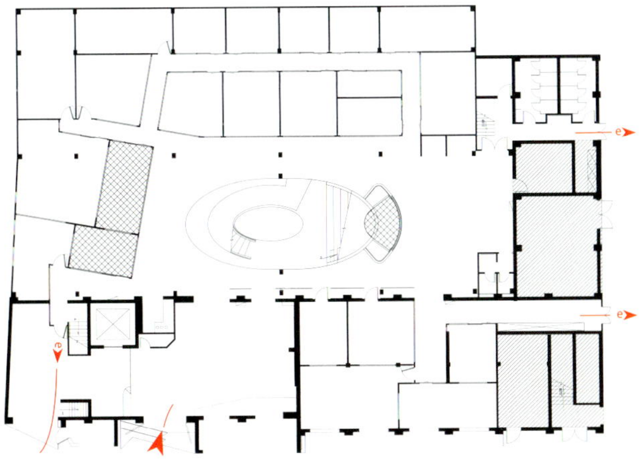

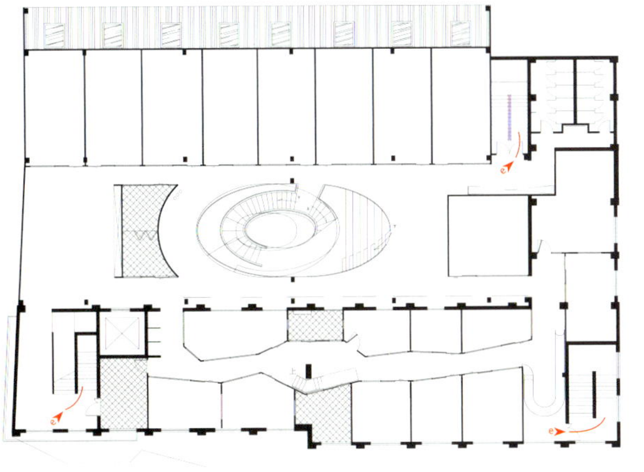

Ground floor plan

First floor plan

06
07
08 09 10

Schematic diagrams of the spiral staircase

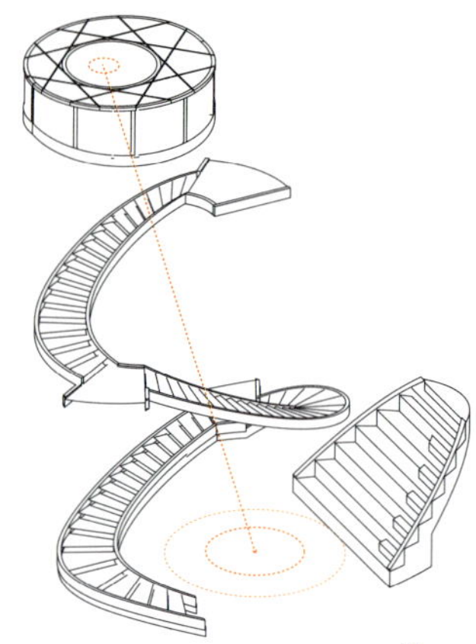

Perspective

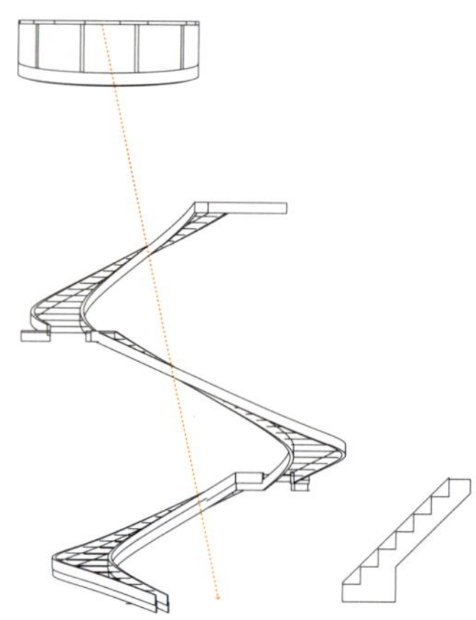

Front

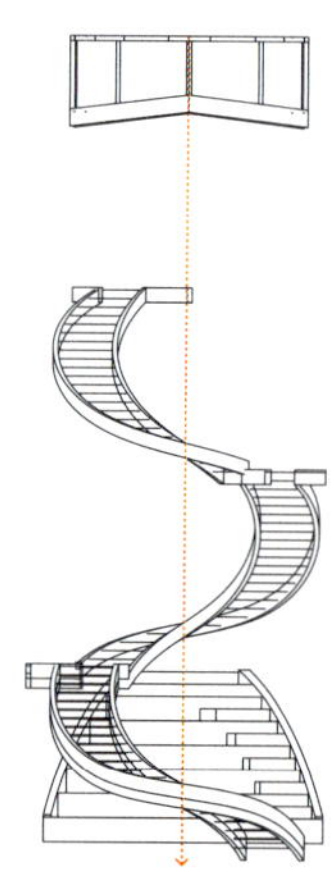

Left

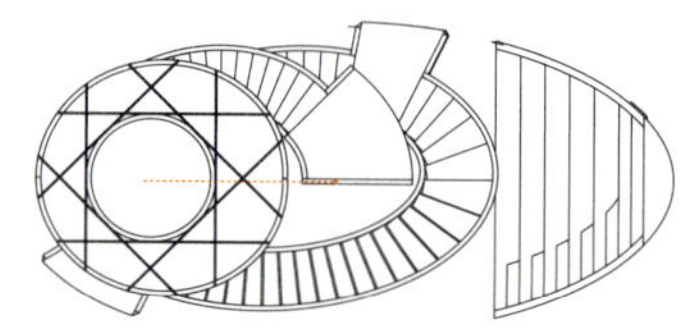

Top

06- Top floor space
07- Circle resting area around the staircase
08- Bright atrium with unique design of staircase
09- Upward view of the staircase
10- Resting area 2

The concept diagram of the project. By bringing the light and inserting the circulation in the center, the space was divided into two parts, creating a gathering space in the meantime.

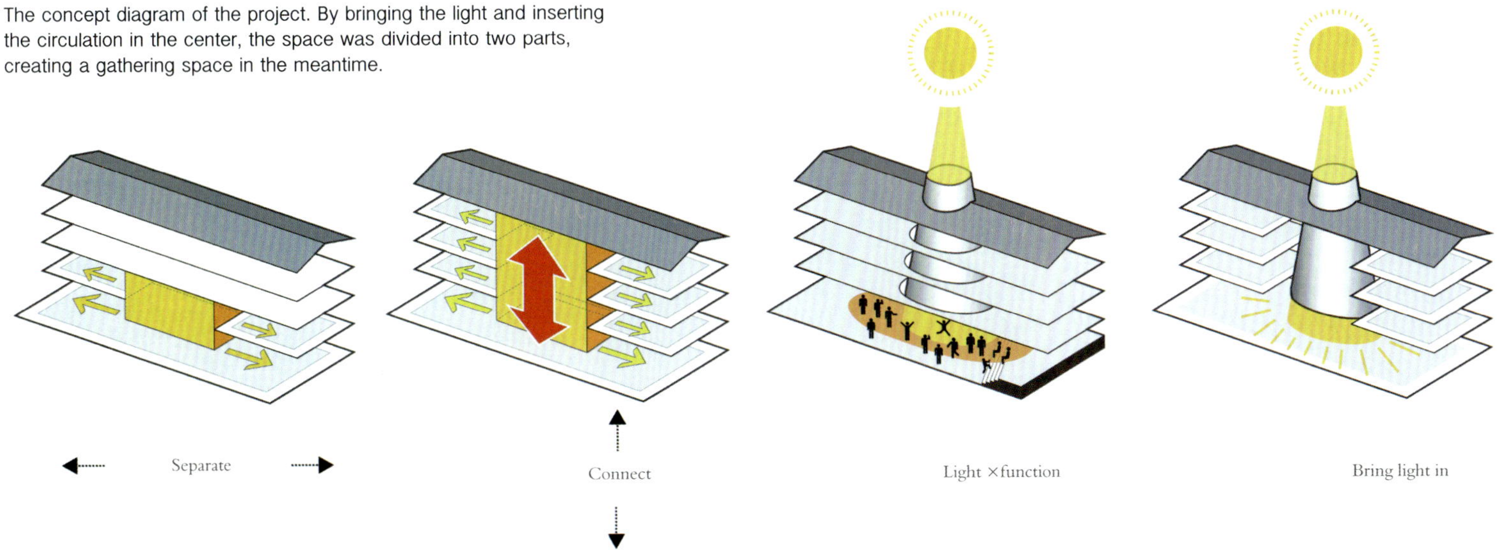

11- Sharing area
12- Café area on the ground floor
13- Working area

11
13
12

An atrium flooded with natural light and a strikingly white spiral staircase is the focal point of this co-working space. It demonstrates how a thorough understanding of lighting conditions generated a dynamic insertion that draws natural light four stories down into the ground level of an existing factory building.

Casa Mediterraneo headquarters

Refurbishment of the old Benalúa Station

Location-Alicante, Spain
Architect-Manuel Ocaña del Valle
Area-33,368 square feet (3100 square meters)
Completion-2012
Photography-David Fruto
Client-Casa Mediterráneo

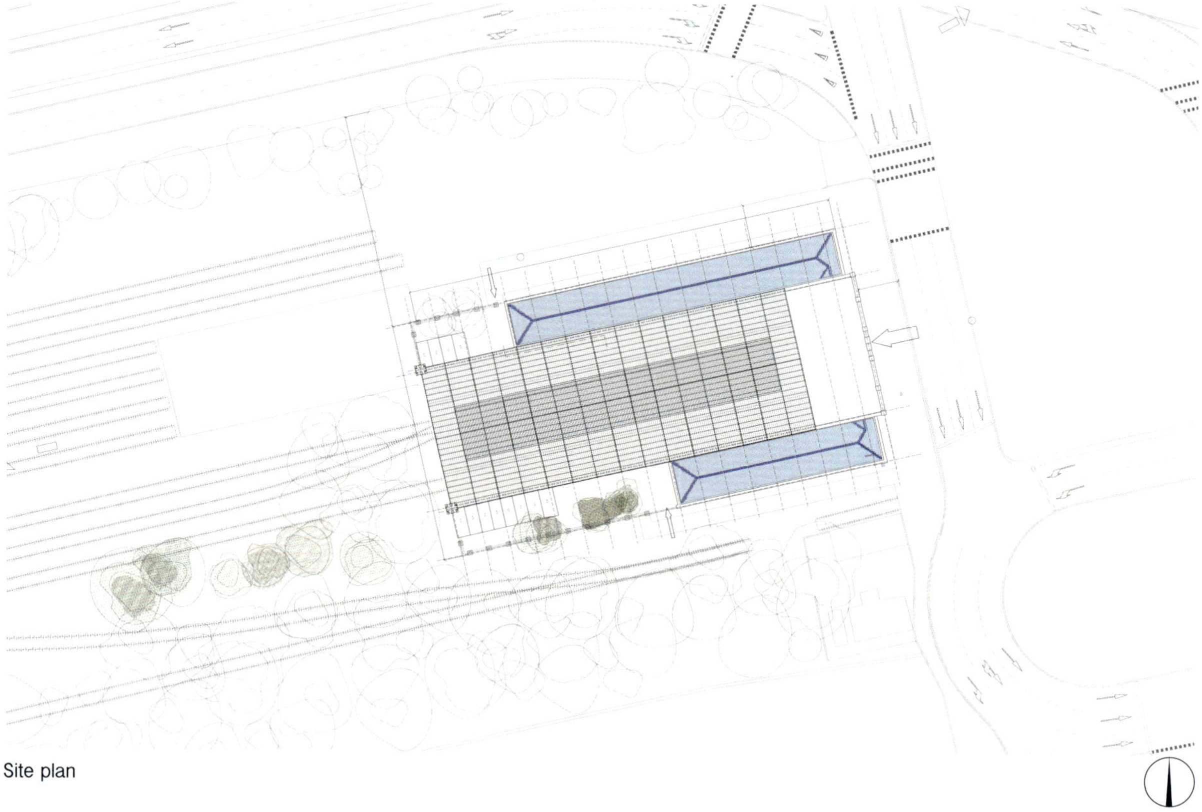

Site plan

In the Mediterranean city of Alicante, Spain, an old railway station was transformed into a vibrant office for Casa Mediterráneo. This non-profit institution is committed to fostering a common identity among the Mediterranean villages. This transformation helped its new headquarters equip the existing station with the spaces to develop the organization's program and offer a beautiful example of how the organization can reinvigorate old perceptions.

The brief emphasized the importance of preserving the building appropriately for the program, but in a way that honored the heritage of the building. Therefore, the architects decided against any large modernist intervention, and they went for a straightforward and sophisticated renovation that emphasized the bold lines of the old train station, which was spread over a surface of 33,368 square feet (3100 square meters).

The architects separated the spaces into smaller individual pavilions surrounding a larger 16,146-square-foot (1500-square-meter) hall. The 16,146-square-foot (1500-square-meter) longitudinal space was intended to become an experience hall. The large hall was once dark and dank. A Klein-blue, translucent roof filters the incoming sunlight, which, after reverberating through a vibrant, circular-patterned aluminum lattice, dyes and excites the old walls and floor, flooding the space and turning it into a sea of blue shadows. So, the hall was changed into a multicolored, ever-changing stage for events, parties, and exhibits.

The conventional program is fitted into an array of small pavilions scattered along the perimeter aisles. These are equipped and climatized, and enable any eventual worker or onlooker to enjoy and understand the original structure and space. The rest of the building is not climatized. Though sheltered, the spaces are not closed, allowing a constant flow of fresh air inside. The floors were cast of compact sand, and the gardening was distributed in glossy ceramic pots.

The result was a new occupation and transformation protocol for heritage buildings; a new scenario in which the old buildings and the citizens empathize, feeding the flame of memory while avoiding any nostalgic concession.

01

01- The architects separated the space into several smaller individual pavilions

02- The old railway station before transformation
03- A Klein-blue, translucent roof filters the incoming sunlight

02
03

Section

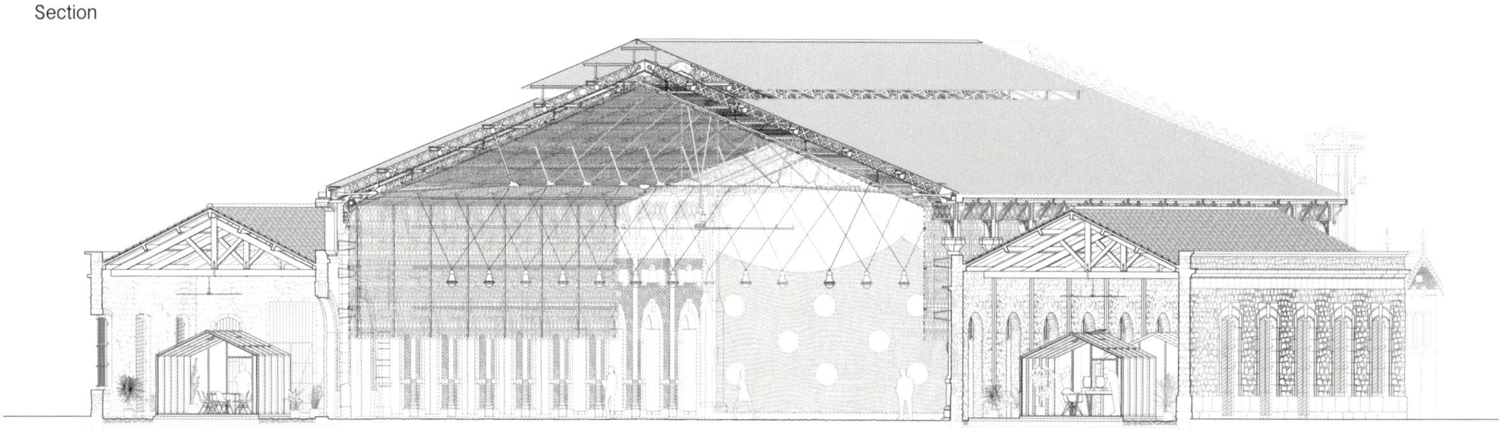

Climatically-controlled working pavilions were inserted into the large open perimeter spaces of this former railway station, while a bright translucent blue roof and circular white lattices create a dazzling light effect in the main hall.

Master plan and plant scheme

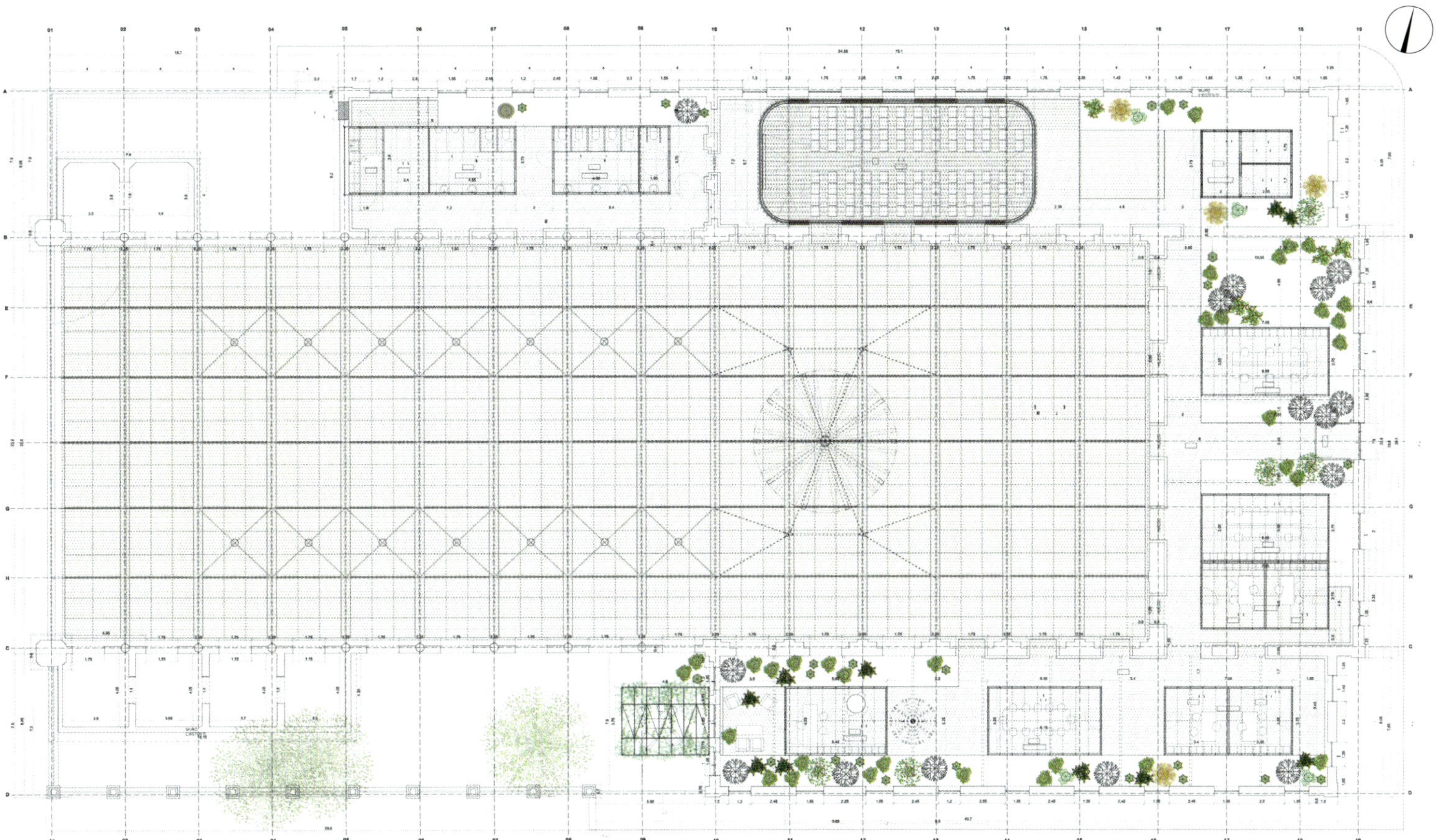

04- The improvements made to the old railway station lie at the intersection of modern design and cultural preservation
05- Inside the pavilions
06, 07- Echoing roof, blue is used as the dominant tone throughout the project

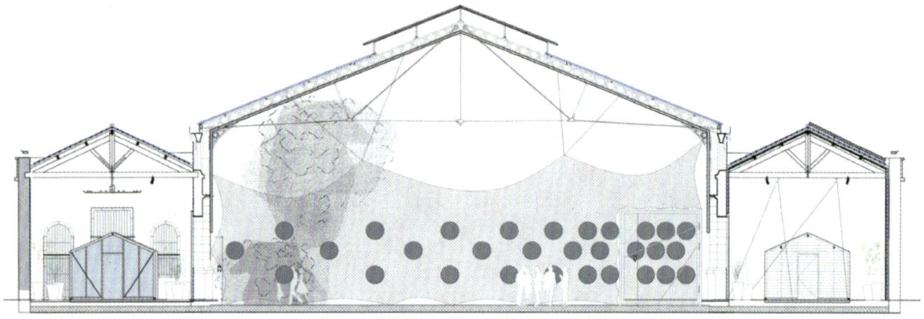

Transverse section

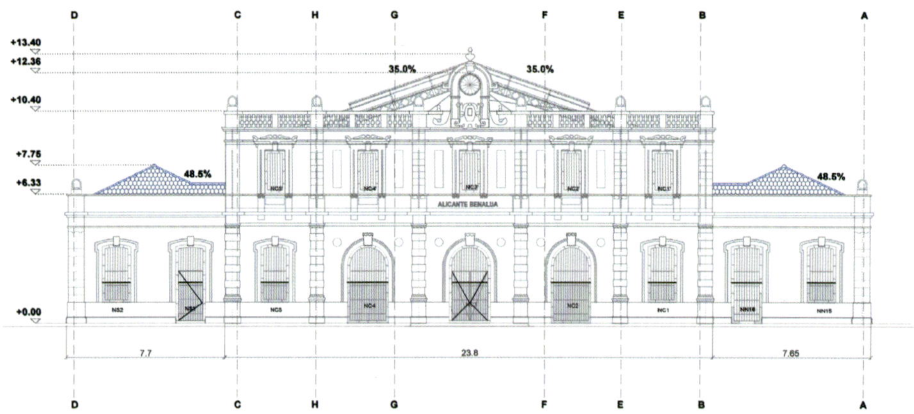

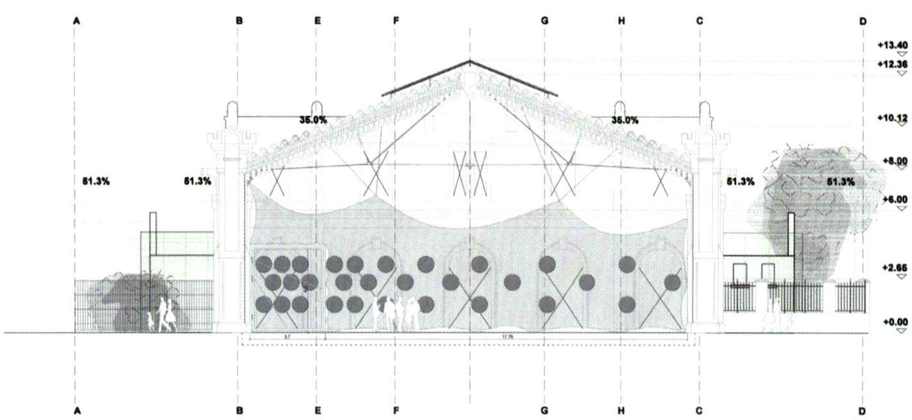

East and west elevations

05
04 | 06 07

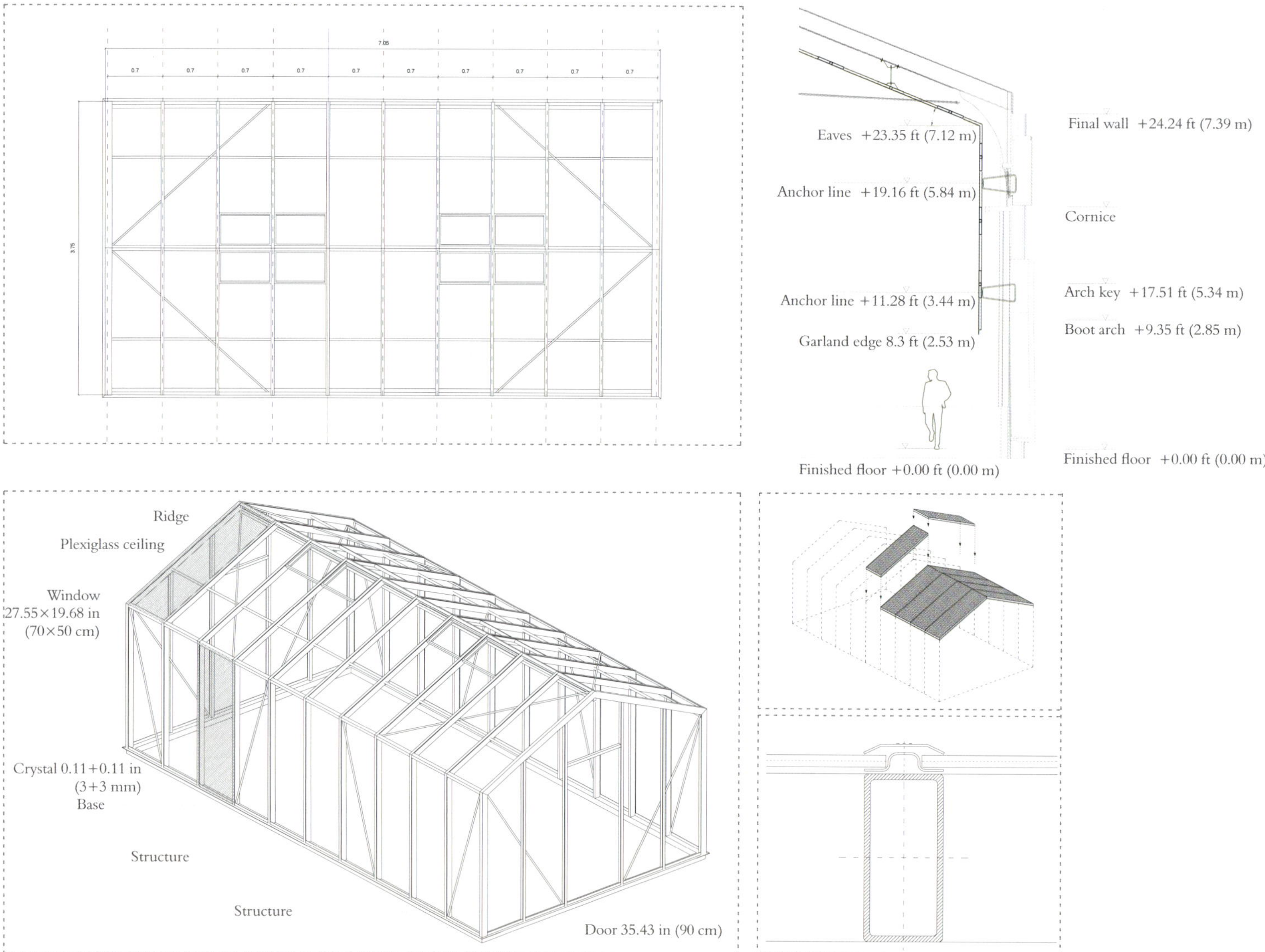

Micropaviliions' detailed drawings

09 10
08 11

Five modular greenhouses [2498.51 ft^3/house (70.75 m^3/house)]
12,466 ft^3 (353 m^3) total climatized volume

Axonometric

08- The daylighting within the office space is brilliantly white, while the large hall dances with colors at different times of the day
09, 10- The pavilions within the railway station are daylit, naturally ventilated, and surrounded by vegetation
11- The night view of the pavilion offices inside the train station

Grupo SUD headquarters

Conversion of an old perfume factory

Location-Santiago, Chile
Architect-57STUDIO
Area-16,146 square feet (1500 square meters)
Completion-2015
Photography-Caco Oportot
Client-Grupo SUD

General sections

The Grupo Sud project involved the conversion of an old perfume factory into an open work space for a holding of four companies that are fully integrated in marketing, production, design, and communication areas. The building is located in the city of Santiago, in the 'Italia' neighborhood that encompasses design, art, and decoration luxury stores.

The site, 66 feet wide by 246 feet deep (20 meters wide by 75 meters deep) comprised a series of warehouses constructed at different points in time that had been expanded and subdivided throughout the years. The project entailed the restoration of the sequence of spaces and their reorganization so as to serve the needs of the companies—mainly offices for a workforce of about 100 people.

Two main actions were proposed: to remove what was useless and to reuse what existed. Removing and reusing the elements of subdivision restored the communication between the different warehouses and resulted in more fluid and brighter spaces—the ideal environment for an integrated and teamwork approach.

The intervention aimed to reveal and contrast the old and the new. Longstanding thick walls, textures, and high ceilings are contrasted against to the new, lighter, and transparent elements, minimally scaled to satisfy the user's needs. The color palette chosen was neutral to maintain the sense of quietness and to highlight the ample spaces. The white background, which varies from a matt to a gloss finish, was used as a foundation to unify and revalue the spaces through light. The floors were kept gray while some accents were incorporated on walls through the use of color or by revealing the brick layer.

The new divisions were made of glass, seeking to dilute boundaries and to contrast these new elements of straight and defined edges to the imprecision of the old. The new climate and electricity control panels were highlighted in galvanized metal, moving in an orderly fashion through the neutrality of the white background. Both the furniture and the lamps were designed by the architects, following the same premise of identity and contrast over a recycled space as a backdrop.

01

01- View of kitchen

vampiros en la habana
AL PACINO SCARFACE
dogs

02

03 04

01 Access and parking
02 Showroom
03 Warehouses
04 Management offices
05 Restrooms
06 Service area
07 Kitchen
08 Offices
09 Multi-space
10 Open workspace
11 Backyard

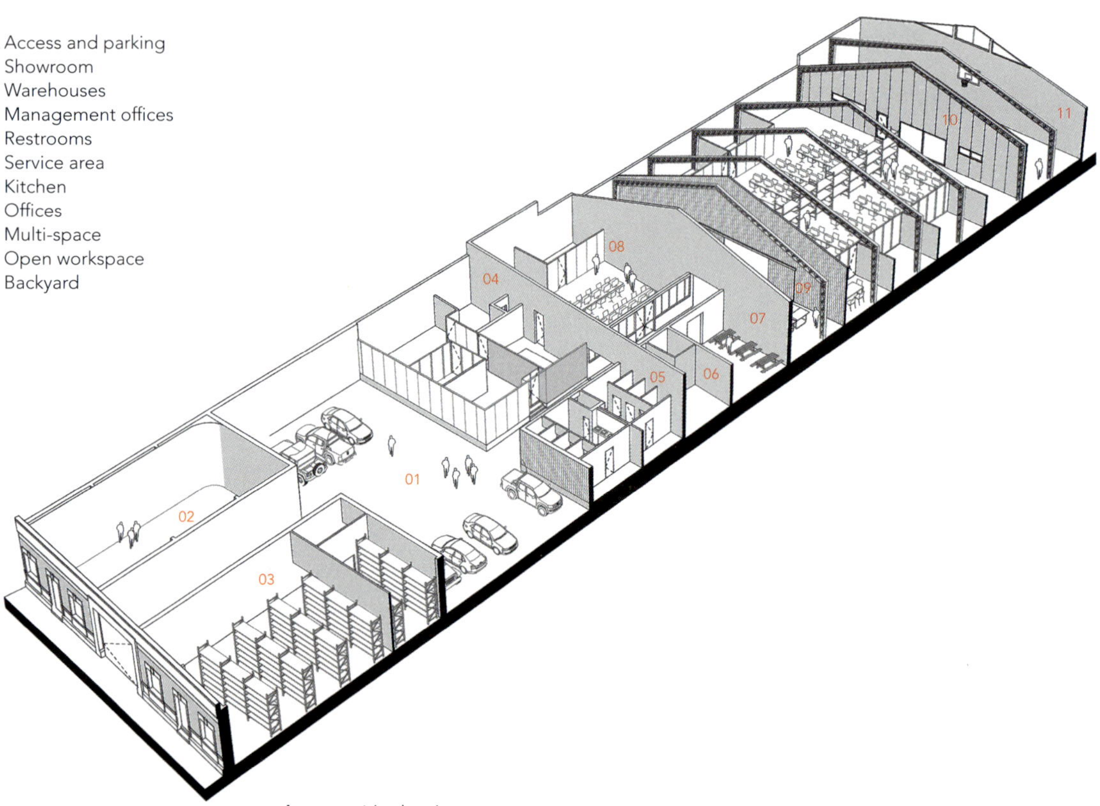

Axonometric drawing

02- Exterior view of the façade
03- Original picture
04- Picture during construction

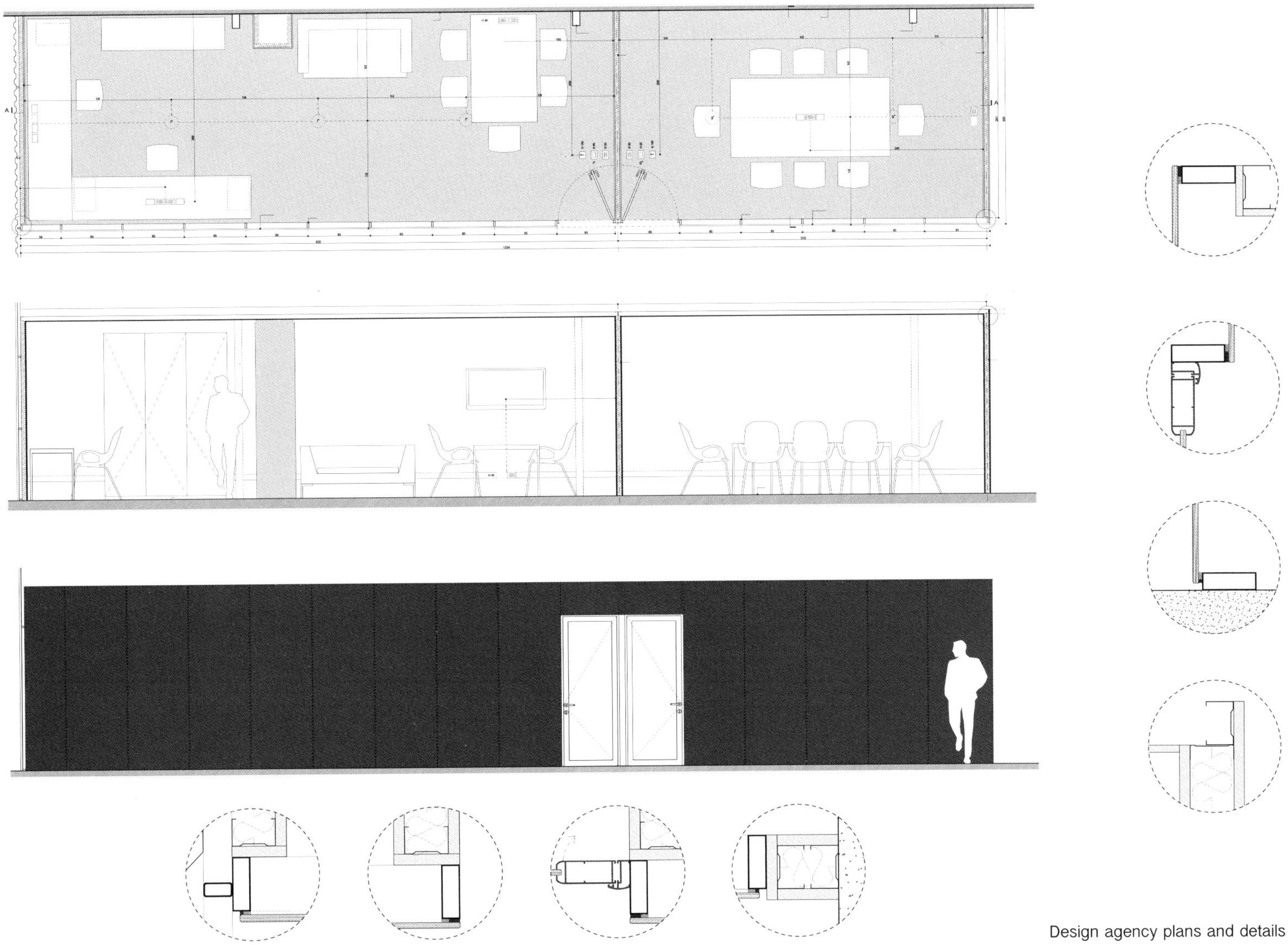

Design agency plans and details

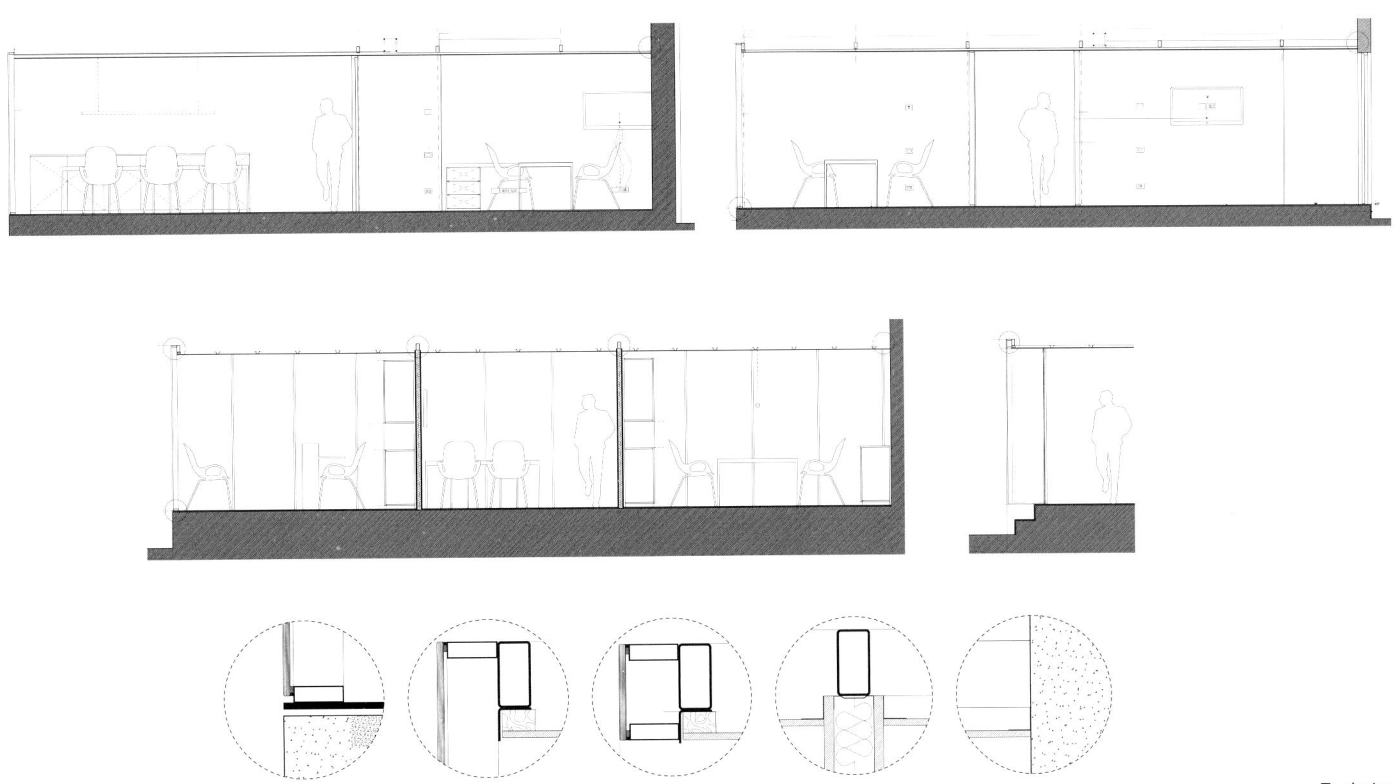

Technical details

05 06 | 07
08 09

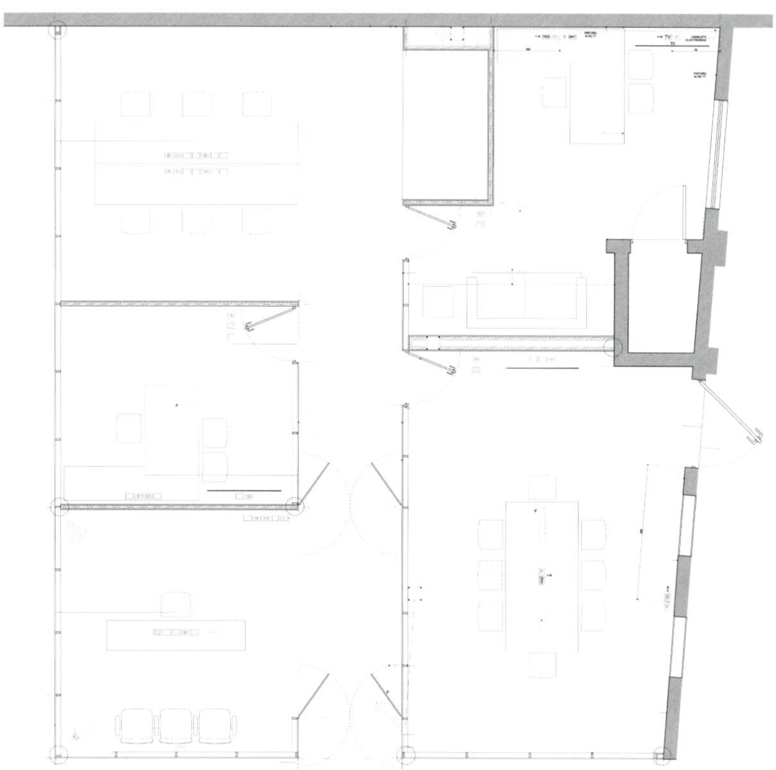

Management offices detail plan

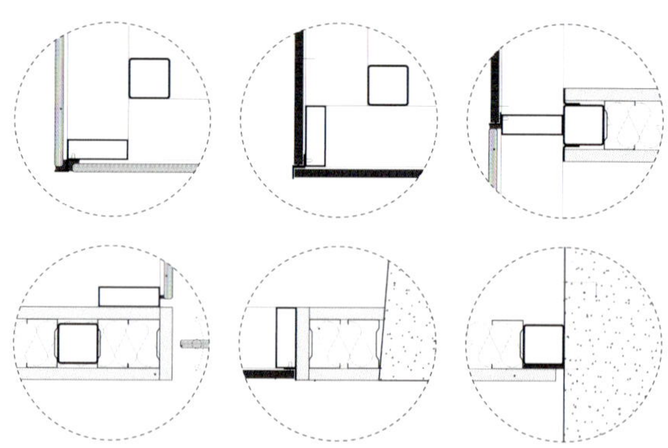

Details

05- Recreational area
06- Public restrooms
07- Media agency access doors
08- Media agency meeting room
09- Design agency open workspace

A sequential arrangement of a series of spaces emphasizes the sense of threshold as one moves through the building, and this movement is echoed by the accentuated service runs that flow along a similar route.

Master plan

01 Access and parking
02 Showroom
03 Warehouses
04 Management offices
05 Restrooms
06 Service area
07 Kitchen
08 Offices
09 Multi-space
10 Open workspace
11 Backyard

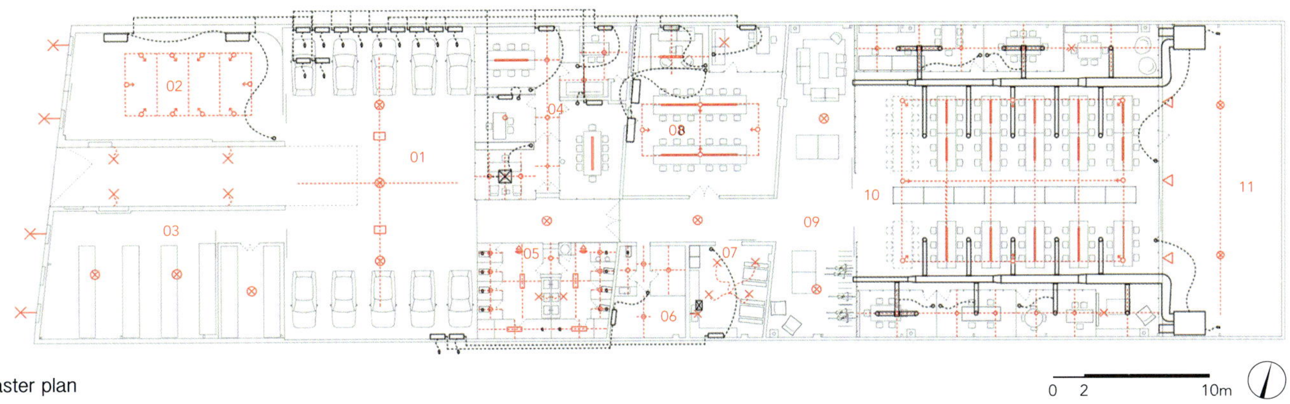

Master plan

10
11 | 12 13

10- Production agency manager office
11- Media agency public space
12- Media agency manager office
13- Recreational area

Dream Factory

An old glass factory transformed into a creative incubator

Location-Rotterdam, the Netherlands
Architect-Studio Roosegaarde
Area-10,764 square feet (1000 square meters)
Completion-2016
Photography-Willem de Kam, Studio Roosegaarde
Client-Studio Roosegaarde

Dating back to 1937, a derelict building—a former glass factory located near the Rotterdam harbor—was about to be demolished until it caught Roosegaarde's eye. The 11,764-square-foot (1000-square-meter) structure was saved from demolition and overhauled by Roosegaarde and his team of designers and engineers to create its new Dream Factory offices.

Inspired by Roosegaarde's fascination for the Dutch skies, this new design opened up the space to Dutch light to fully soak up its magic, transforming it into the dream lab of the 21st century. The main artery of the building was used for the building of prototypes, visible from the above offices and balconies at any time of the day. The building's main center stage is malleable to its dream functions such as open lab sessions and educational activities.

Special features include the dream library, which houses an extended collection of antique and new books. Wall divisions in the space are made of glass, enabling new ideas to be drawn on the walls directly as an open sketchbook, inviting team members to contribute and develop concepts together. A unique laboratory is housed on the ground floor, in the former garage, to cultivate live bio-organisms in the dark. The furniture, such as the team desks, were directly inspired by large boats and float like islands in space. From the top floor, the studio offices provide stunning views over the harbor and river.

The grounds surrounding the Dream Factory are part of Rotterdam's Innovation District program and house leading design studios as well as warehouses converted into creative incubators, cafés, and shops. The area is set to become the next Dutch design hub of tomorrow.

01 | 02 / 03

01- Rotterdam innovation district home of Roosegaarde's Dream Factory
02- The Dream Factory
03- The Dream Factory seen from the backyard

ROOSEGAARDE

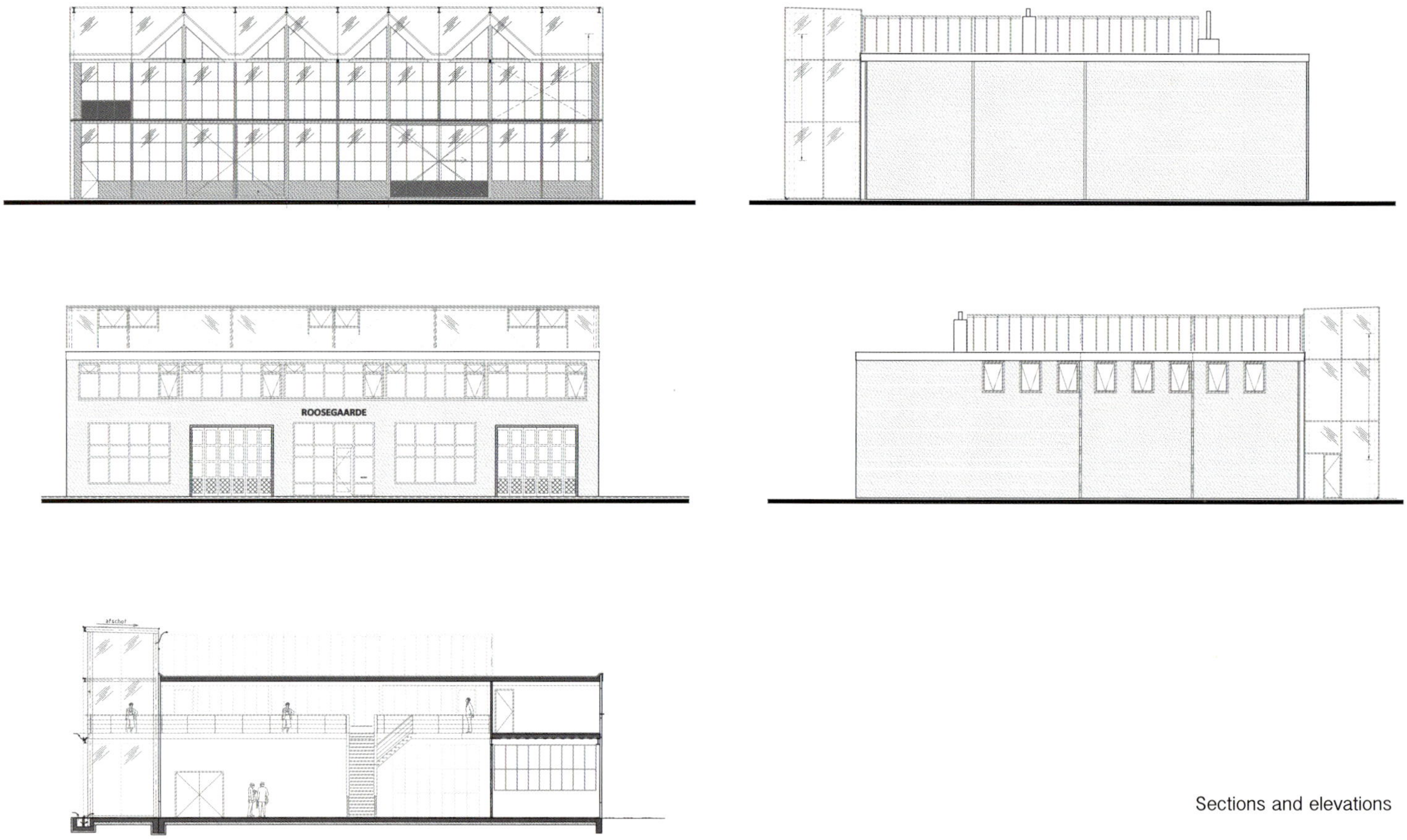

Sections and elevations

05 06
07 08
04

Extract Cadastral Map

0 10 5m

04- Front door
05, 06, 07, 08- Construction status

Floor plans

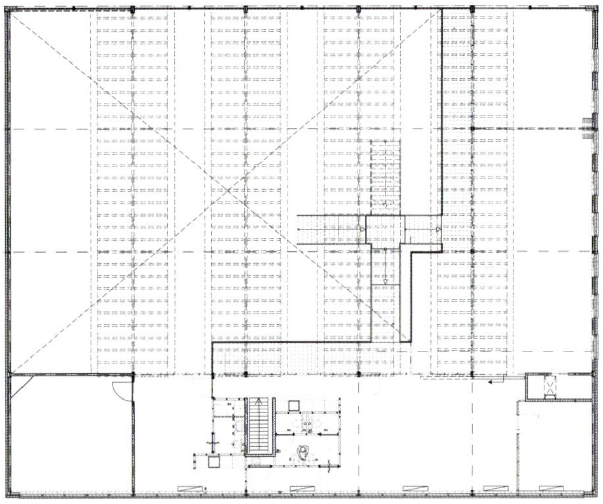

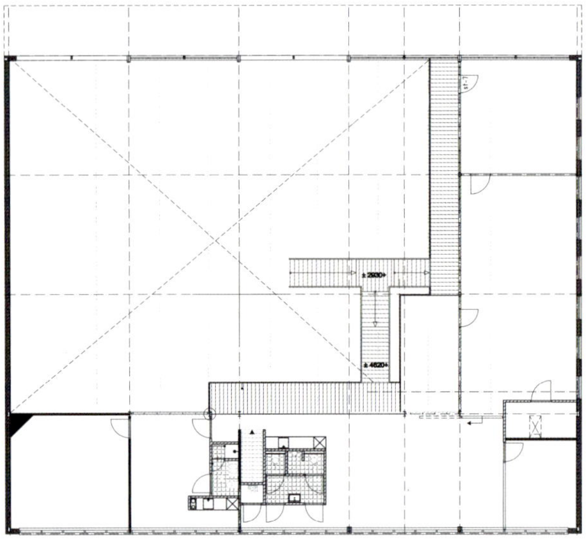

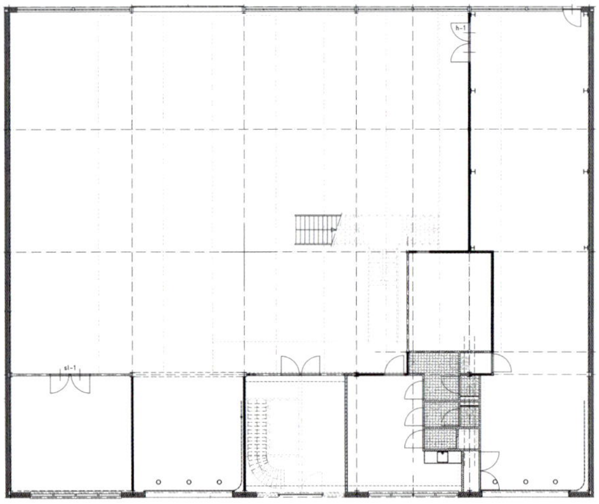

09- The central staircase
10- The transparent roof
11- The designers' and engineers' offices featuring large windows facing out over the harbor and the river
12, 13- The offices on the second floor

The large central open space of this building retains its industrial character through the use of an exposed steel structure; its glazed roof and large glass façades ensure that almost every part of it is flooded with natural light.

09 11
10 12 13

The Pennovation Center

Adaptive reuse of a paint factory

Location-Philadelphia, USA
Architect-Hollwich Kushner Architecture, KSS Architecture
Area-59,125 square feet (5400 square meters)
Completion-2016
Photography-Michael Moran
Client-The University of Pennsylvania

The Pennovation Center is the centerpiece of the University of Pennsylvania's new campus: Pennovation Works

The Pennovation Center is a 21st century idea factory transformed from an old paint factory. The building is the centerpiece of a new development at the University of Pennsylvania, known as Pennovation Works.

To create a dream space for innovators and entrepreneurs, the architect wanted to celebrate the rawness of the former factory and place emphasis on creating a diverse mix of environments suitable for privacy, collaboration, socializing, and the business side of growing a company.

Entrepreneurs thrive on invention. It means a lot of dedicated time spent in labs hunched over workbenches and computers. While much of the building is occupied by shared dry and wet labs and efficient co-working areas, key social spaces tempt entrepreneurs to leave their desks and engage with their colleagues. These spaces are tucked into the new angular façade that reaches outward towards the Schuylkill River, featuring a conference room, a co-working counter with a view of campus and the city, and bleacher seating where inventors can share ideas, pitch to investors, and gain crucial perspective.

On the exterior, the architects cut a large, glazed triangle into the main façade, which announces the building's primary entrance. The façade is fronted by a plaza with a series of benches, and black-and-white pavers that form an artistic pattern. Throughout the building, casement windows were replaced with energy-efficient glass set within a metal grid. Inside, the architects created an industrial-style atmosphere, with concrete flooring, exposed structural elements, and long communal tables.

This adaptive reuse project maintains an industrial aesthetic. It inspires creativity within, while simultaneously telling the world outside that Penn is committed to putting knowledge into action for the greater good. A beacon for the next generation of entrepreneurship in the region, the Pennovation Center will advance the dynamic role of the university as both an inspiration for and a facilitator of cutting-edge invention. The design creates a truly iconic landmark for Penn's innovation ecosystem and a dynamic hub for Penn's culture of innovation and interdisciplinary collaboration.

01
02

01- The adaptive reuse project transformed a 20th century paint factory into a 21st century idea factory
02- A new public plaza welcomes visitors

PENNOVATION

PENNOVATION

03 | 07
04 05 |
06 | 08

A robust steel and concrete interior allows for flexibility of use on the inside, while dynamic cantilevered extrusions serve as a beacon and provide a connection with the outside world.

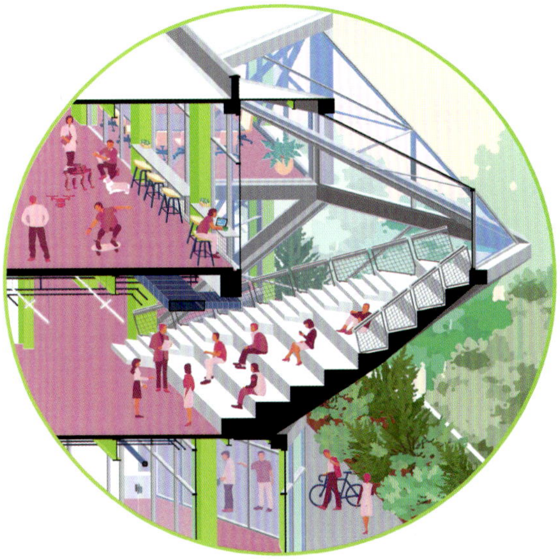

A triangular bleacher for pitching to investors creates a spatial focal point

03, 04, 05- The old factory before renovation
06- The addition of modern programming is gestured through the new crystalline façade
07- Stairs to the second floor double as bleacher seating
08- Key social spaces tempt entrepreneurs to leave their desks and engage with colleagues

Floor plans

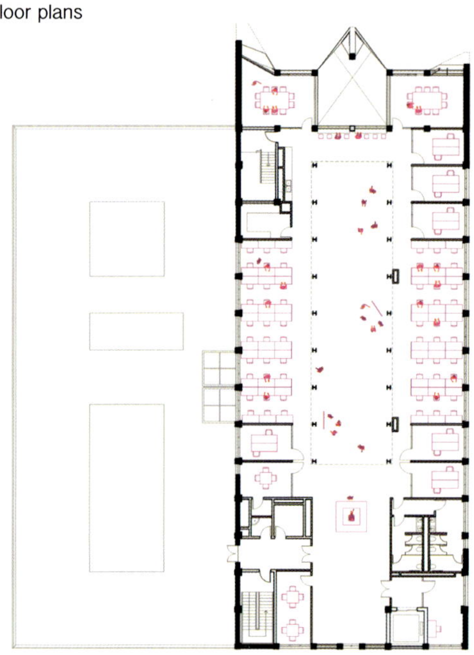

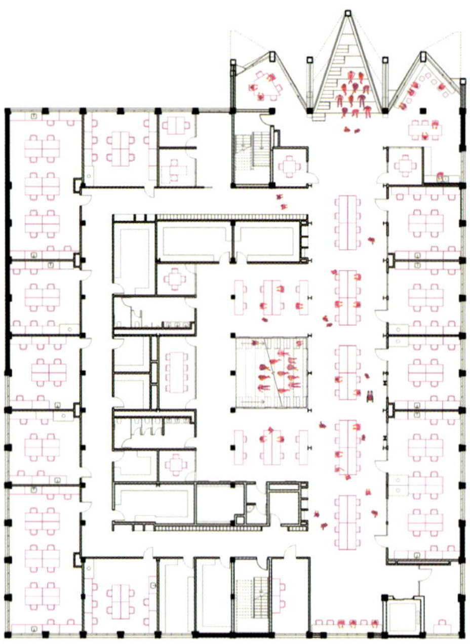

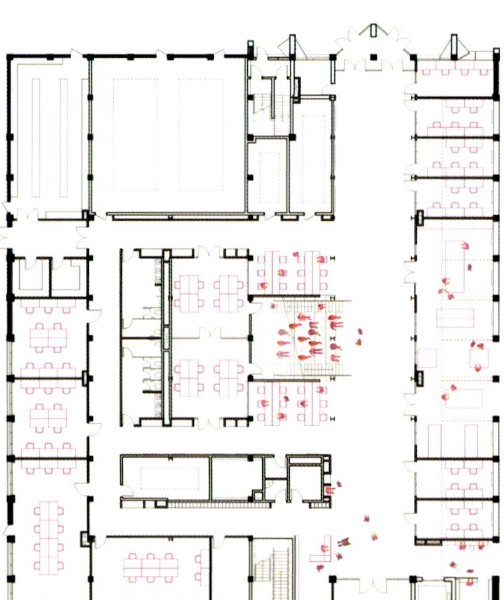

09- Third floor conference rooms and workspace are visible from the pitch bleacher
10- Large circulation corridors double as co-working and event space
11- The crystalline façade reaches out over the Schuylkill River towards Center City Philadelphia

10
09 | 11

12- Communal spaces act as testing grounds for new inventions
13- Central workspaces promote collaboration
14- State-of-the-art lab space
15- The project's exposed concrete and duct-work maintains an industrial aesthetic

12
13 14 | 15

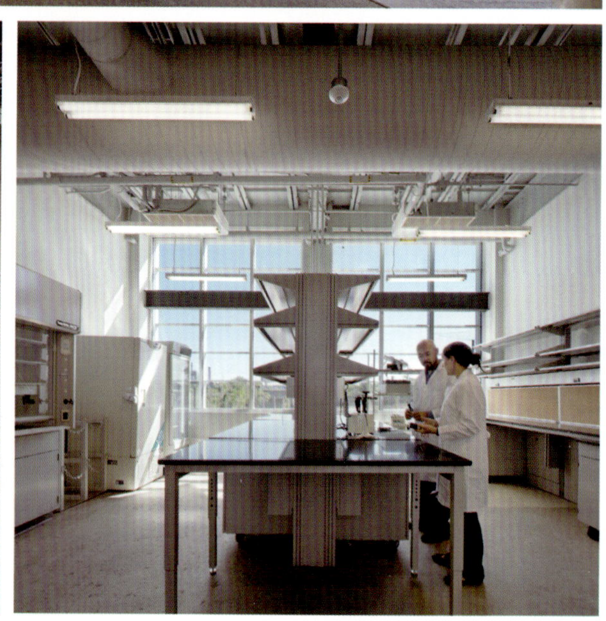

Renovation of Wuzhen Beizha silk factory

From factory to exhibition space

Location-Tongxiang, China
Architect-Design Creates Atelier
Area-91,514 square feet (8502 square meters)
Completion-2016
Photography-Ai Qing, Wu Qingshan
Client-Wuzhen Tourism Co. Ltd

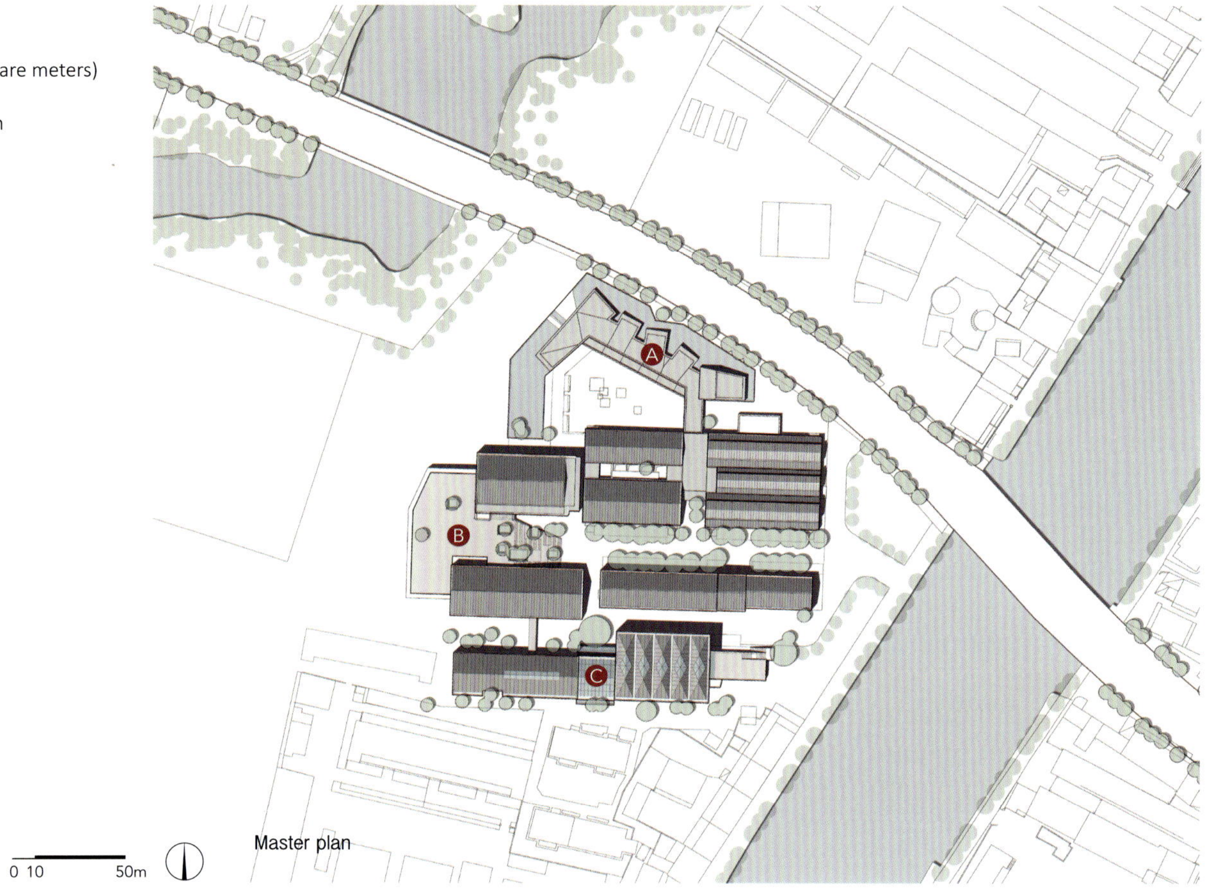

Master plan

Wuzhen is a typical ancient water town in southern China. Wuzhen Beizha silk factory was built in the 1970s and declined in the 1990s. The factory, which witnessed the development of the old town's industry, had been abandoned for more than 10 years. In the renovation, the original layouts and spatial features of the site were transformed to adapt to the new program—the venue of the 2016 International Contemporary Art Exhibition.

Structural reinforcement and roof refurbishment were integral to the reconstruction. In the old factory, as a result of technological requirements, there were a lot of windows to ensure natural ventilation, but this was not suitable for an exhibition space. Some of the excessive windows were blocked because of this, while the window recesses were kept to preserve their memory. All suspended ceilings were removed to expose the slim roof structure and provide suitable spaces for the exhibition. The mottled façades of the old buildings were kept. Only the tallest building was wrapped with a dark grey stretched aluminum mesh, which brought an obscure image mixed with modern and traditional features.

All existing trees were mapped and preserved in the reconstruction. Specific care was taken to consider the dialogue between trees and buildings; hence, a new status that combines the buildings and the environment emerged. Three different means were adopted to integrate three new buildings with the old ones to form a single entity:

- Apposition: Building A served as entry and small galleries, and was set up along the new road with floating boxes above a pool, which echoes the water town image of Wuzhen. It also encloses the outdoor exhibition area with the old workshops.
- Insertion: Building B was inserted between two-story buildings. The first floor accommodates gift shops and cafés, which serve both the venue and the community. A roof platform connects the second floor of the buildings on both sides and becomes the recreation and communication space during exhibitions.
- Connection: The second-floor circulation was established by a bridge, which links building C and the old buildings. The transparent hall in the middle connects the eastern and the western parts of the building. In the second floor of the eastern part, a spacious indoor exhibition hall with skylights is created by folded large-span roof truss.

01
02

01- Outdoor exhibition area
02- Night view of the main entrance

NORTH
北栅
SILK FACTORY
丝厂

03 04 | 06
05

03, 04- Before and after renovation
05- Entrance towards Building C
06- North entrance view of Building C through two factory-transformed galleries

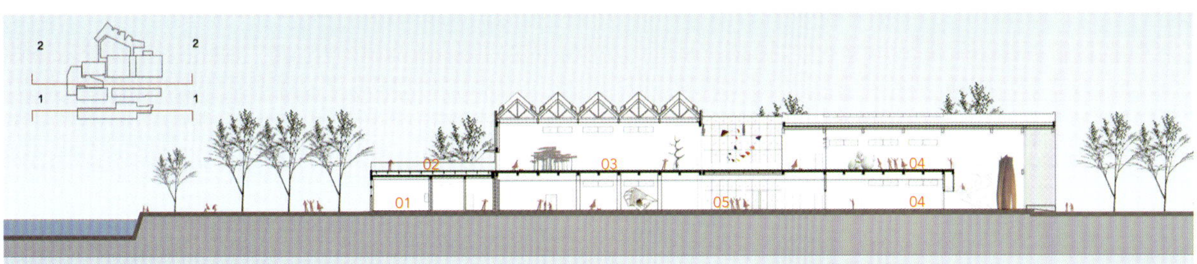

Section 1-1

01 Restroom
02 Terrace
03 Grand exhibition
04 Exhibition hall
05 Lobby

Section 2-2

01 Cafeteria
02 Terrace
03 Exterior grand stair
04 Outdoor exhibition area

Ground floor plan

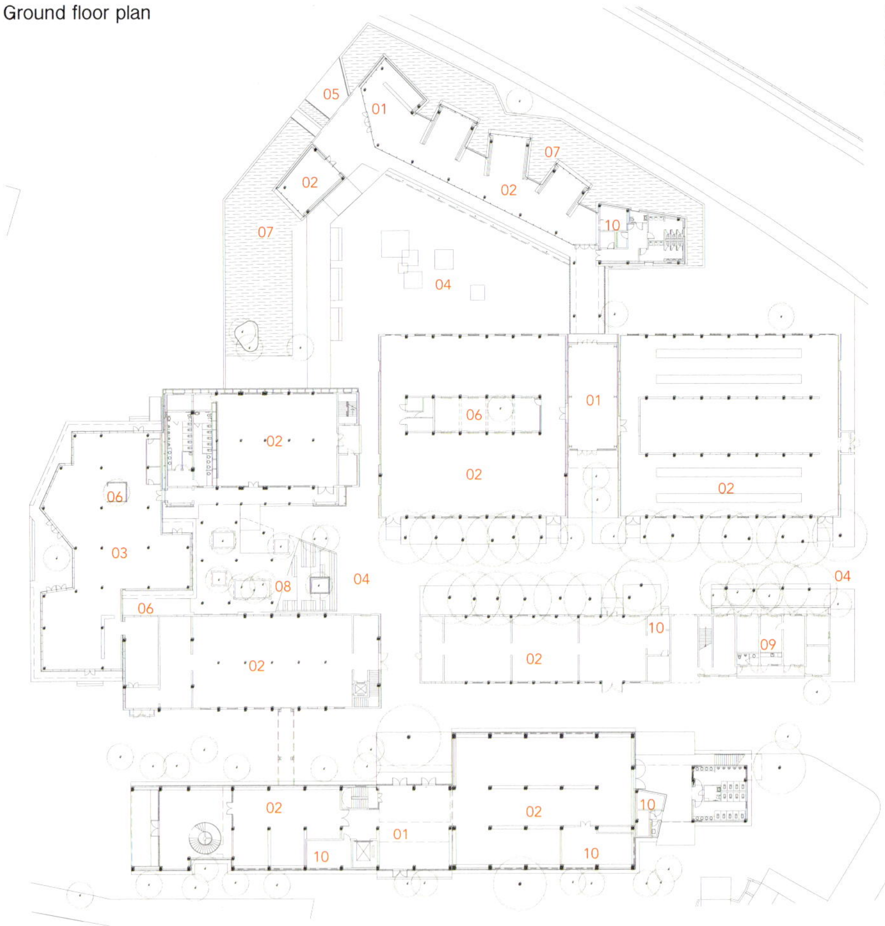

07- Sky bridge over the atrium of Building C
08- Exhibition hall on the second floor of Building C
09- The corridor connecting Building A and the existing factory building
10- The western lobby of Building C

01 Lobby
02 Exhibition hall
03 Gift shop & café
04 Outdoor exhibition area
05 Entrance ramp
06 Courtyard
07 Pond
08 Terrace
09 Office
10 Equipment

0 10 50m

08
07 09 10

Contemporary insertions that pay homage to the buildings of an ancient water town complement the refurbished older buildings' scale and façades, which in turn retain their original finishes and traces of their former openings.

Yingliang Stone Archive

Between stonework and architecture

Location-Beijing, China
Architect-Atelier Alter
Area-5081 square feet (472 square meters)
Completion-2016
Photography-Atelier Alter
Client-Beijing Tian Cheng Ying Liang Stone Co., Ltd.

Elevation

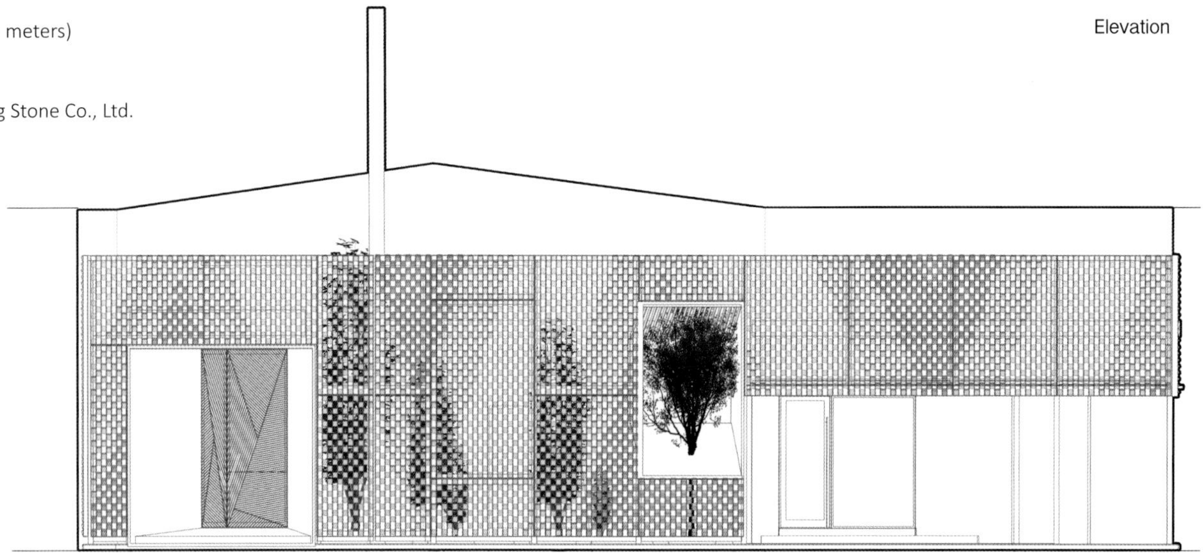

This rehabilitation project entailed the conversion of an old storage space into a stone archive: it served to showcase the diversity of stone craft and to create a space for architects to contemplate their designs with stone.

As the most primitive construction material, stone comes with dignity and authenticity. However, as construction becomes more and more visually dominated, stones are crafted to be light and polished. The spirit within stones seems to be lost, as stones are gradually substituted by other superficial materials. This project attempted to propose a critique for modern construction.

From rough to fine, stone processing begins when drill bits measure the landscape and enormous cubic volumes of natural stone are cut from the mountains. The project started from this notion by imagining the 23-foot-high (7-meter-high) storage space as a complete piece of stone. By dissecting the volume with angular plates, the architect created solid and void spaces: while solids are for exhibition, meeting, and archive spaces, the voids become the circulation space. The cutting plates were also materialized as different stone shelves for the separation and mediation between spaces.

Three layers of stone shelf walls were arrayed from exterior to interior to create a narration of stone processing in space. The stones used in the shelves were recycled materials from different stages of stone processing. The first layer that separated the architecture from the street was a perforated stone wall made from thousands of 3.9-inch (10-centimeter) stone cubes cut directly from leftover dimension stones in the quarry. The three trapezoidal openings punched through the perforated stone walls are the entrance, the clerestory window, and the opening to the restaurant.

Between the perforated skin and existing wall, there is a garden that brings light and breezes into the space. The second layer of stone shelf was set apart from the inside of the existing wall and creates a residual space that prepares visitors for entering the gallery. The outwards-tilted stone shelve in the second layer was composed by the stacking of mountain skins cut away from dimensional stones. The trace of chisel and the roughness of stone unveil the life of the material. The third layer of stone shelves is a zigzag stone screen that separates the exhibition space, meeting hall, and stone archive within the double-storey gallery space. The stone screen was made of small flagstone slabs sliding between a structural net of welded steel. The space above and space below were connected and separated simultaneously by the stone screen.

As the material processing impacts the internal logic of the architecture, the architecture also becomes a reinterpretation of the material. By inventing new construction methods based upon levels of local craftsmanship, the architects strove to find coherence between the architectural scale and the detail scale of the work. They combined steel and stone construction in perforation, suspension, and inclination to represent the authenticity of stone in a new way. Stone becomes the subject but also the background of the show.

Small restaurants, bars, and cafés are situated next to the gallery. The catering space is enhanced by a library and an internal courtyard. The furniture and lighting of the space were designed with polished slabs and super-thin complex stone veneers, which represent the finest degree of stone processing. A stone carpet made from parametrically arranged slabs brings the three spaces together.

01

01- Café

02, 03, 04- Before reconstruction
05- Façade
06, 07- Front yard

02 | 05
03 04 |
| 06 07

Sections

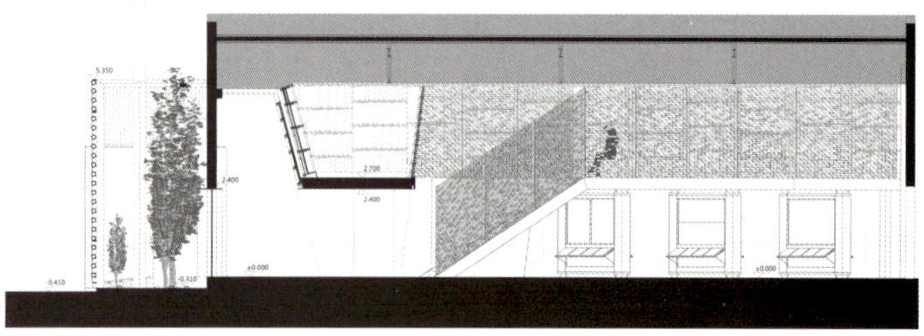

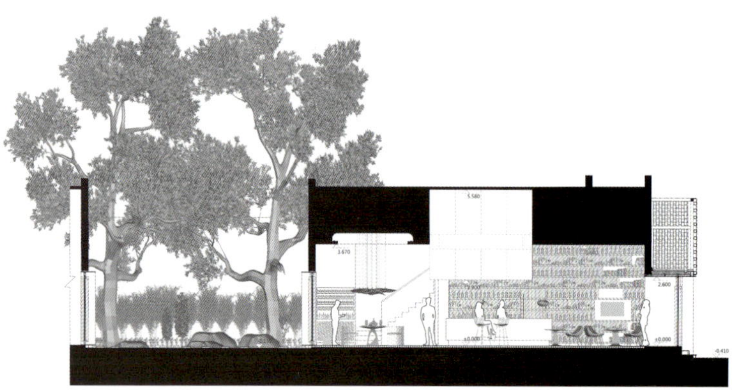

Diagrams

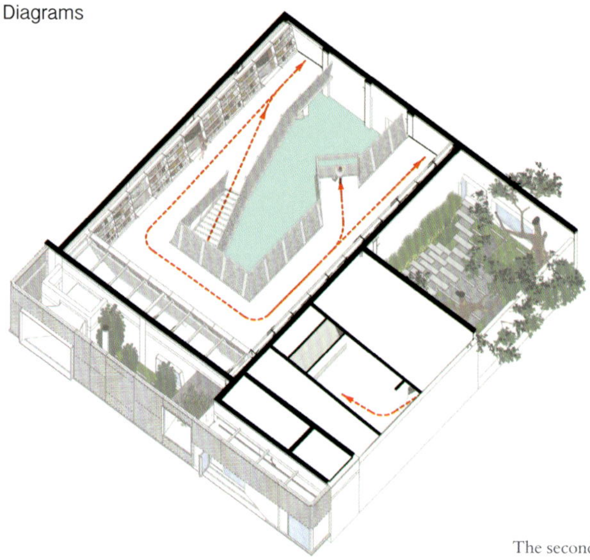

The second floor route

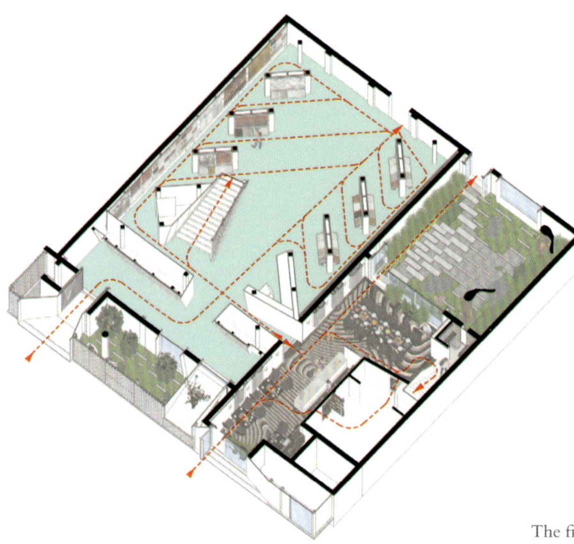

The first floor route

This celebration of stone combines the memory of traditional craftsmanship within an old storage facility with contemporary design and manufacturing techniques.

08- Main hall
09- Stone liberary
10- Front hall

08
09 10

First floor plan

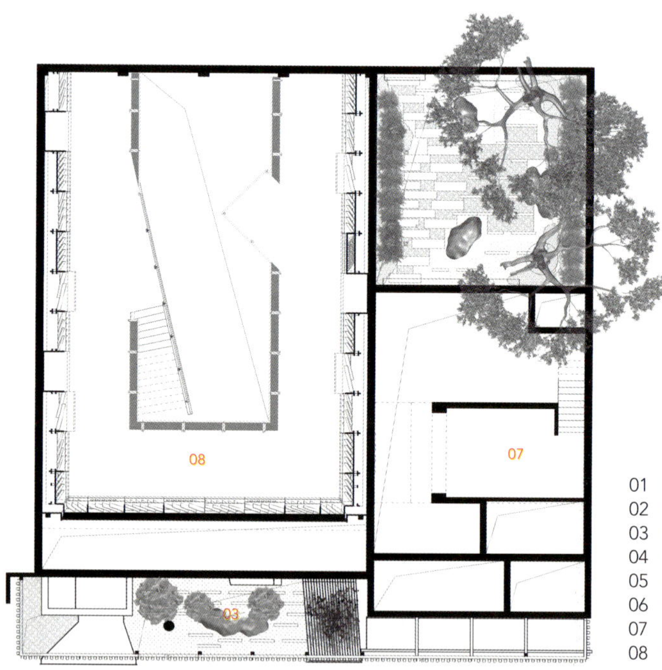

Second floor plan

01 Exhibition entrance
02 Restaurant entrance
03 Courtyard
04 Café
05 Lobby
06 Kitchen
07 Restaurant
08 Exhibition

0 1 5m

Exhibition Isometric on the second floor

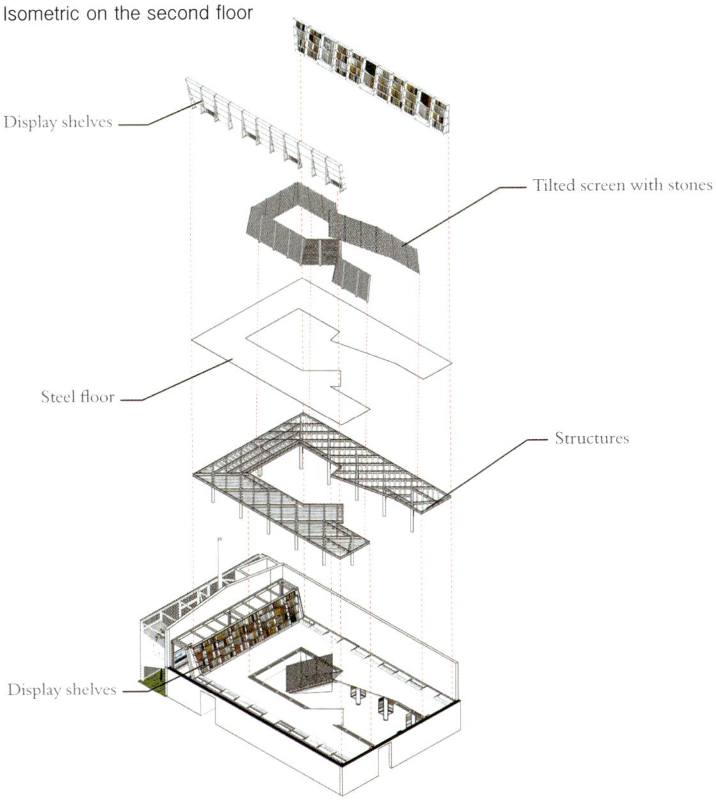

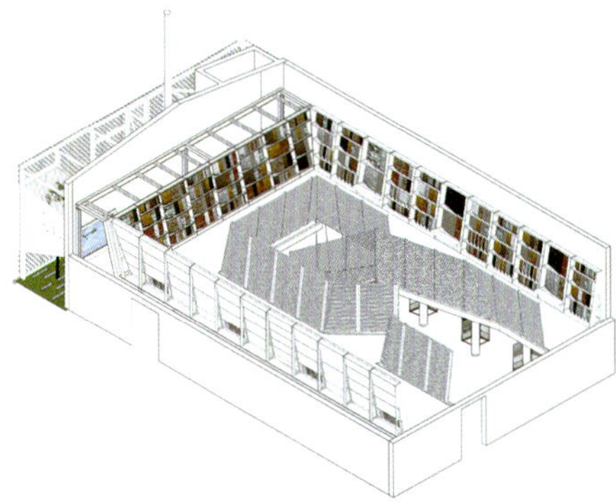

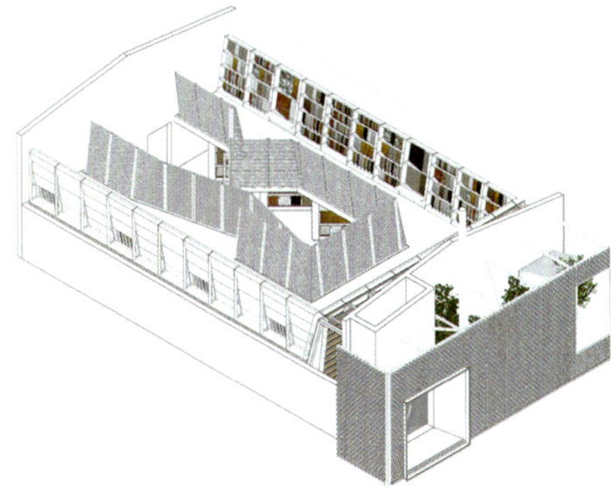

Exhibition tilted screen on the second floor

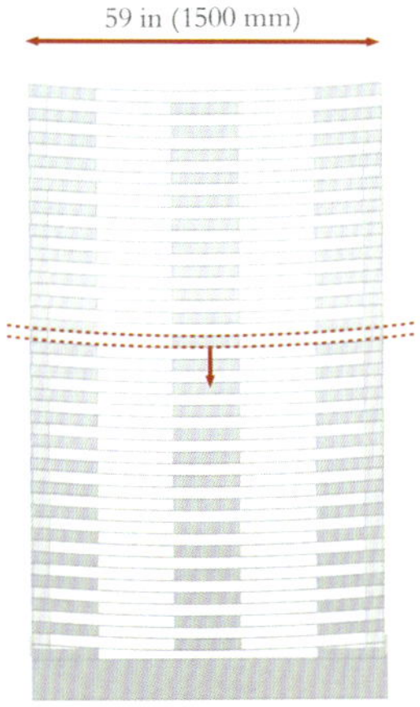

Deviation

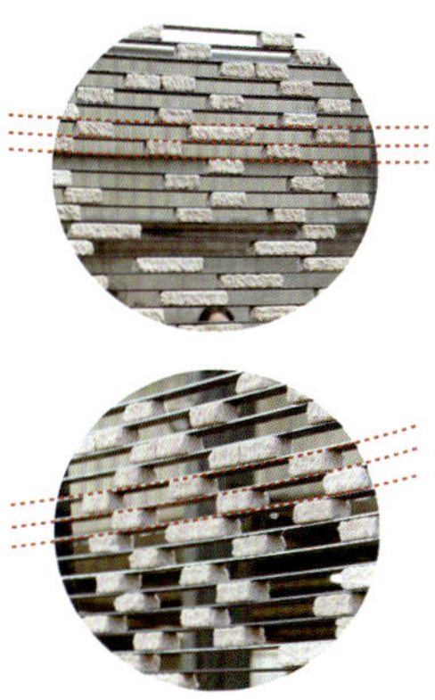

Experiments

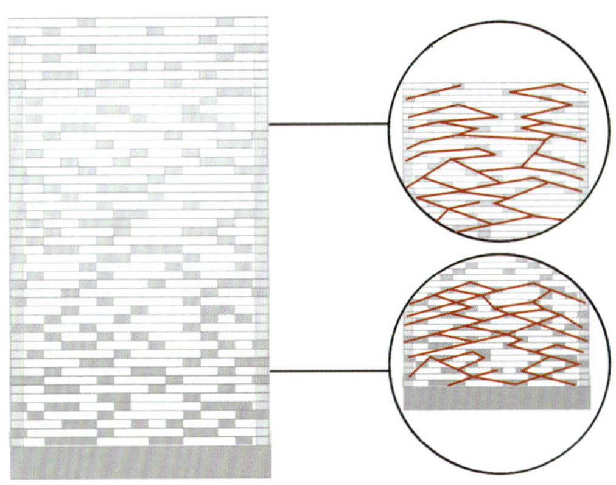

Forces pattern

11
12

11, 12- Cafeteria

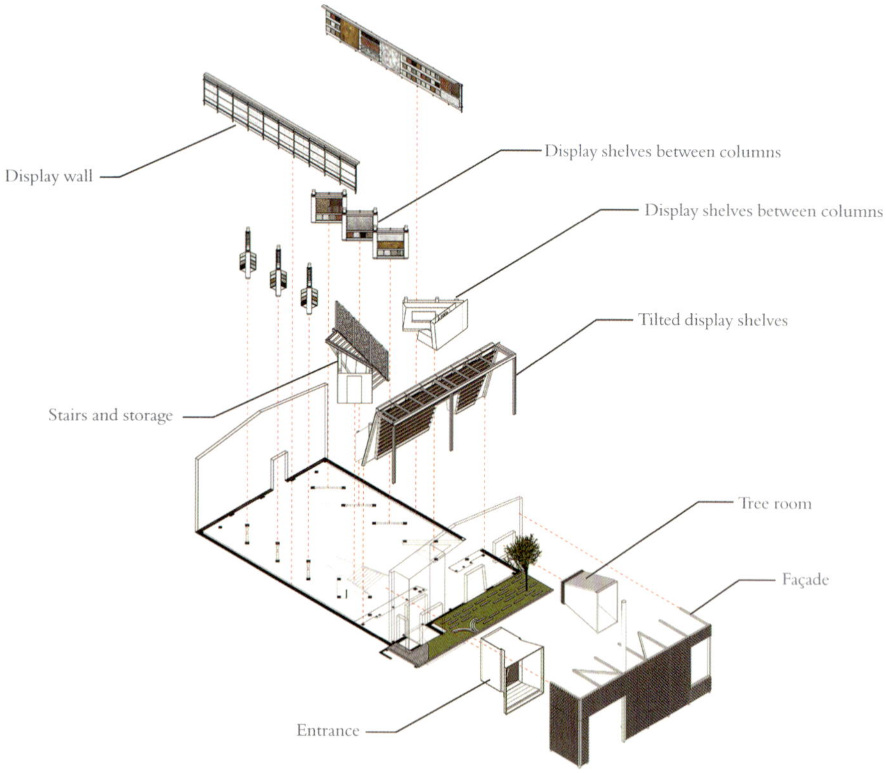

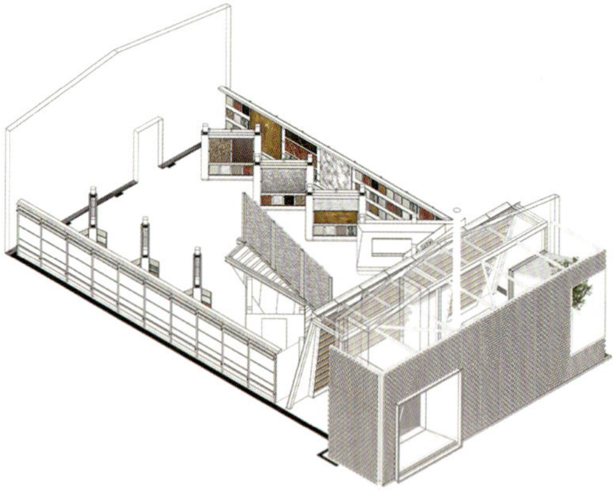

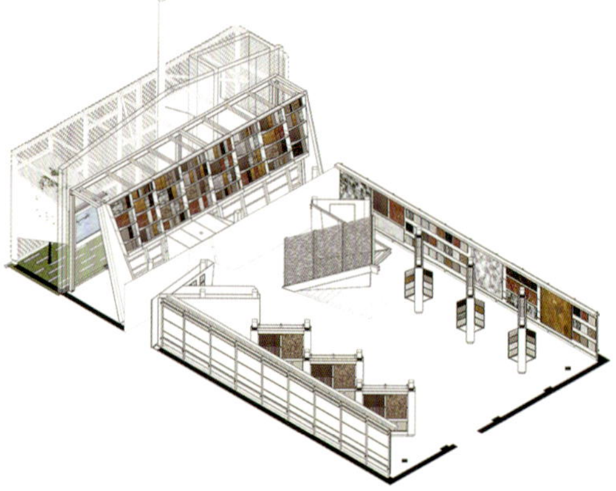

Exhibition Isometric on the first floor

Zi Bo the Great Wall Museum of Fine Art

Ancient and modern transformation

Location-Zi Bo, China
Architect-Archstudio
Area-40,849 square feet (3795 square meters)
Completion-2015
Design team-Han Wen qiang, Cong Xiao, Huang Tao
Photography-Wang Ning
Client-Zibo Yongquan Calligraphy and Painting Academy

Site plan

The dilapidated industrial factory was located behind the bustling downtown, not far from Zibo train station. Established in 1943, the building was originally a pharmaceutical factory. With the development of urbanization, the factory was forced to stop and move to a new district. All the equipment had been removed, leaving only an empty building. After being abandoned for years, the factory experienced the turn of fortune's wheel. Featuring a long-span structure and earthy texture, the factory was an ideal place for artists to visit; hence, it was decided that it should be transformed into a contemporary art museum.

The reconstruction area had a rectangle shape of about 40,903 square feet (3800 square meters), which included three workshops and a few warehouses of varying sizes. Few trees and plants could be found there, as there is a civil air defense facility under the concrete floor.

Based on the decentralized structure of the industrial factory and of its characteristically enclosed exterior, the design laid emphasis on the relationship between exterior and interior to enhance people's interaction with the artistic environment and endow the factory with life by publicity, openness, and flexibility. By creating a pedestrian path through a translucent hallway that connects the interior and exterior, it changed the mechanical impression of the old factory, forming a dialogue between the old and the new.

The sensually curved glassed hallway became a multi-functional media center, that includes a bookstore, a tea room, an art studio, and a few discussion rooms, making the daily activities of the art museum a part of exhibition. This hallway, made of coated glass and gray patterned steel panels, laid on the interior and exterior floor, creates a harmonious, horizontal, and continuous line. As visitors walk into the hallway, they will see the scenarios that can evolve alternately and repeatedly. Inside, the building maximally retains the original characteristics of its industrial design, and is interspersed with modern lighting and display walls. Outside, the cobblestone-paved ground and the newly-planted bamboos complete the exterior environment, which acts in cooperation with the interior space.

With the rapid expansion of urbanization in China, many old traditional buildings are being demolished to make space for new buildings. However, there could be a variety of methods to reuse the old buildings to explore their realistic meaning to the city. A contemporary art space should not only serve as a gallery, but also needs to be a space that embodies multi-functional activities and serves more people. This type of transformation can make the old industrial buildings more livable and brings art closer to public life.

01
02

01- Bird's view
02- The courtyard

Lightweight modern additions and insertions that successfully contrast with the rough industrial finishes of this former factory provide this building with a sense of lightness and transparency.

Axonometric

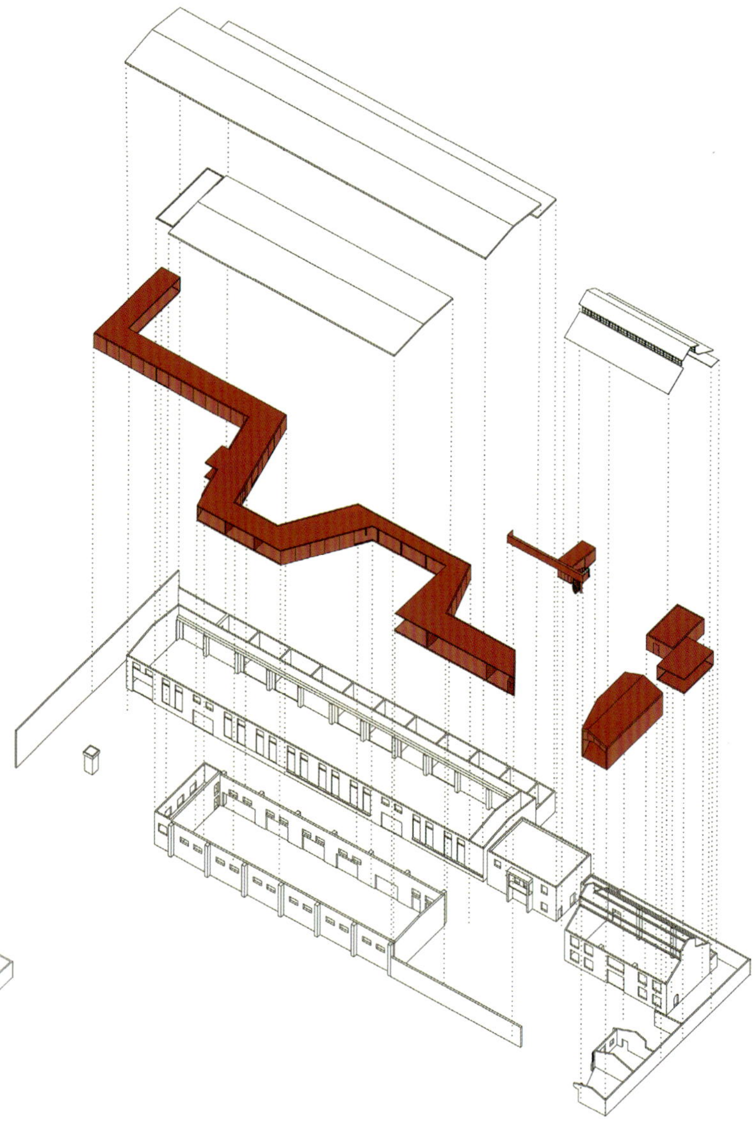

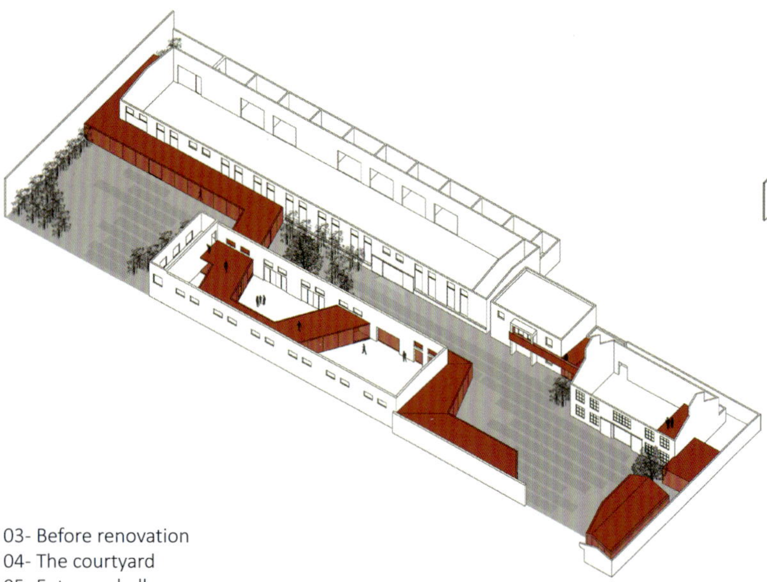

03- Before renovation
04- The courtyard
05- Entrance hall
06- Workshop hall

03 | 04 | 05 06

Sections

01 Ceramics hall
02 Calligraphy and painting
03 Hall corridor
04 Indoor courtyard
05 Artist studio

01 Corridor
02 Exhibition hall
03 Storage
04 Reception room
05 Finanical office
06 Open working office
07 Artist studio
08 Seminar
09 Negotiation room

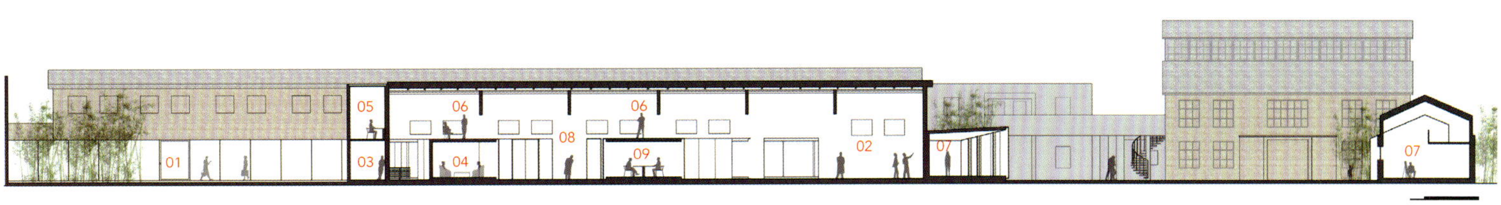

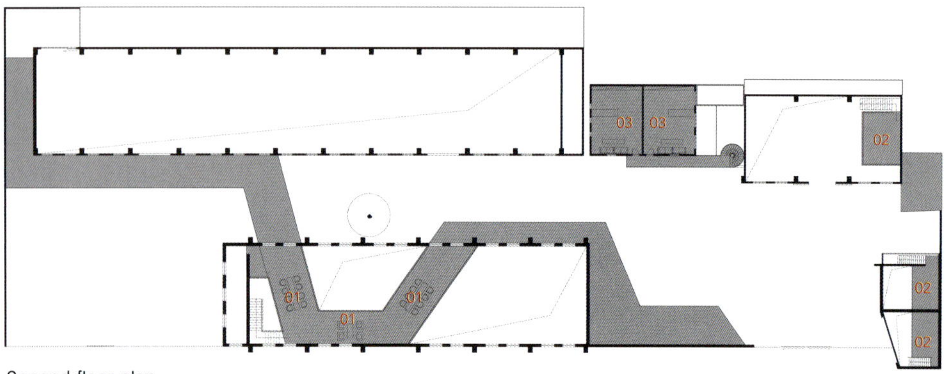

Second floor plan

01 Open working office
02 Artist studio
03 Office

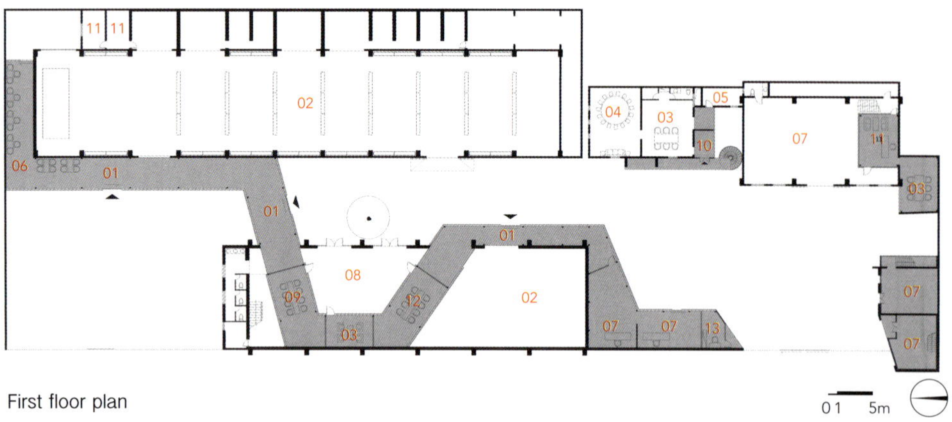

First floor plan

01 Entrance porch
02 Exhibition hall
03 Tea room
04 Restaurant
05 Kitchen
06 Tea bar
07 Artist studio
08 Seminar room
09 VIP room
10 Hall to restaurant
11 Office
12 Meeting room
13 Guard room

07 08 09

07, 08, 09- The gallery

Stella Matutina Museum

Recapturing the factory

Location-Saint-Leu, Reunion Island, France
Architect-L'Atelier Architectes
Area-9.2 acres (3.7 hectares)
Completion-2015
Photography-Hervé Douris
Client-Region Reunion

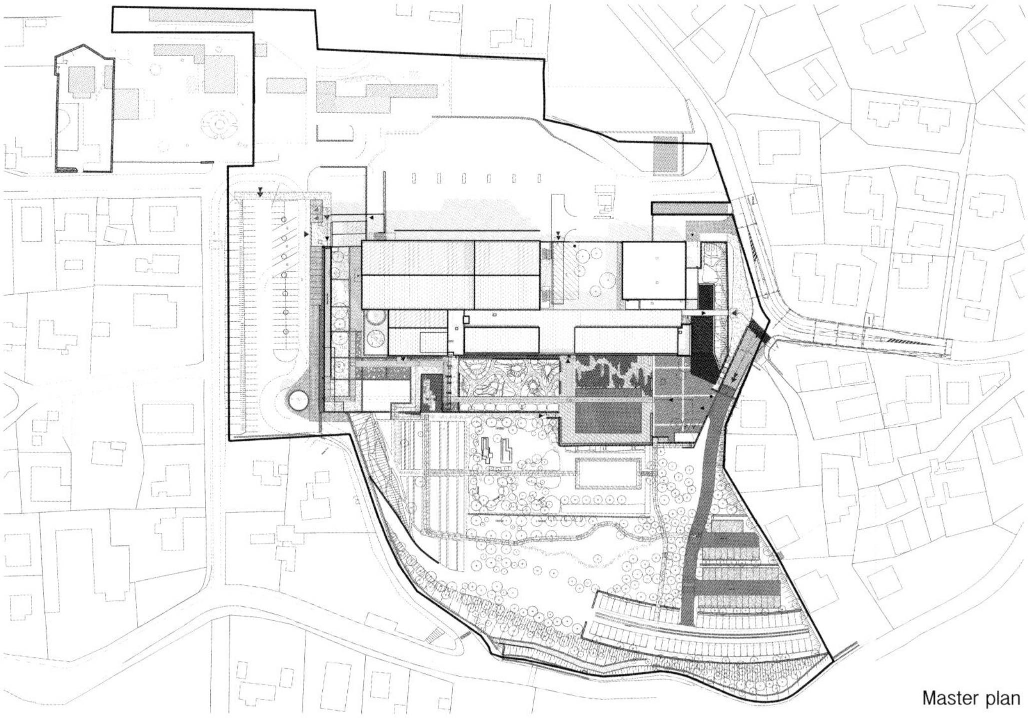

Master plan

Driven by a new scientific and cultural program, this project focused on both the buildings of the original sugar factory and the museum trail, with a set of enriched collections and the use of innovative multimedia and interactive technologies. The project implementation covered the rehabilitation of the buildings, restoration of the collection items, and the museographical aspect. The architects were in charge of all operations onsite, including environmental remediation, restoration of machines, and transport of heavy collection items from their locations in situ.

The architects moved to the site of the old factory for the duration of the design phase. An important task of appropriation of the site, its environment, and its history was undertaken by the architectural team. A special insight was also made possible, thanks to the cooperation with former workers of the factory. This enhanced the understanding of the site and its environmental conditions, the integration of the factory in the landscape, and the history of the region and its inhabitants.

The challenge was to restore the original area and enhance the factory, which had a strong symbolic trait. The museum was essentially only the old factory, which was revealed through the removal of gateways and multiple split levels that rendered it unreadable. The factory was imbued with new life and its original sense of grandeur could be experienced once again.

The modification was deliberately light on the exterior of the factory. It was limited to the change of the outer part of the building in order to identify it better as a museum, marking its transition from an industrial into a cultural building. A slightly nobler treatment was chosen with the use of copper cladding.

The northern façade was cladded with louvers. This large horizontal cladding ventilates the building while protecting it from sunlight. In addition, it provides a beautiful natural light inside, which varies according to the time of day. From far away, the façade vibrates and sparkles in the sun 'like sugar.'

The additions and extensions, which met the client's desires of having an archive center, a temporary exhibition hall, and an amphitheater, were placed in such a way that Stella's silhouette remained unchanged. The extensions were hidden in the contours of the existing building and they do not alter the perception of Stella in any way, especially its silhouette as it emerges. It can be discovered gradually from La Route des Tamarins—the main highway that connects the north to the south of the island.

About 60 machines were refurbished and staged in the museum. Some, by their large size, were restored in situ, with all the precautions that this job required, on a site under construction. More generally, the restoration of nearly 600 collection items allowed local actors to take advantage of skills transfer from experienced personnel.

Endemic plants, fruit trees, shrubs, aromatic herbs in the landscaping of the gardens created an educational, leisure, and heritage space for visitors. The gardens and outdoor spaces, completely renovated, consist of several pathways as well as external spaces dedicated to diverse events.

01

01- Large-scale landcaping

Sections

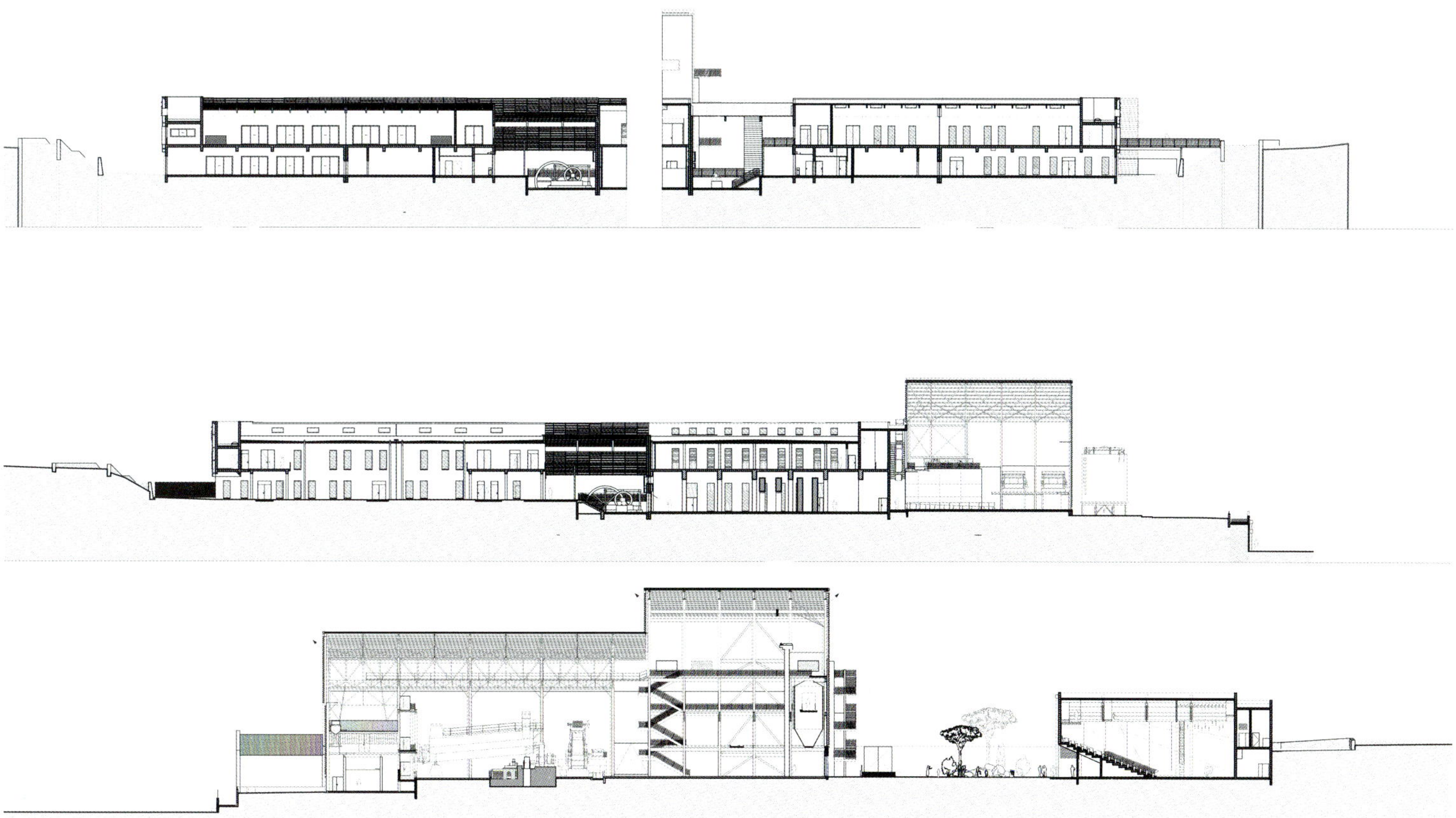

02 03
04
05 06 07 08

02- Existing building
03- Construction site
04- Large horizontal cladding ventilates the building
05- Old machine parts, like wheels, were kept to create an educational and heritage landscaping space
06- A new skin dresses the building
07- Moving and restoring machinery
08- Interior of the existing building

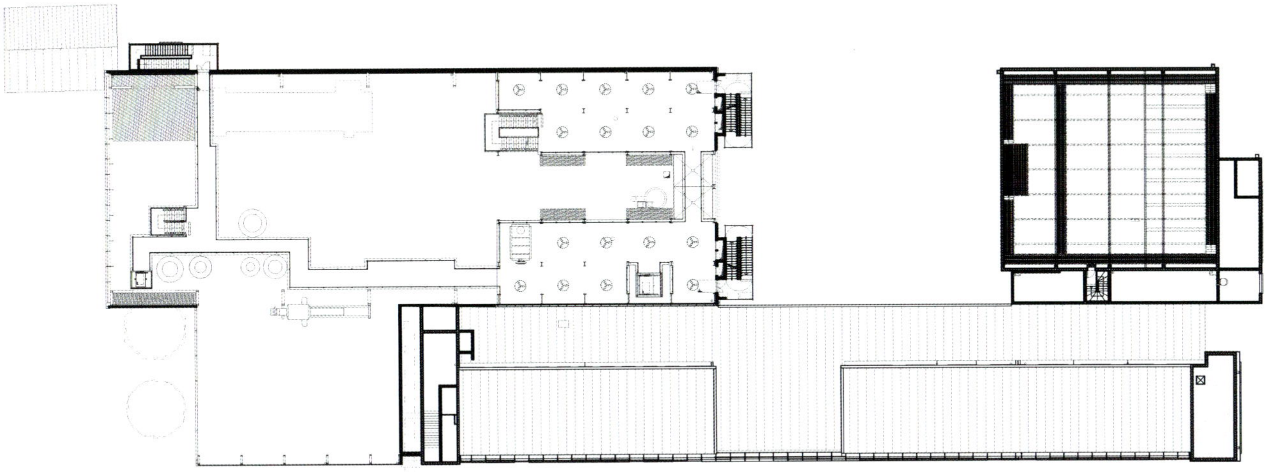

Third floor plan

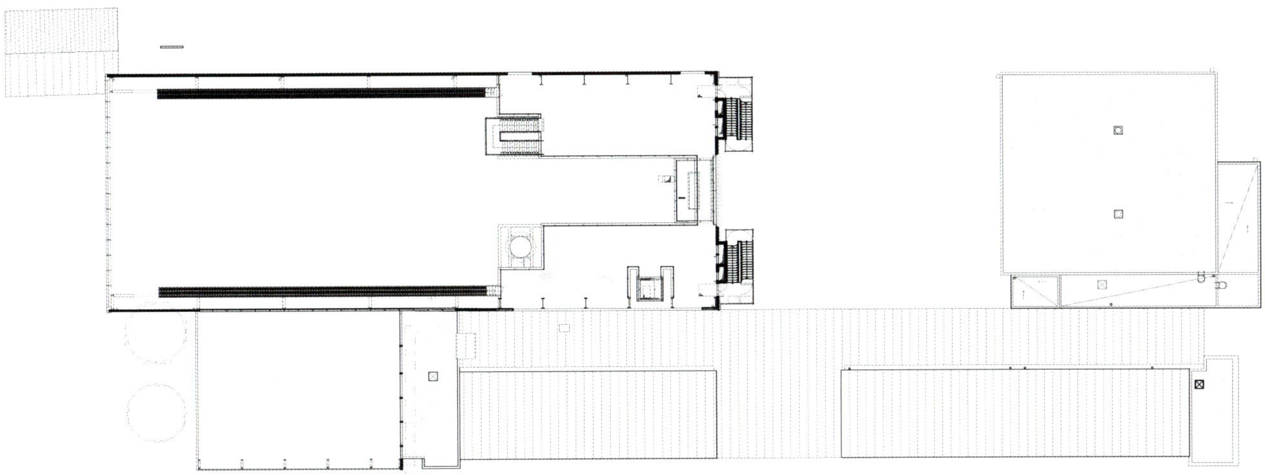

Second floor plan

The architects of this project took on a range of different roles and immersed themselves into its context. Uncovering the stories of past employees and allowing for the transfer of specialized knowledge helped to facilitate the preservation of both tangible and intangible heritage.

09

10 11

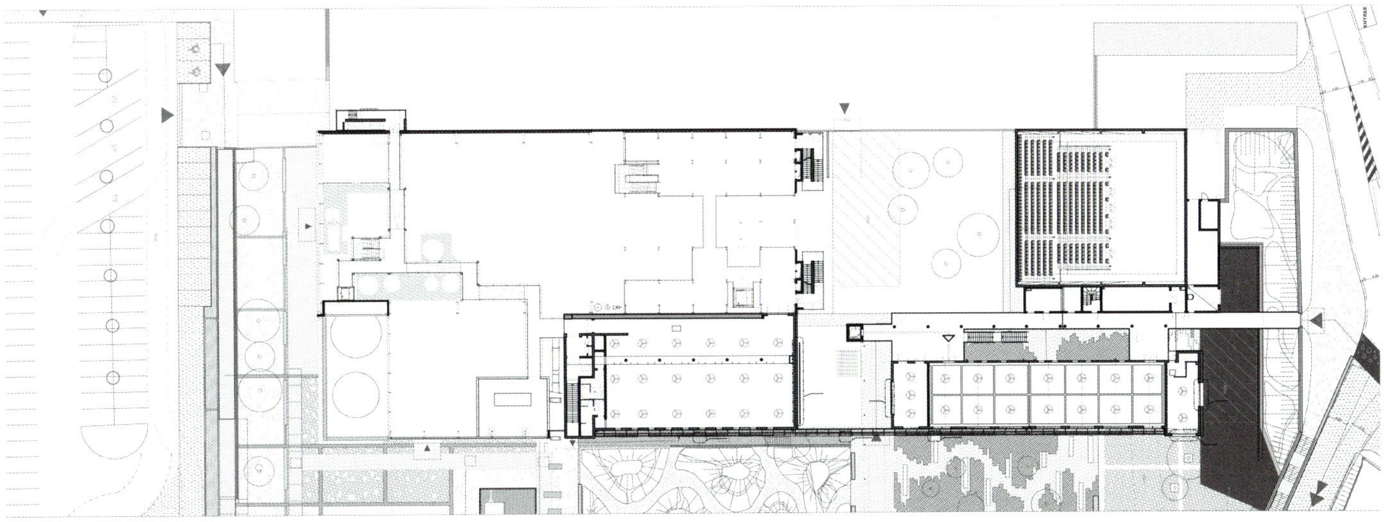

First floor plan

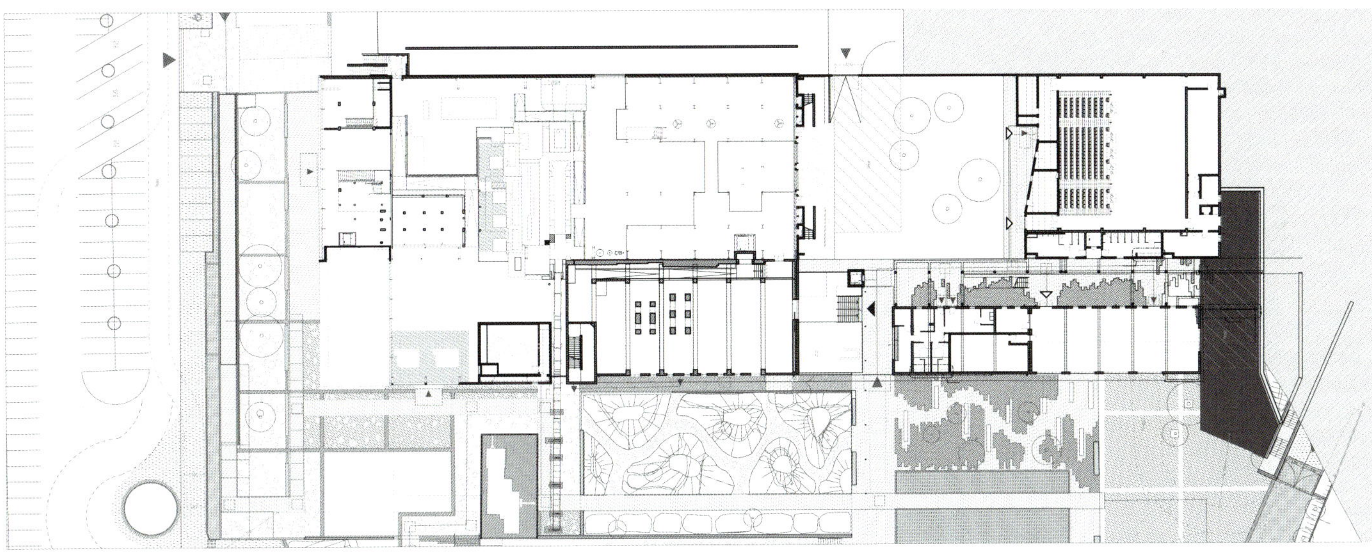

Ground floor plan

09- The factory—the main collector's item
10- 60 industrial machines in situ
11- Collection items

Royal House Recording

Manufacturing warehouse reuse

Location-Royal Oak, USA
Architect-Saroki Architecture
Area-5,450 square feet (506 square meters)
Completion-2015
Photography-Jared Chulski
Client-Royal House Recording

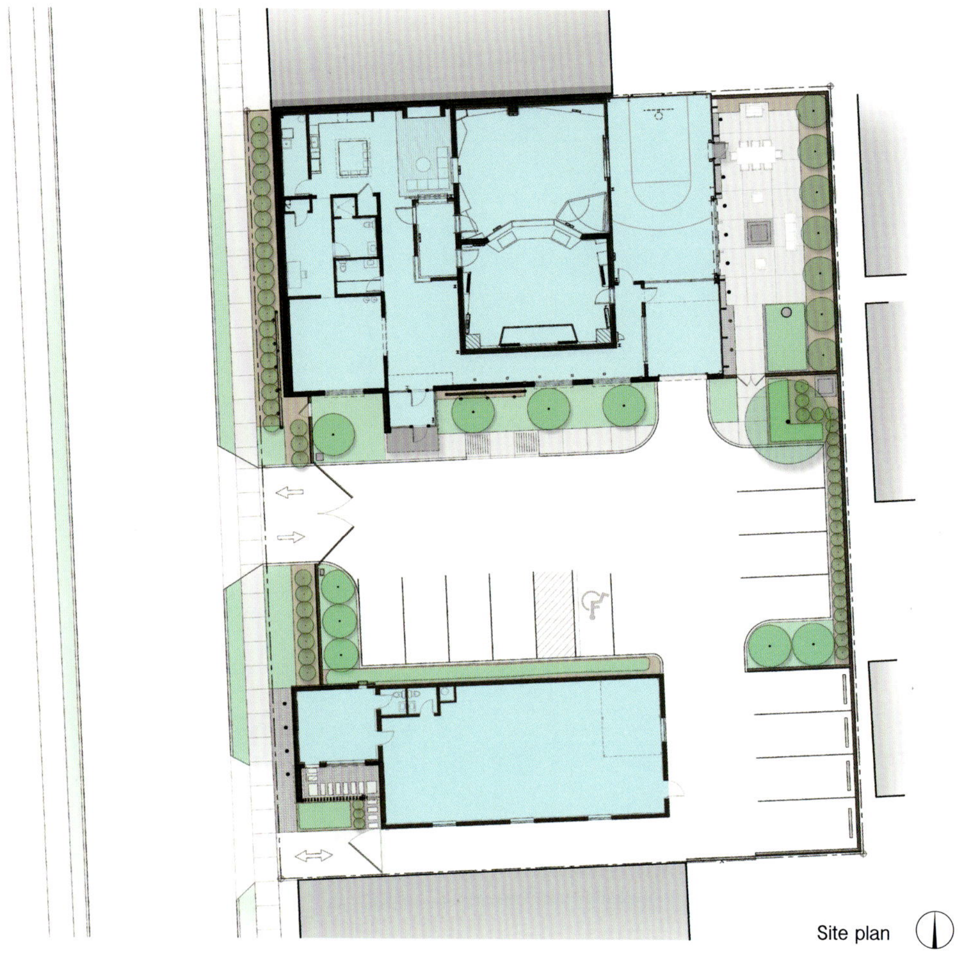

Site plan

Royal House Recording represents a new approach to inspiring the creativity of today's recording artists. It functions as a small campus with an array of amenities and private courtyards that help artists break from the generic confines of a typical studio. This adaptive re-use project is situated along Delemere Avenue in Royal Oak's primary industrial corridor, providing the privacy and flexibility required for its users. Built from the remains of an old manufacturing warehouse, Royal House Recording intended to help bring back the status of Greater Detroit's legendary past in the music industry.

This fully equipped studio accommodates every need of its artists for intense recording sessions. It is supplemented with a kitchen, lounge, exercise room, basketball court, and outdoor patio. These amenities allow the artists to work with an uninterrupted creative flow. The campus is entirely enclosed with a perimeter wall, creating a private environment for the high-profile artists.

The building's exterior took cues from the original industrial aesthetic, yet it is accented by a glass entry, custom steel doors, and a large glass and steel bi-folding hanger door. Free-standing red cedar screen walls provide warmth and contrast, while lush trees and shrubs soften the courtyard landscapes. A pierced brick privacy wall serves to shield the entrance of the secondary office and storage building from the street and creates yet another private courtyard.

The interior of the project carefully blends industrial elements with custom-stained cedar walls and a theatrical 'Hollywood glam' selection of finishes. Much of the interior was built as separate structures within the original warehouse because the existing building had a limited structural capacity. These new structural frames and beams were left exposed to identify with the original architectural character. Luxurious finishes and nuanced details coexist harmoniously with concrete block and raw steel to create an environment that stimulates the senses and encourages creativity.

01

02

01- Perspective view from street
02- North elevation—interior private courtyard looking at main entrance and private garage

West elevation

03 04
05

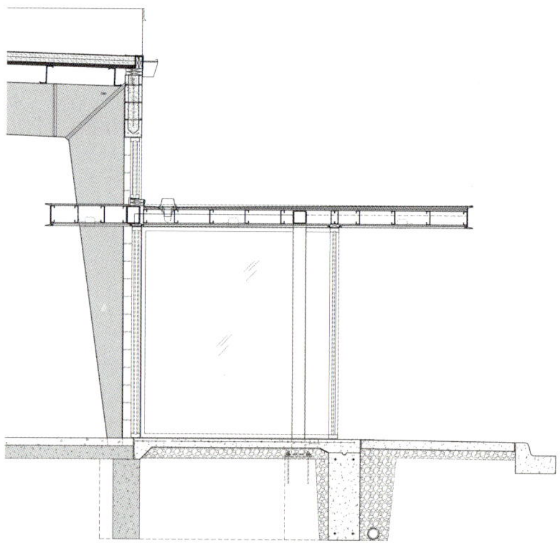

Section through the main entrance vestibule

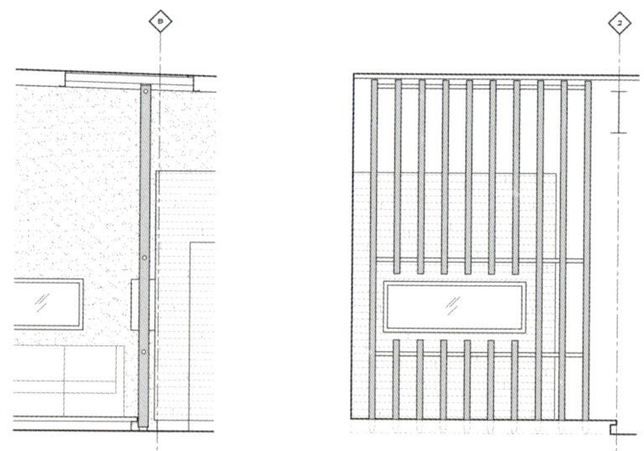

Interior cedar wood screen wall section and elevation in lounge

03, 04- Street view of the original existing manufacturing warehouse
05- Evening view of the west elevation showing the recording studio complex on the left and the annex studio on the right.

South elevation

Original south elevation of existing manufacturing warehouse

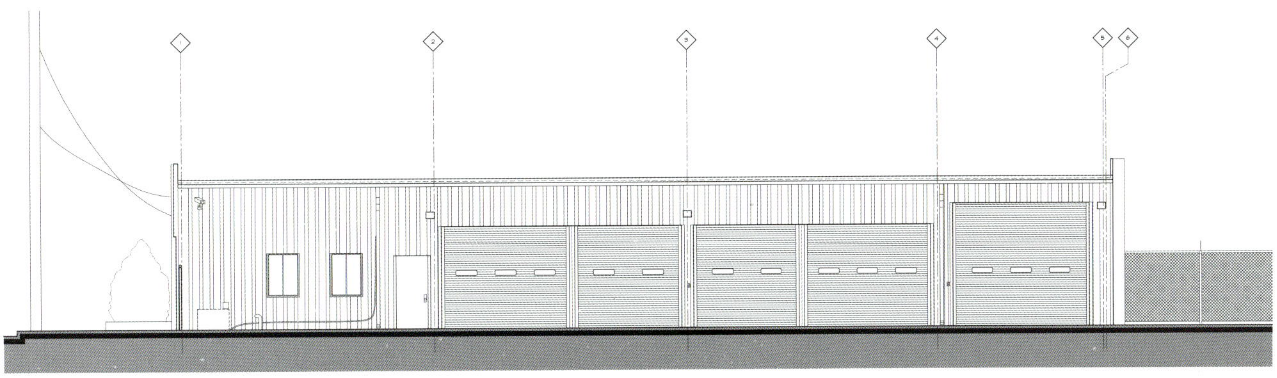

06- Aerial view of patio and bi-folding hanger door
07- Main entrance vestibule for recording studio
08- Brick screen wall and courtyard for annex studio
09- View from basketball court looking into the garage
10- Kitchen

06 | 09
07 08 | 10

An exposed industrial material palette contrasts with the plush finishes expected by this building's clientele. These same finishes have been used on planar exterior elements, which, through their layered application, have helped to enrich the original building's low-slung nature and simple rectangular form.

11- Lounge
12- Gallery
13- Control room
14- Live room

Hall within the cloud
Renovation of a metal materials factory

Location-Beijing, China
Architect-office PROJECT
Area-8611 square feet (800 square meters)
Completion-2016
Photography-Sun Haiting
Client-Xu Hongquan

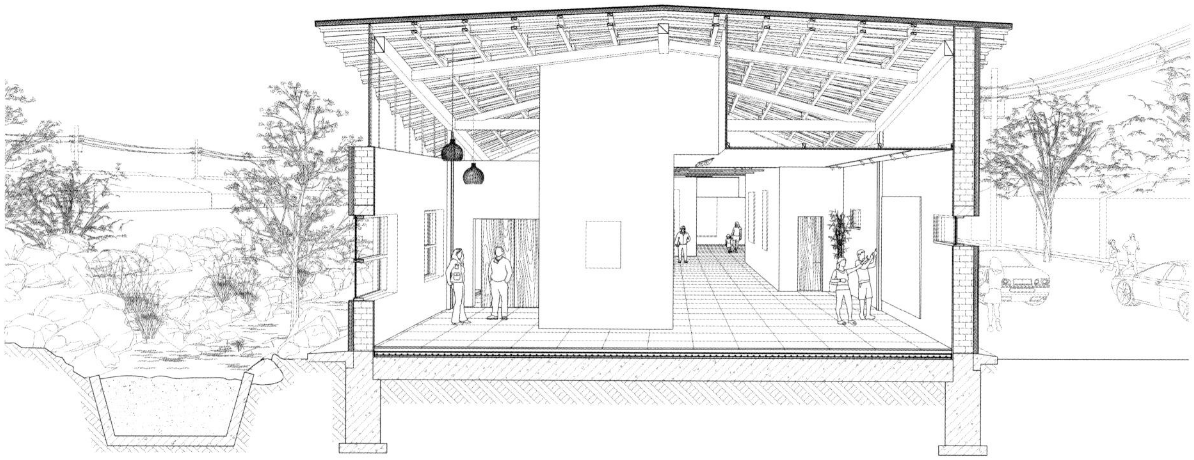
Section

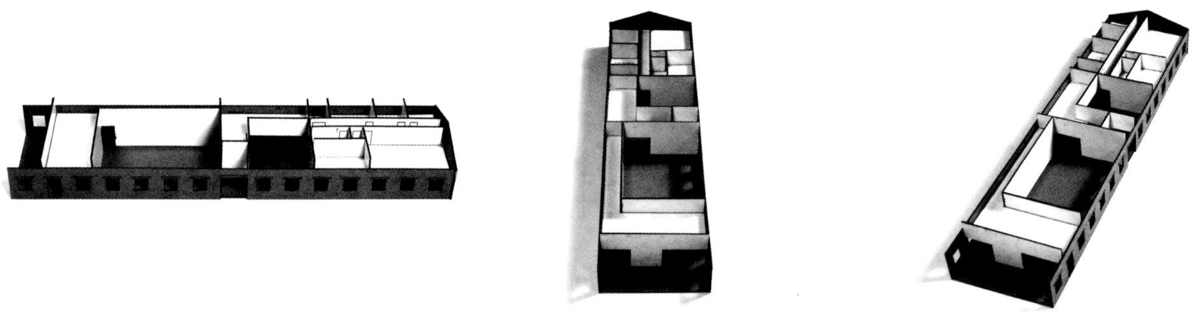
Models

The old factory building of a metal materials plant at Huairou District in Beijing was converted into Xu Hongquan's atelier, with the typical configuration of an artist's studio, including an office, a tea room, a bedroom, a reading room, and so on. Before reconstruction, the metal materials plant was a typical linear brick factory building with a sloped roof. The building was about 19.5 feet (6 meters) tall, kept in good condition, and included a triangular steel roof truss structure.

Based on basic needs, such as sleeping and dining, the middle area was transformed into a space for meeting and exhibiting, and the outermost area for studio space for the painter. The architect created a nested progressive space structure. People can walk from one room into another room through the exit at the corner of room. The openings at corners form a visual corridor running through the building. Events that happen in each space can be watched by another space, which thoroughly eliminates the need for corridors at the same time.

Since the site is surrounded by a mass of forest land, Mr. Xu wanted to move the bedroom and study to the second floor, so that the beautiful surroundings can be appreciated. It was decided not to use the double-pitched roof on the second floor since it would have made the structure too high and it would have made the junction with the existing roof too abrupt. At the same time, it was felt that this would not have resulted in a sympathetic dialogue with the existing roof form.

01

01- Entrance

02 03
04 05
06

Construction diagram of roof

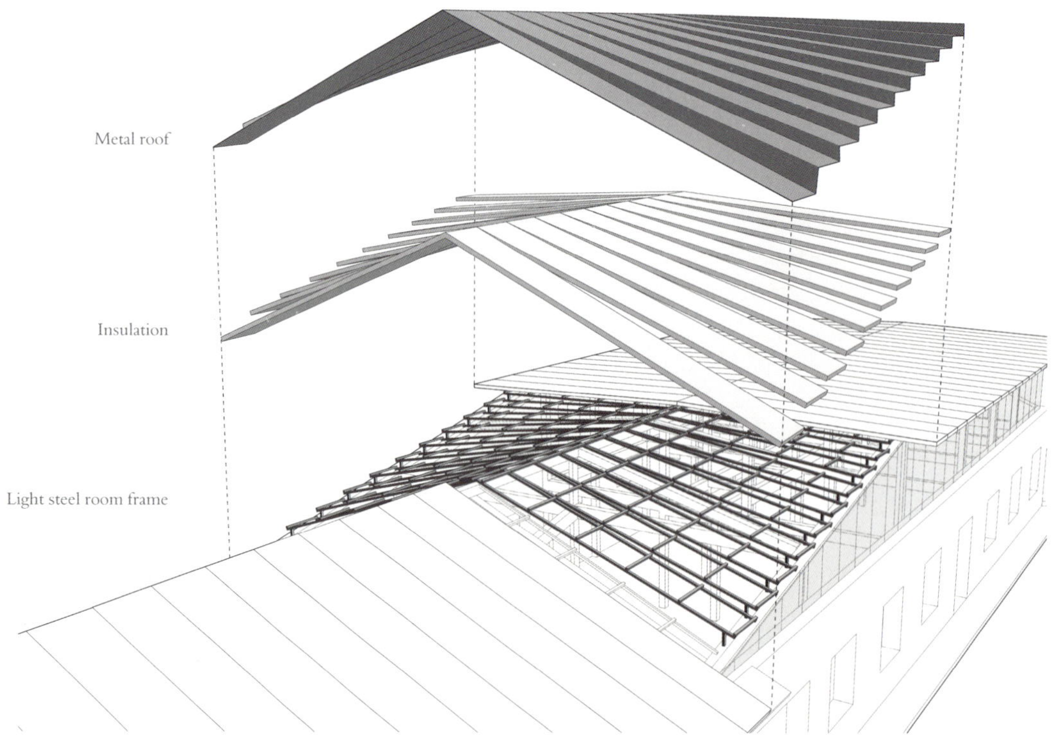

02, 03, 04, 05- Building process
06- The yard

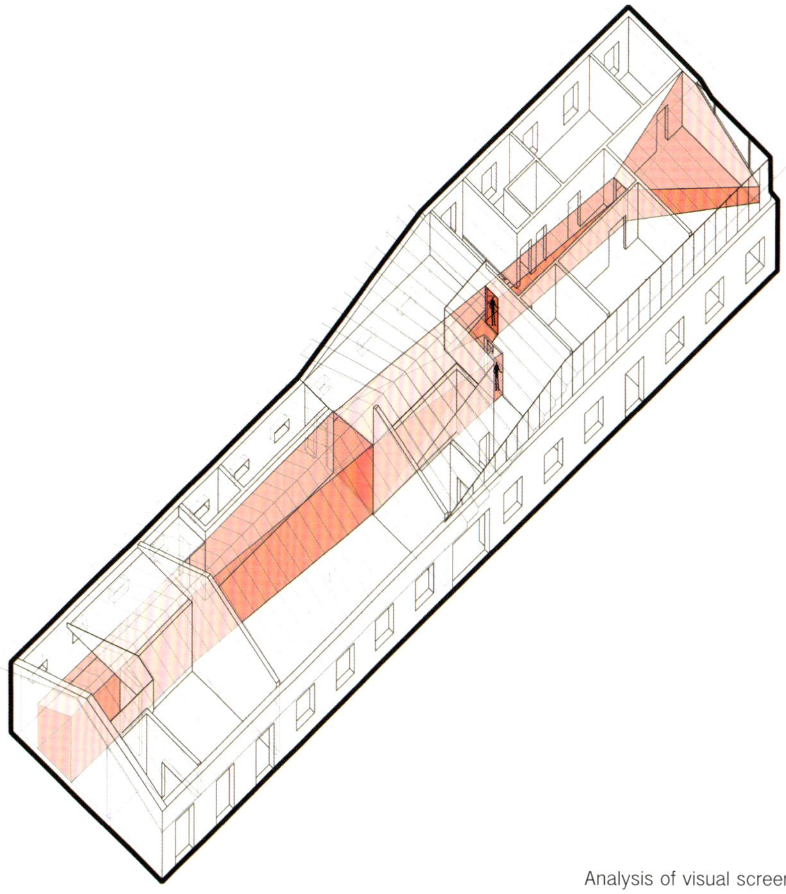

Analysis of visual screen

Construction diagram

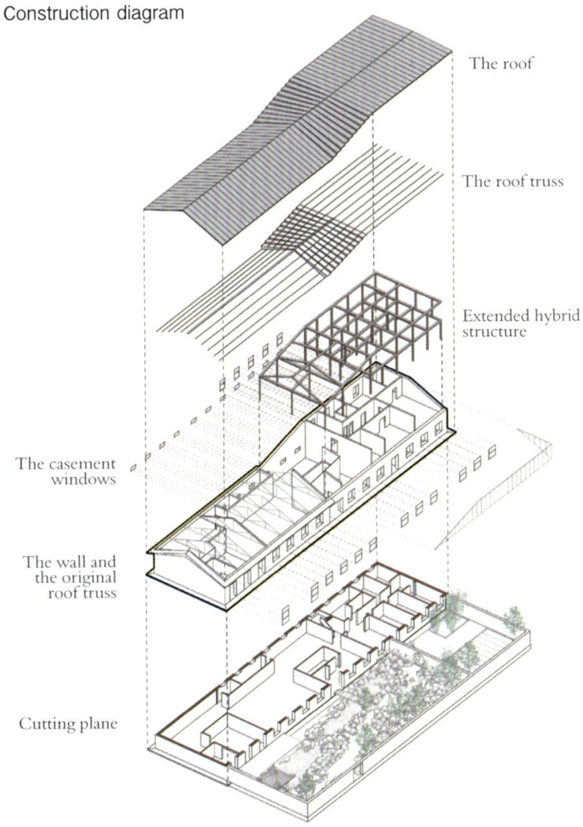

07- Exhibition area
08- Gallery at the entrance
09- The exhibition area imitates the effect of 'painting of the painting,' like the Double Screen Chess Painting by Zhou Wenju (Song Dynasty)
10,11- The interior design accentuates a transparent effect throughout the whole exhibition hall

07 09
08 10 11

This artist's studio has a fluid spatial arrangement with a distinctive segmented roof that emerges out of an existing double-pitched roof structure; this allowed for the insertion of large glazed panels that admit light into the exhibition space below, and provide panoramic views from the main bedroom and studio on the first floor.

13
12

Second floor plan

01 Storage
02 Bathroom
03 Video room
04 Bathroom
05 Master bedroom
06 Studio
07 Ceiling
08 Dormer

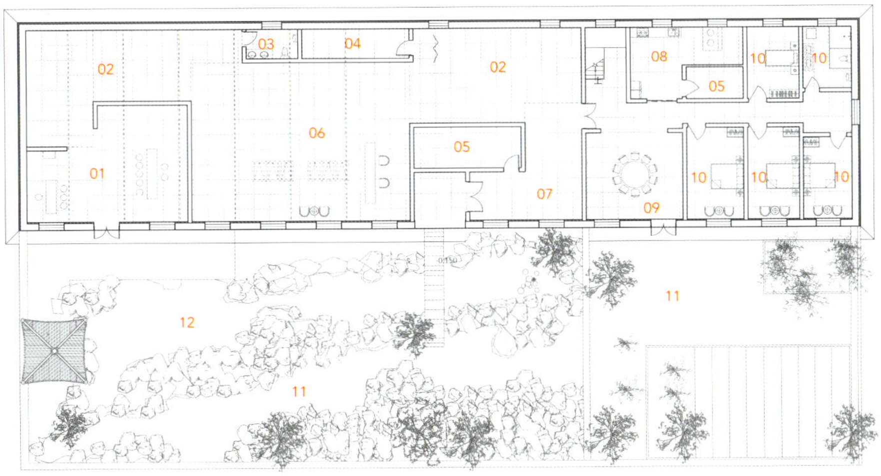

First floor plan

01 Tea room
02 Exhibition area
03 Bath room
04 Bathroom
05 Storage
06 Painting/exhibition area
07 Foyer
08 Kitchen
09 Dining room
10 Bedroom
11 Yard
12 Pond

12- Foyer
13- Tea room

Ruhr Museum

Rehabilitation of a UNESCO World Heritage Site

Location-Essen, Germany
Architect-HG Merz GmbH
Area-51,667 square feet (4800 square meters)
Completion-2010
Photography-Brigida González (Museum), HG Merz (original building)
Client-Zollverein Foundation

Section

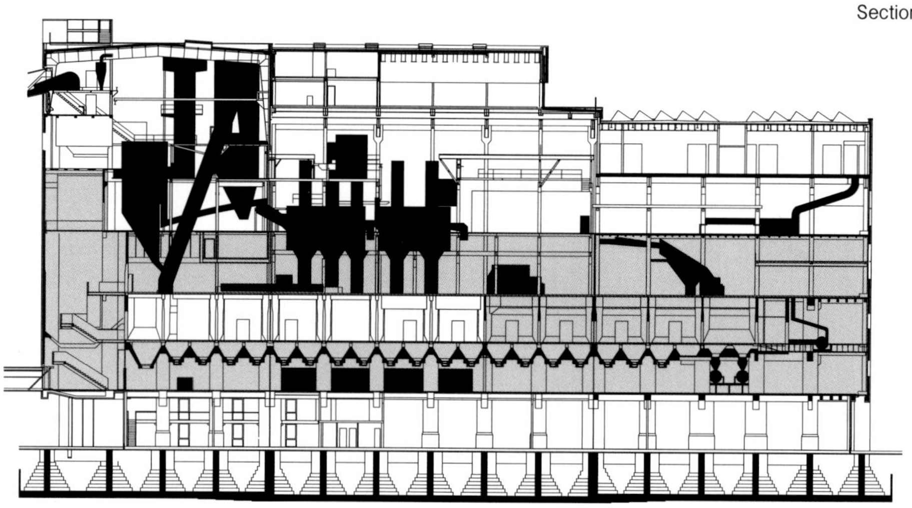

The Zollverein coal mine in Essen may be seen as a symbol of the region's transformation process. Erected around 1930 by Fritz Schupp and Martin Kremmer as a unified whole, the complex is recognized today as a World Heritage Site.

Starting in 1989, it was rehabilitated step by step. At the heart of the former coal mine, the monumental coal-washing plant posed a particular challenge for developing an appropriate museum concept and exhibition design. The cultural significance of the landmarked building complex led to a sensitive and creative handling of the spaces filled with historic machines. Heinrich Böll Architects and Office for Metropolitan Architecture (OMA) refurbished the building and added a grand new escalator that marked the metamorphosis of the architecture. HG Merz developed a museum concept and visitor center as well as a 'monument's path' and implemented it into the landmarked building.

Rather than competing with the building, the exhibition unfolded in a distinct, chary character. A lucid guiding system and an intuitive physical structure reacted precisely to the building, which is seen more as a machine. The result is a museum that is as unique as the structure it is placed in. About 80 percent of the machines were kept in place for reasons of conservation, a fact that posed something of a challenge for the museum designers, who were forced to lay out the various collections and exhibitions around the existing objects.

The exhibition itself is divided into three main chapters: Presence, Memory, and History. The three main chapters are located on different levels at heights of the 56 feet (17 meters), 39 feet (12 meters), and 20 feet (6 meters) level. The levels were added for the museum, since the coal washing facility was a machine and nobody was supposed to walk through it.

At the 56 feet (17 meters) level, which is reached via the grand OMA escalator, visitors encounter the Ruhr Area as it is now. The open structure and the bright and white appearance stand for the light of the present, but also for the laboratory setting the Ruhr Area became after heavy industry mostly left the region. The clear and abstract exhibition design builds a stark contrast to the 14 mighty bucket conveyors that reveal the original function of the building.

The exhibition design of the 39 feet (12 meters) level answers to the complex spatial structures with 12 coal bunkers and the surrounding original technical equipment of the building. In the bunkers, objects of high aesthetic quality are presented like in an art gallery with the outer walls encrusted with coal dust. The 20 feet (6 meters) level combines a viewing storage space with scenographic interventions. It tells the story of the development of the Ruhr Area as an industrial region and the massive restructuring of Europe's most densely populated region. The exhibition design on this level incorporates on a spatial level the depth and ramifications of historiography.

The design of the new Ruhr Museum was awarded numerous prizes. Where once 'black gold' was washed and sorted by complex and highly rationalized industrial processes, the natural and cultural history of the Ruhr area is now presented on three levels in a new integrated concept. Today, it is the center of the redeveloped area of UNESCO's World Heritage Zollverein.

01

01- Kohlenwäsche (coal washing plant) at UNESCO World Heritage Zollverein

02, 03, 04, 05- Original building, retrofitted by Heinrich Böll Architekt
06- Media shows highlights and explains the machines without interfering with the monument
07- Exhibition and building go hand in hand
08- The whole coal washing plant is open to public tours
09- Historic artifacts of collections from the region inside the machine/building
10- Info point for the industrial heritage of the region

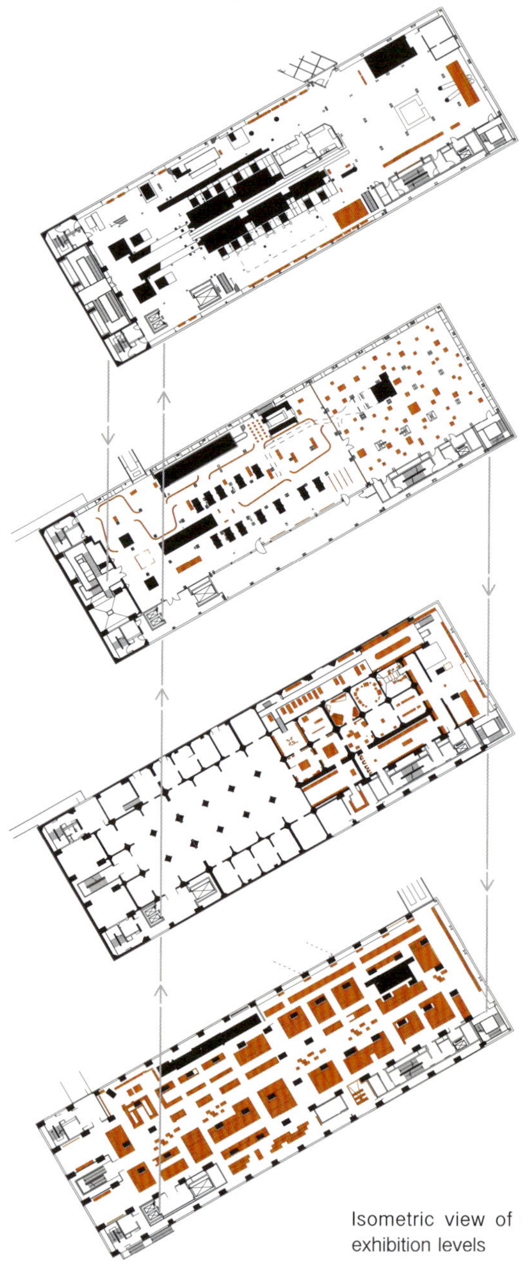

Isometric view of all exhibition levels

02 03 04 05	08
06 07	09 10

11 | 12 | 13

11- Cultural heritage of a former heavy industry region
12- Archaeology and natural history
13- Movie sequences revive live work in the Ruhr Area

PHENOMENA
GEGENWART | THE PRESENT
STRUKTUREN

A well-conceived processional route flows through a former coal-washing plant, which is reminiscent of a futuristic movie set. Illuminated museum displays provide dramatic highlights inside the dark, moody interior, which was allowed to retain its sense of drama, atmosphere, and monumentality.

14 | 15 16 | 17 18

14- Models of the cultural regeneration of the Ruhr Area, a former heavy industry region
15, 16, 17, 18- Prehistory, work life, spirituality, nature: the Ruhr Museum combines a variety of subjects inside the industrial monument

Wine Experience Hotel

From vineyard to tourism center

Location-Amarante, Portugal
Architect-FCC Arquitectura
Interior design-Paulo Lobo
Area-55,972 square feet (5200 square meters)
Completion-2015
Photography-Fernando Guerra, FG + SG
Client-Quinta da Lixa

Cross section of the main house

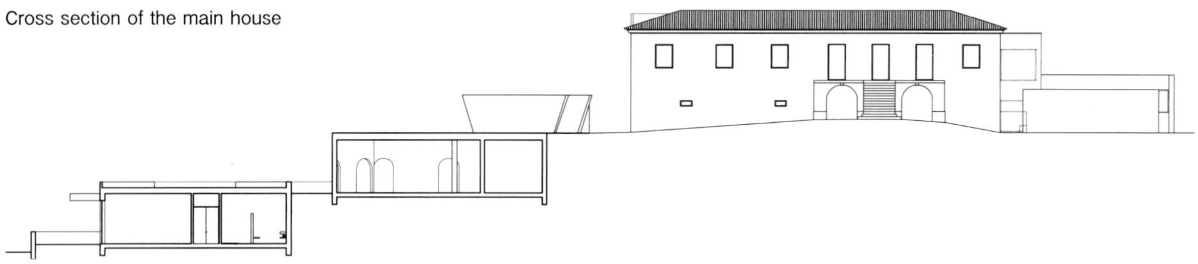

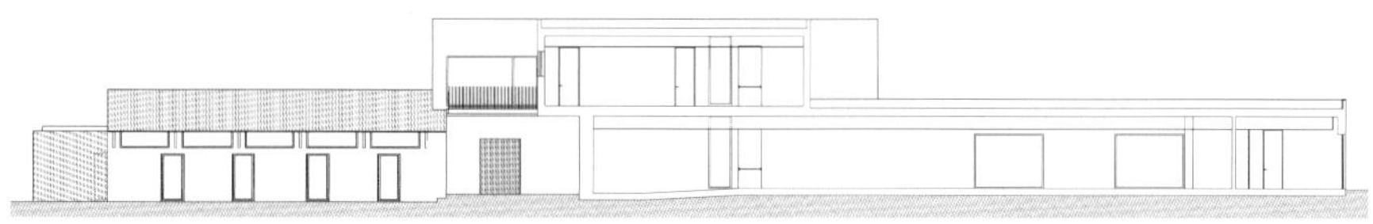

Cross section of the west house

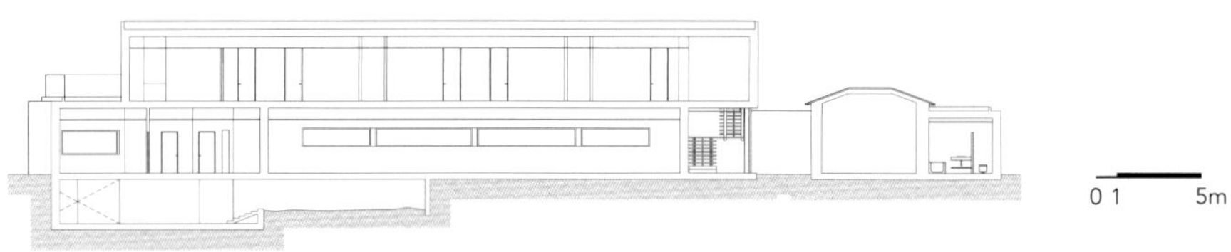

Cross section of the east house

Located in northern Portugal, this project aimed to transform a space that used to produce wine into a rural hotel devoted to wine tourism. The main thrust of the project was to refine this space by adding a luxury touristic component, fully integrated in and framed by the pre-existing physical environment. The key aim was to make the vineyard and its wine the centerpiece of the enterprise, connecting visitors to the cultural heritage and landscape of wine production.

The scheme included accommodation (30 rooms) and catering services, winery tours, a spa, indoor and outdoor pools, wine-tasting rooms, and events and conferences facilities. There are footpaths around the property that seamlessly connect its various buildings, while the visual link between the building's interior spaces and the surrounding environment helps define an intimate atmosphere with a strong rural character.

The pre-existing built-up area was insufficient for the optimum investment program. It was, thus, decided to embark on an effort to rebuild and expand this area, guided and inspired by the key features of the old buildings and infrastructure. The old buildings, with the exception of the main house, all had a rural character, but were in a state of disrepair and degradation. The formal and functional regeneration of this space, and the expansion of the built-up area, sought to preserve its architectural legacy, respecting the natural environment and the cultural heritage of the setting. It revitalized the whole of the infrastructure, while retaining its identity, fostering a dialogue between contemporary architecture and rural surroundings.

The project aspired to go well beyond offering luxurious accommodation and catering. It intended to create a truly unique experience for its visitors through a harmonious, mutually-reinforcing interaction of the various physical elements that make up the whole architectural setting—an engaging, exclusive space, where each element is perfectly integrated into a coherent whole.

01

01- Aerial view of the buildings

02
03 04 | 05
06

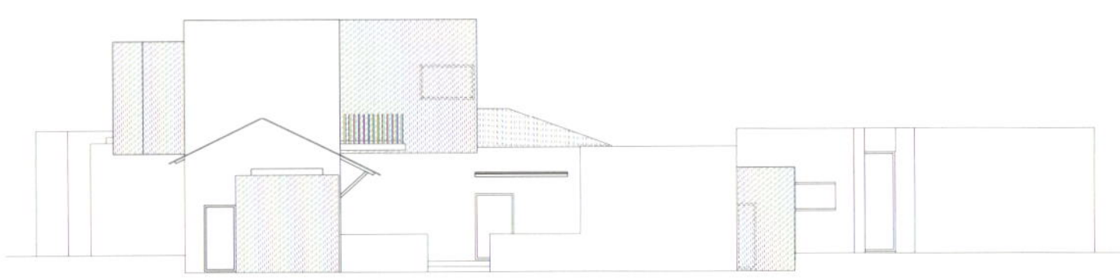

West house—north elevation

West house—west elevation

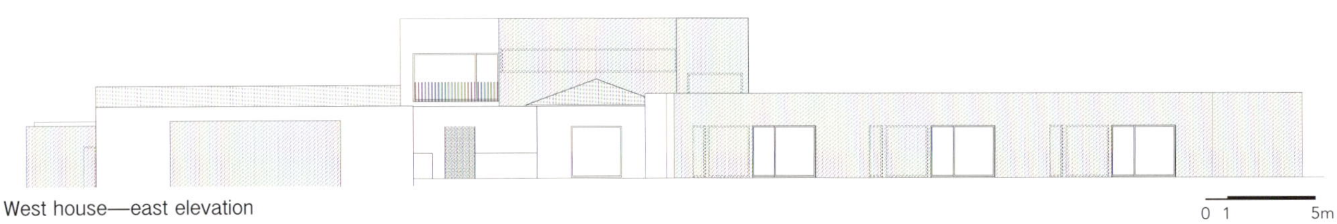

West house—east elevation

02- Aerial view of the site
03- Main house pre-existence
04- West house pre-existence
05- View of the east house
06- View of the south façade

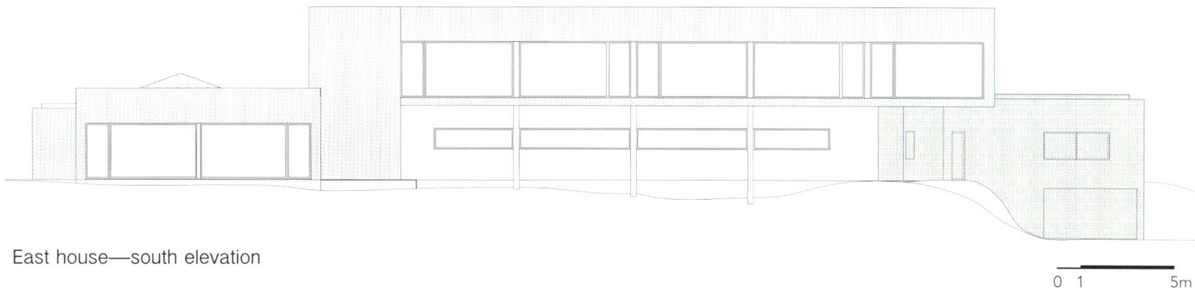

East house—south elevation

07
08 09 10

Contemporary additions and materials selected for their capacity to weather over time are in a constant dialogue with the older, refurbished farm buildings; the combination of stark geometry and rusticity creates a striking counterpoint to the hotel's natural setting.

07, 08- View of the west house
09- View of the main house
10- View of the pool

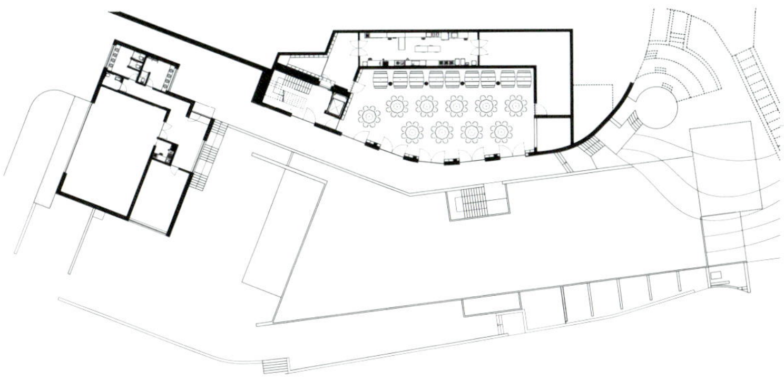

Underground first floor plan

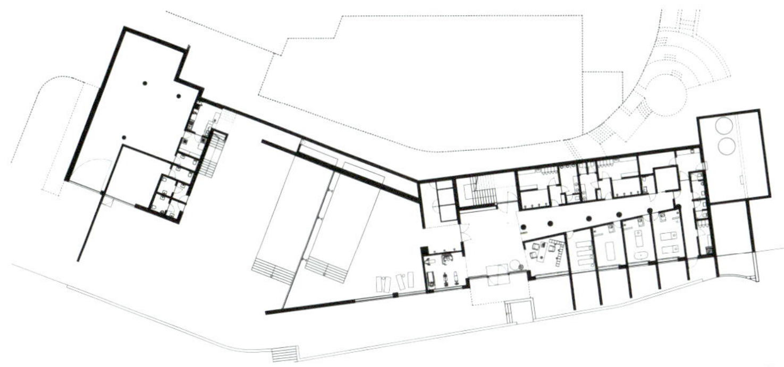

Underground second floor plan

0 1 10m

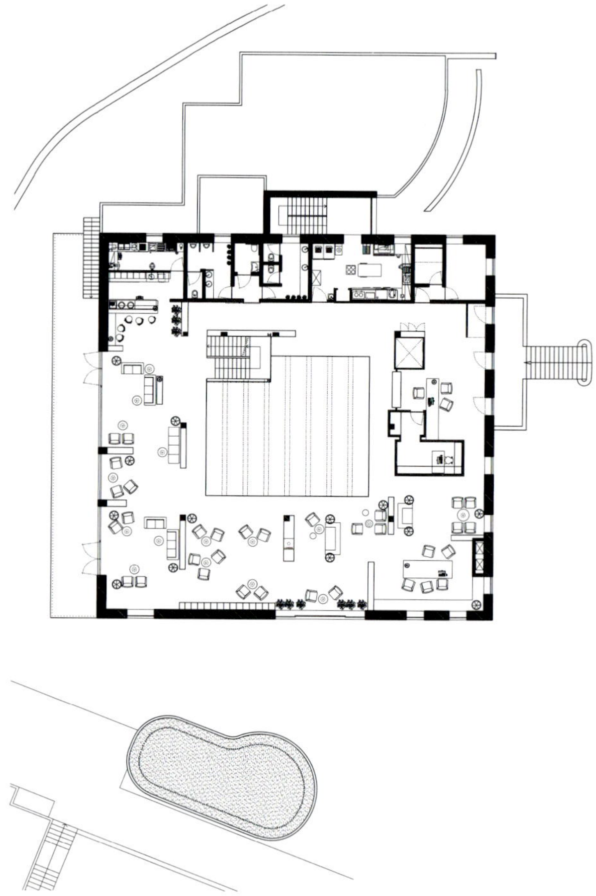

First floor plan of the main house

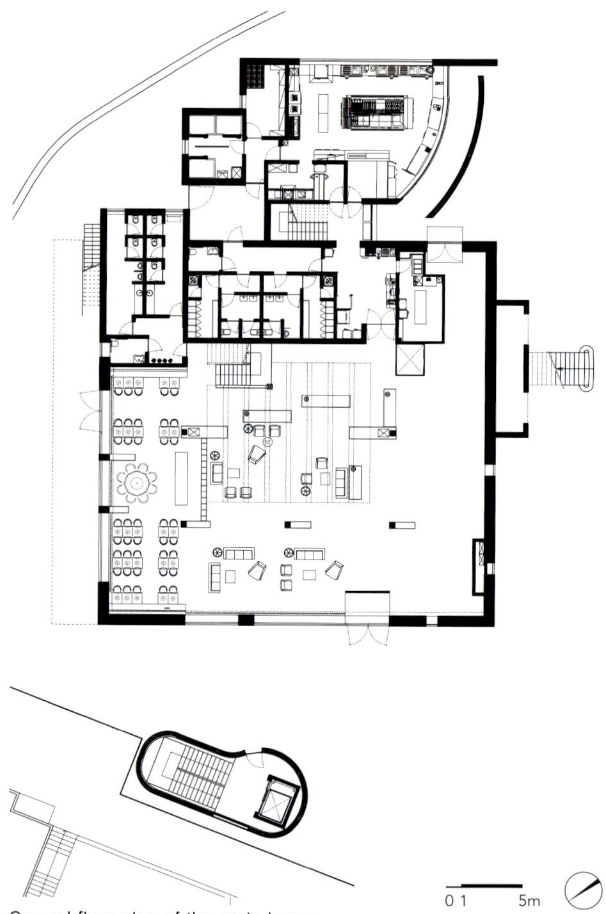

Ground floor plan of the main house

11 13 14 15

12

11, 12- Lobby of the main house
13- Bathroom
14- Bathroom and guest room
15- Guest room

Ground floor plan of the west house

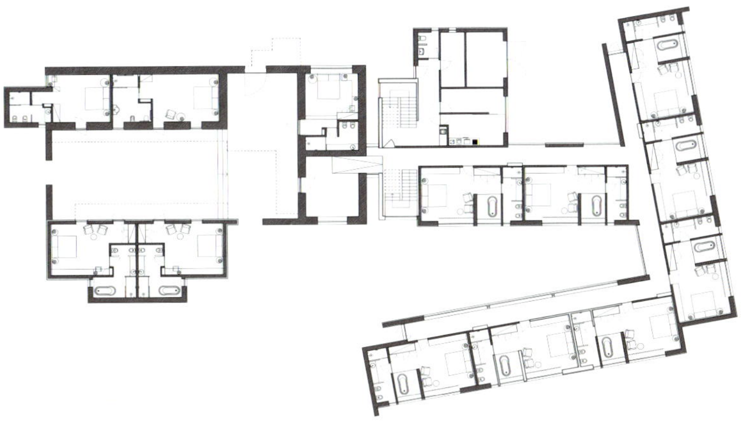

First floor plan of the west house

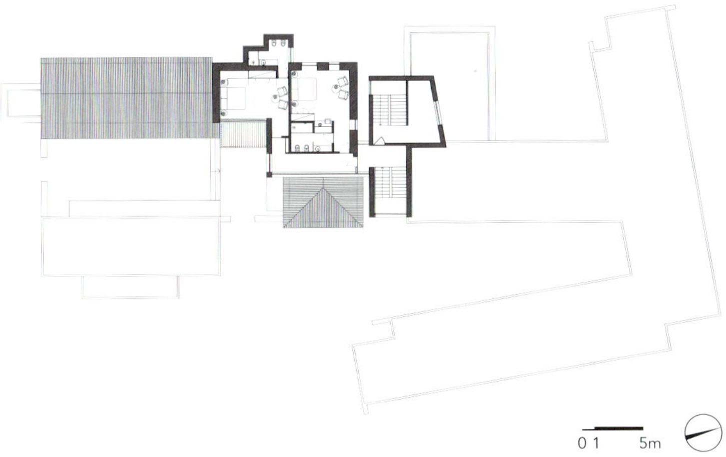

The Silo
Residential apartments

Location-Nordhavenen, Copenhagen, Denmark
Architect-COBE
Area-2.5 acres (1 hectare)
Completion-2017
Photography-Rasmus Hjortshøj – COAST
Client-Klaus Kastbjerg and NRE Denmark

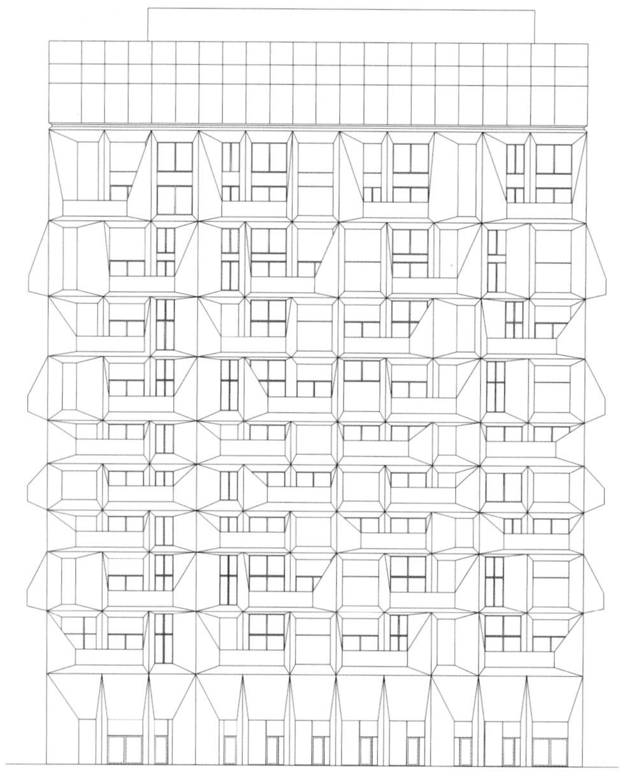

East façade

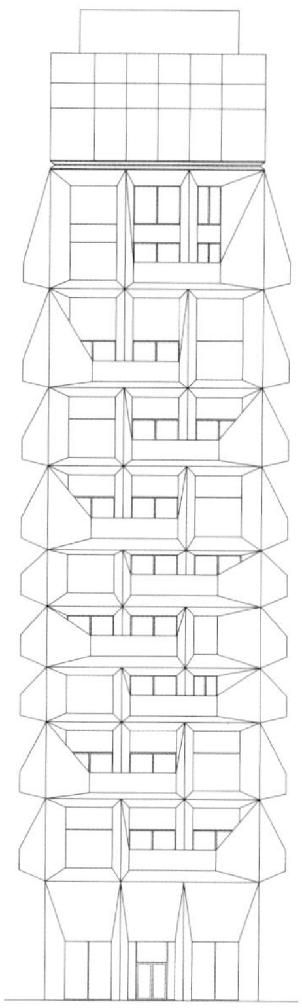

North façade

The Silo is part of the transformation of Copenhagen's North Harbor—a vast post-industrial development, which is being transformed into a new city district. From concrete storage containers to urban anchor points, the 17-story former grain silo —and the largest industrial building in the area—was transformed into 'The Silo,' offering residential apartments and public function spaces.

The architects wanted to retain the spirit of the silo as much as possible—both in terms of its monolithic exterior and majestic concrete interior. In order to bring the building's industrial concrete façade up to current standards, the exterior of the existing silo was retreated, while the interior was preserved to be as raw and untouched as possible. The aim of this inside-out transformation was to convert this industrial building in such a way that its new inhabitants and the surrounding urban life would highlight the structure's identity and heritage. An angular faceted exterior façade made of galvanized steel was installed to serve as a climatic shield. This retained the original harbor character and material feel, lending a roughness and raw beauty to the area, as in its industrial past.

The spatial variation within the original silo was immense due to the various functions of storing and handling grain, creating space for 38 unique apartments. Single and multi-level apartments range from 1141 square feet (106 square meters) to 4316 square feet (401 square meters) in size, with floor heights of up to 23 feet (7 meters). All apartments have panoramic, floor-to-ceiling windows and balconies, and several have been preserved in raw concrete. The window frames are hidden on the outside of the existing concrete walls, offering expansive views of the city skyline and the Oresund coast.

Private housing and public functions ensure that the building remains active all day. The public functions at the top and bottom also ensure a multidimensional experience for the various users of the building. Both the top and lower levels have public access. The top floor consists of a mirrored glass box housing a public restaurant with a 360-degree view of the city and the sea. The glass façade mirrors the surroundings in the daytime, and at night it is reminiscent of a lantern. The ground floor was designed as a flexible event space.

The Silo will be inhabited, but will also be a destination—an urban focal point for the new development at North Harbor by revitalizing the industrial heritage, offering new potential, and highlighting historical traces.

01

01- The external view of the whole building

HIMMEL OG HAV!

02, 03- The building under construction
04, 05- The silo and its surroundings—it will be an urban focal point for the new development at North Harbor, highlighting historical traces
06- The angular faceted exterior façade made of galvanized steel retained the original harbor character and material feel, lending a roughness and raw beauty to the area, as in its industrial past

02 03
04 05 06

A striking faceted galvanized steel façade envelopes this former grain silo. Its pre-manufactured modules reflect the spatial variation of the apartments inside and they create an abstracted finish that is both rendering and reality.

07- The majestic concrete interior
08, 09- The interior was preserved to be as raw and untouched as possible
10- The panoramic, floor-to-ceiling windows and balconies

07
08 09 10

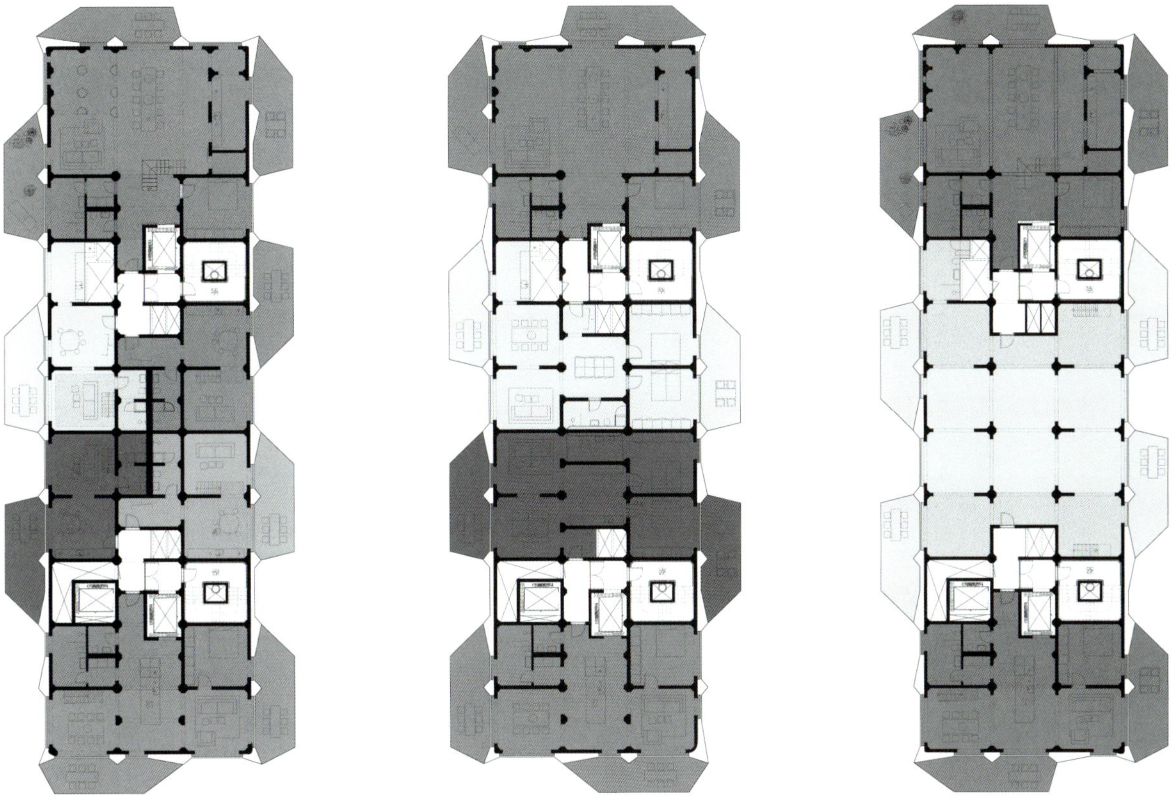

Floor plans

The Turbine Boutique Hotel and Spa

Transformation of a power station

Location-Knysna, South Africa
Architect-CMAI Architects
Area-21,528 square feet (2000 square meters)
Completion-2010
Photography-Ian Fleming
Client-Next Leisure Group

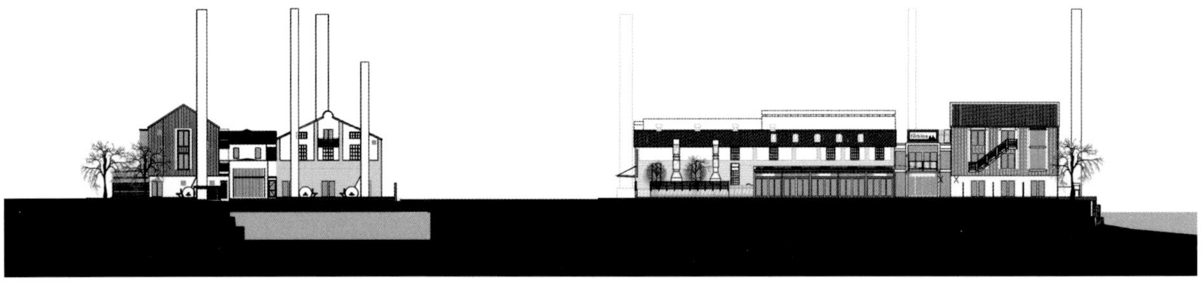

East elevation South elevation

One of the oldest industrial structures retained for adaptive re-use on Thesen Islands, this project involved the transformation of the old power station into The Turbine Boutique Hotel and Spa.

The power station was a building of approximately 21,528 square feet (2000 square meters), which used to be part of the Thesen Sawmill. It consisted of a number of structures that were built and added onto over a long period of time, the largest of which were built about 60 years ago, but some of the equipment inside was more than a 100 years old.

It used to provide electricity for the whole of Knysna and Plettenberg Bay by burning woodchips left over from the cutting of locally harvested timber logs. Decommissioned approximately 10 years prior to this project, it was estimated to have a generating capacity (had it been in working order) of 11,399 horsepower (8500 kilowatt)—which was approximately one third of Knysna's demand.

It was in a very dilapidated state when the project started, so adapting it for re-use was quite a challenge. To fit all the client's requirements into the existing shell between the pieces of machinery, working with a range of different levels, no square walls, and a brittle building envelope all added extra dimension to an already interesting project.

The new hotel, which was designed within and around all the existing structures and equipment, consists of 24 boutique rooms, a spa, conference facilities, a restaurant called The Island Café, and The Turbine Tapas Bar. It incorporates the original turbines, mechanical equipment, operating panels, and extensive sections of piping. In addition, more than 300 smaller pieces of equipment, including numerous gauges, switches, buttons, and dials were allocated specific positions in the new hotel. Meticulously catalogued and detailed by the architects, each piece was removed from the building to be cleaned, repainted, re-glazed and built back into this living museum.

Many of these items were further customized to house new LED light fittings and have been linked to the hotel's lighting circuits.

The turbines, pipework, parts of the boiler, and chimneys were all refurbished and repainted in their original colors, so the layers of paint that were applied over the years had to be carefully removed down to the original layer, to which the new colors were matched.

In addition to recycling the original structure and re-using as much of the existing building materials of the building as possible, numerous energy- and water-saving measures were implemented to minimize resource consumption: solar water heating, heat pumps, energy-saving modules that automatically switch off power in the rooms upon exiting, LED and CFL light fittings throughout, rainwater harvesting and water-saving fittings are just some of the innovations that were incorporated.

New structural members were added to support the new floor slabs that were cast inside the existing shell: since the single volume spaces were all converted to three stories and the existing external walls couldn't be used to support the new slabs on their own, most of the load fell to structural steel that had to be used in conjunction with concrete to support the additional floors. The re-use of much of the existing materials enhances one's experience of the buildings and it brings one closer to the original sense of place—the exterior of the building also responds to the surrounding area by contributing to the industrial aesthetic of Thesen Harbor Town, which includes a number of refurbished industrial structures.

The Turbine Boutique Hotel and Spa demonstrates how previously derelict and obsolete industrial structures can be sensibly adapted to house a variety of functions in order to fulfil a complex brief. It also illustrates how the adaptive re-use of existing materials and structures can preserve the sense of history associated with a building while responding to the surrounding environment in a positive manner.

01
02

01- View from the south across the main canal
02- View from the northeast

turbine

03 04
05 06 07
08 09

Short section through the turbine hall

Long section through the library and lounge

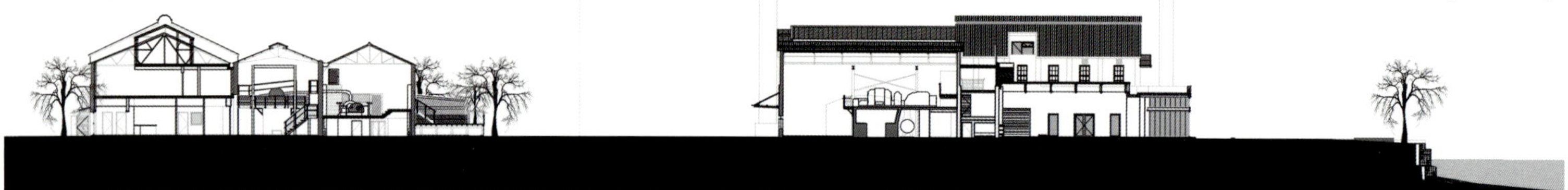

Sketches of existing equipment and machinery

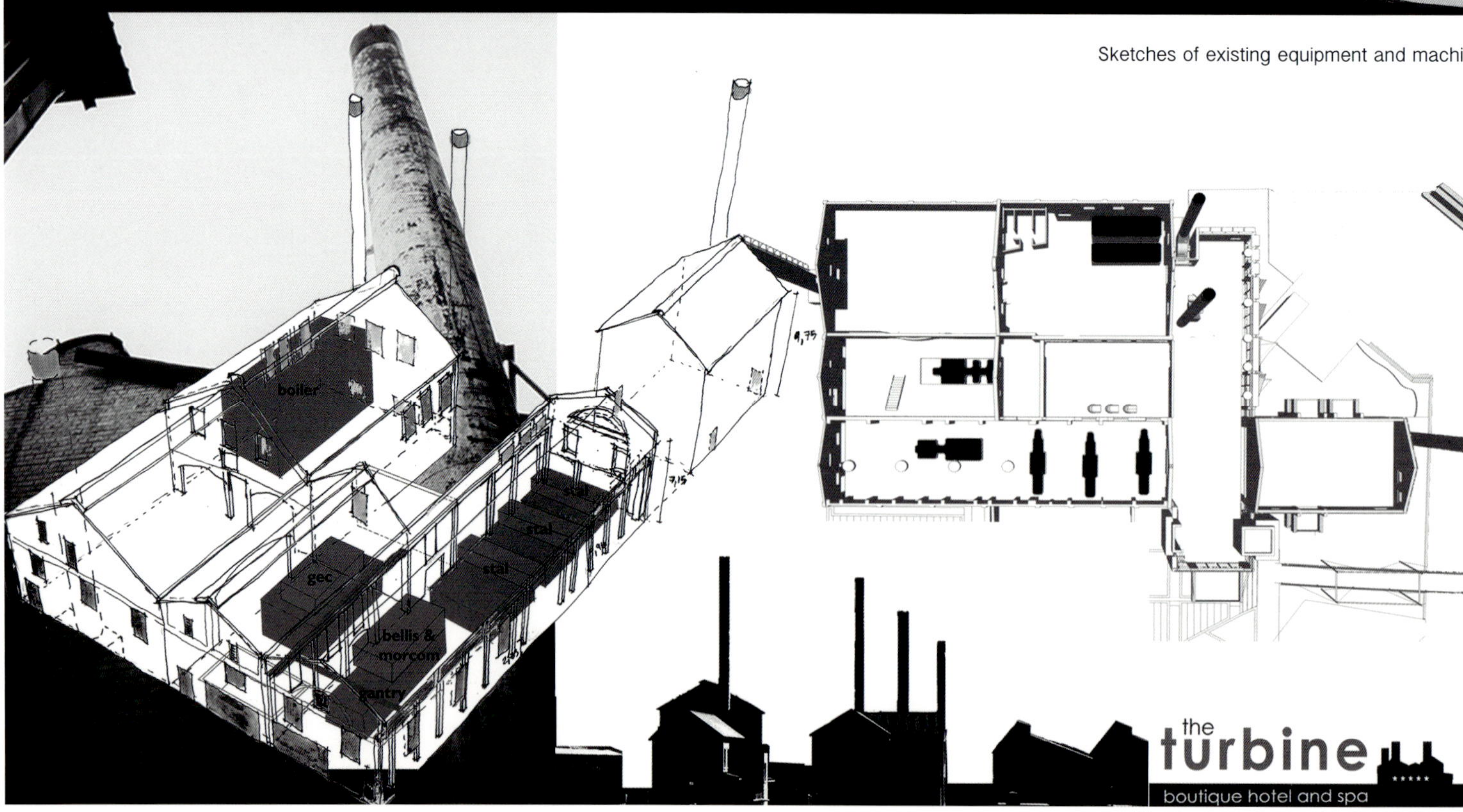

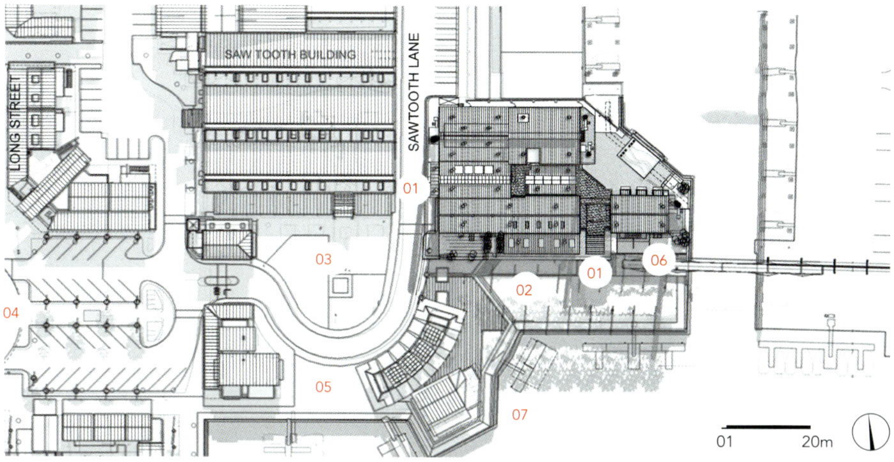

01 Turbine hotel entrances
02 Turbine plaza
03 Sawtooth square
04 Long street
05 Restaurants and retail
06 Monorail pedestrian bridge
07 Canal

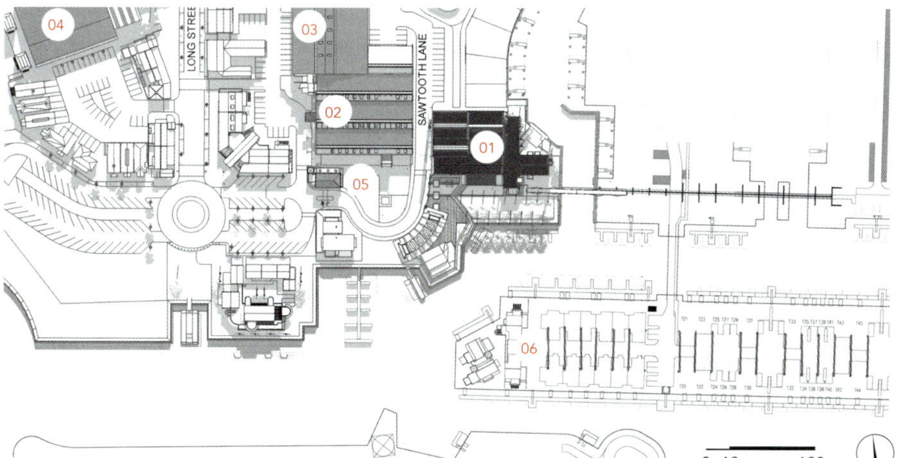

Location plan

01 Turbine hotel (power station)
02 Sawtooth bulding
03 Parking shed
04 The boatshed
05 Old clinic
06 The Dry Mill Marina Apartments

03, 04- Before: northwestern view
05- Before: turbine hall turbines
06- Before: boiler
07- Before: reception lobby
08- View over the pool deck
09- The pool deck

This building demonstrates how a range of new functions can be inserted and distributed inside a small existing power station's shell, whilst retaining most of the existing equipment and piping. Uncovering the original equipment's colors and reproducing those means that the original industrial process can still be followed and understood.

10- The Island Café in the turbine hall
11- The reception lobby
12, 13- Hotel room interiors

10|12 13
11

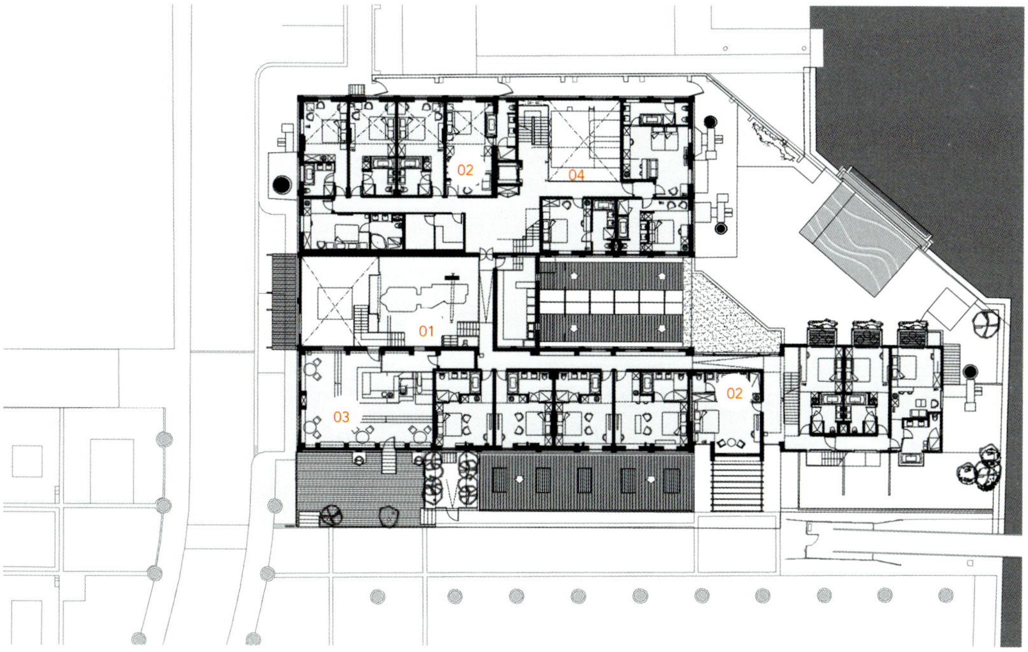

Second floor plan

01 Library
02 Rooms
03 Bar
04 Boiler

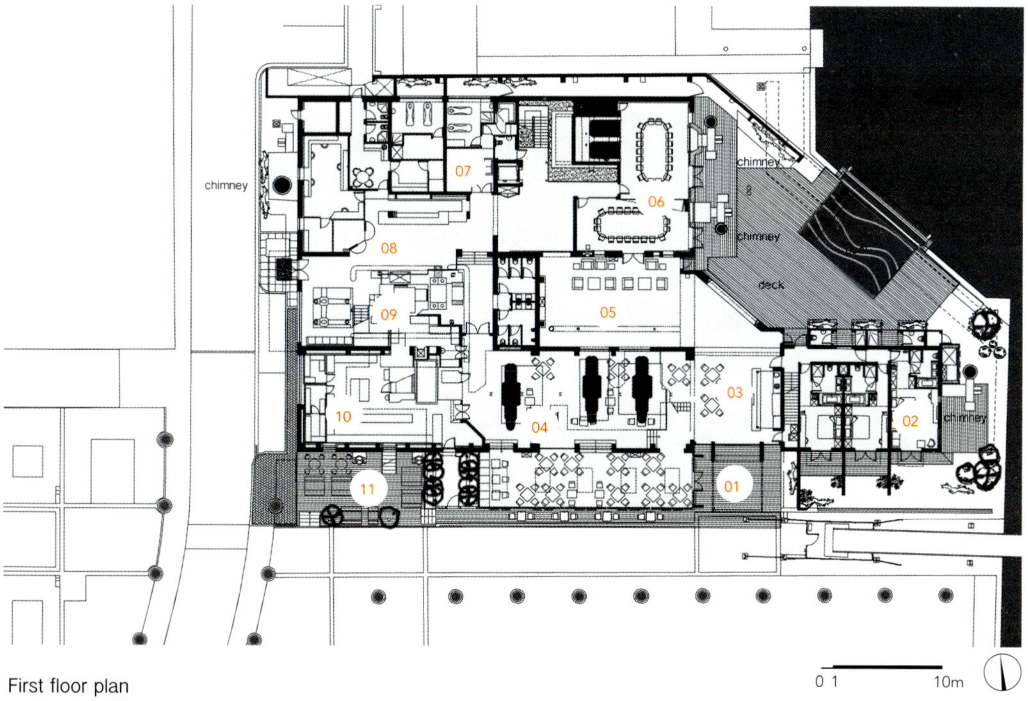

First floor plan

01 Entrance
02 Rooms
03 Bar
04 Café
05 Gallery
06 Conference
07 Spa
08 Reception
09 Store
10 Bar
11 Deck

Conterie Murano

New residential neighborhood

Location-Venice, Italy
Architect-Studio Macola
Area-51,666 square feet (4800 square meters)
Completion-2015
Photography-M. Zanta
Client-Municipality of Venice—Insula S.p.a

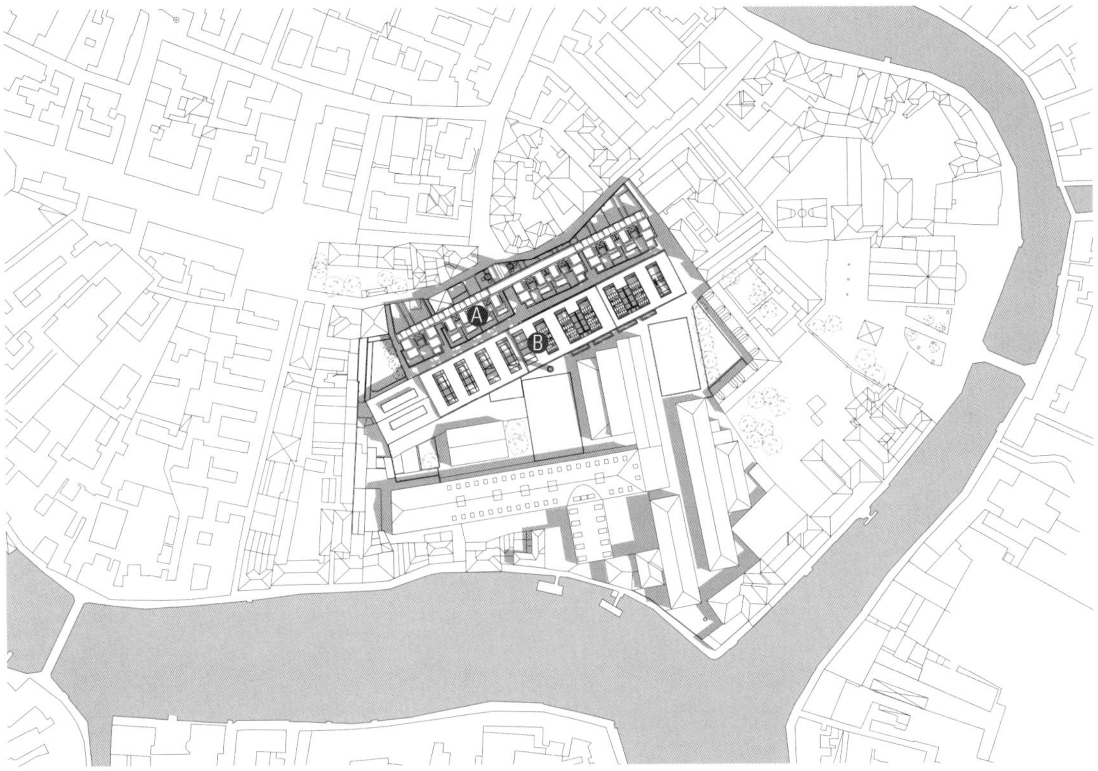

Site plan

This project was part of a plan to revitalize a former industrial site—the Conterie ('small beads')—on the island of Murano. The Conterie was a 5-acre (2-hectare) industrial complex located at the heart of the island. Brought into being between the end of the 18th century, the Conterie's zenith was in the second half of the 19th century. Its decline began in the 1970s, and the factory was finally closed down in 1993.

Two years later, the complex was acquired by the Municipality of Venice. Having lost its original function in the late 20th century, the Conterie became a fenced-off area—a kind of enclosure—the very size of which stood in sharp contrast with the densely built urban space that surrounds it. The tension between the two areas was embodied by the thick wall that encircles the Conterie, making the former industrial complex utterly inaccessible and preventing any kind of exchange between it and neighboring parts of the island.

The regeneration program launched by the Venice Municipality aimed to rectify this situation. Its objective was to renovate the Conterie's industrial buildings by assigning them new functions. The inauguration of new public routes would also contribute to turning the area into an open space, well harmonized with its context.

The new residential complexes (Building A—36 units, Building B—16 units) were built inside the disused factory, parts of which were to be preserved. The project for the residential units spoke to the area's existing urban fabric. The units in building A were shaped by the former factory's north-facing façade (which had to be preserved) and the original window positions were respected during the positioning of the new apartments. The juxtaposition of two duplex units and three simplex units created a comb-shaped structure, which provides ample sunlight from the south, thereby granting the bathrooms both natural light and ventilation. Such a structure means that the distance between the façade of building A and that of the new building varies, generating a sequence of urban spaces.

Building A is completed. According to the renovation plans that are currently being prepared for Building B, it will be built inside the existing industrial complex, which has been duly 'emptied.' The new building is made up of two blocks, each of which comprises eight residential units and a commercial area. It will also make room for the realization of an indoor square, which will become the center of the new development. Building B is equipped with a photovoltaic plant on the roof of the previous building exploiting its arch structure that allows the installation of 20 panels with a gradient varying between 20 percent and 90 percent, south-facing with a rotation angle of 27 degree.

01

01- Entrance to a group of four flats

New apartments with a rhythmic brick façade are in dialogue with a distinctive existing brick wall; the strategic insertion of movement routes and the use of a faceted façade helped to create a dynamic series of spaces that serve to embed the building in its surrounding built fabric.

Present section

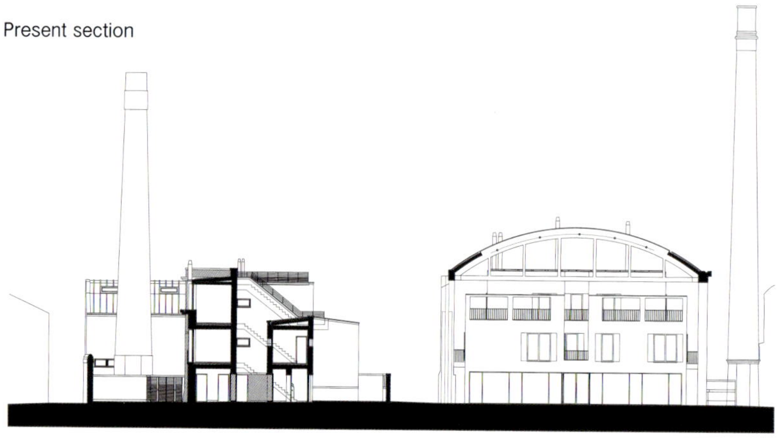

Previous section

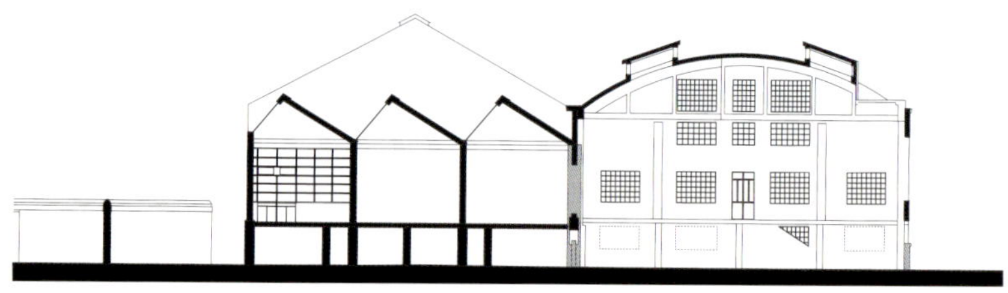

02- Previous building in 1927 (Archive 'Giacomelli photos')
03- Northern façade
04- Public entrance to the area—tiny house between two original chimneys
05- The new roof
06- Southern façade

02 04
03 05 06

South elevation

North elevation

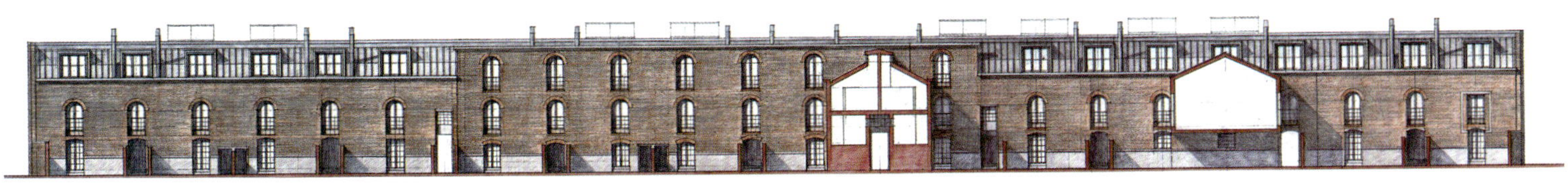

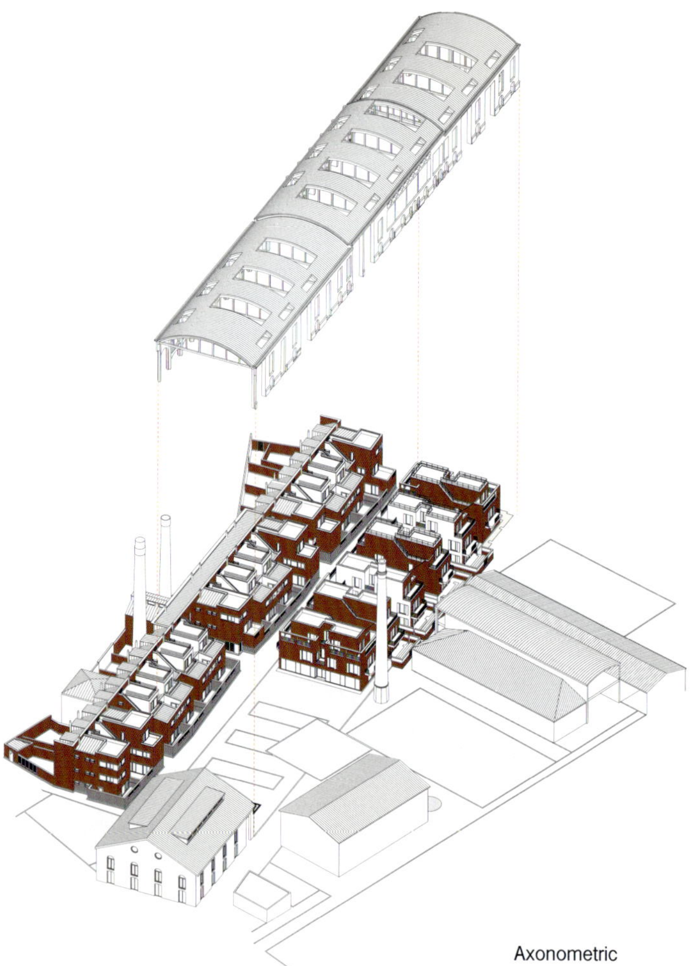

Axonometric

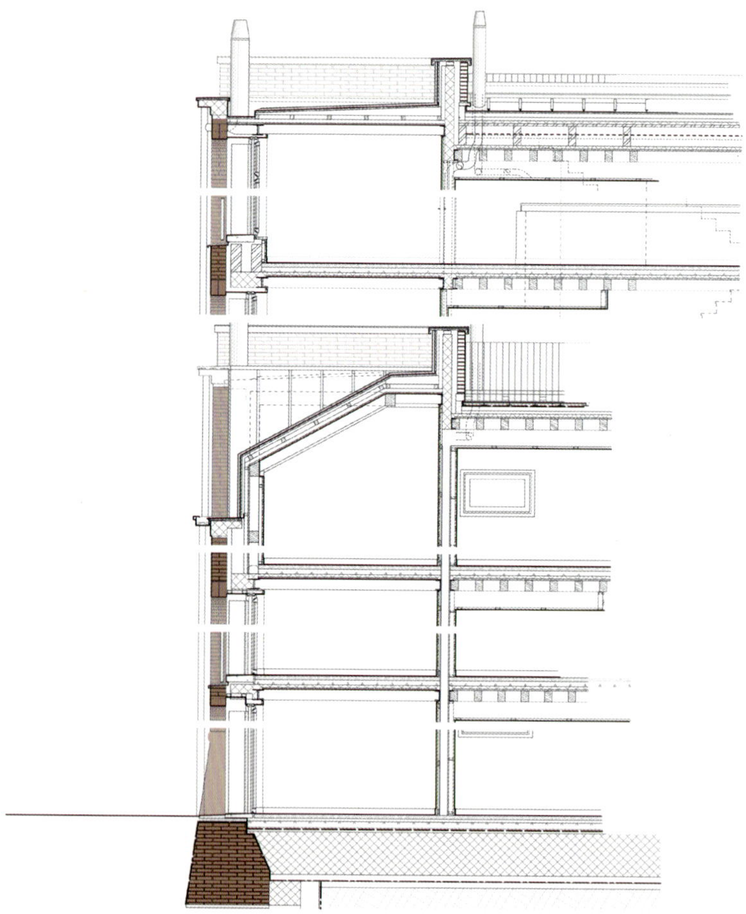

Working details

Second floor plan

First floor plan

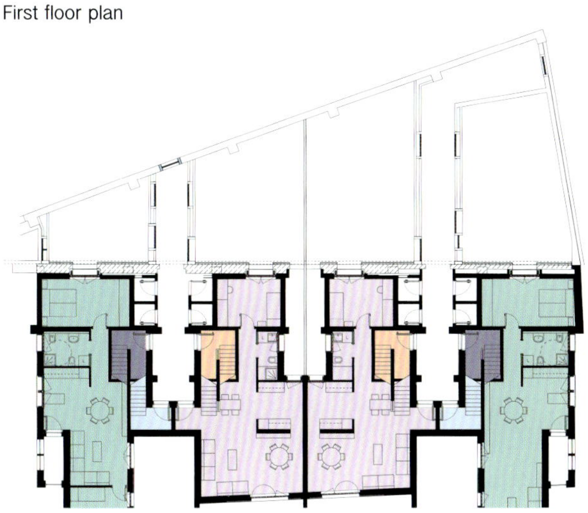

Ground floor plan

07|08
09

07- A 'patio'
08- Interior of tiny house
09- Interior of a first floor flat

XOCO 325

Chocolate factory turned into residences

Location-New York, United States
Architect-DDG
Area-17.3 acres (7 hectares)
Completion-2016
Photography-Bruce Damonte, Robert Granoff
Client-XOCO 325

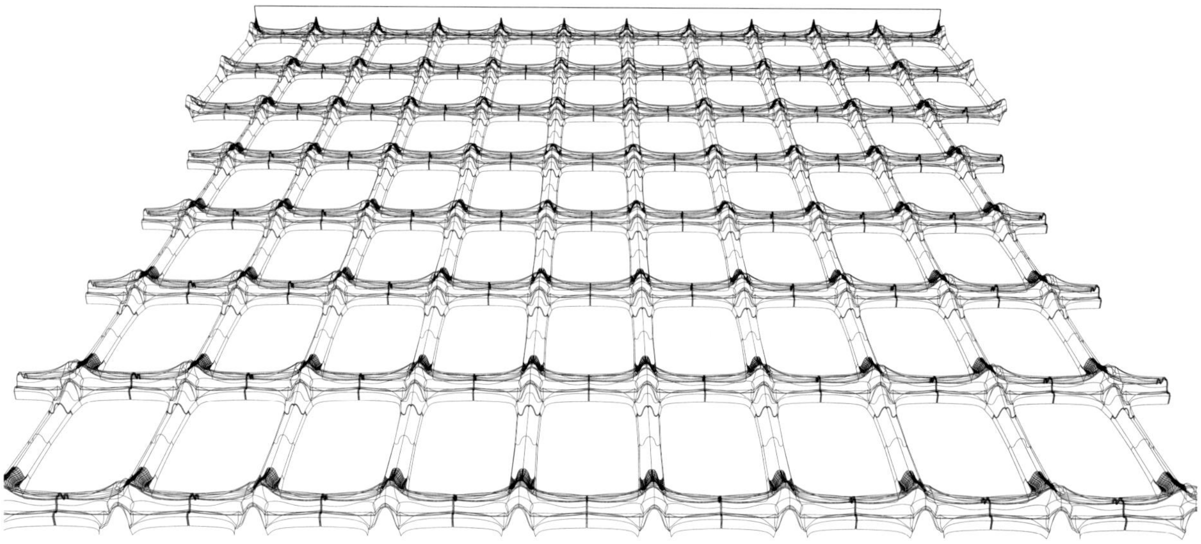

Wireframe screen

Located in New York's iconic SoHo neighborhood, 325 West Broadway, XOCO 325 ('xoco' is the Catalan word for chocolate) sits on the corner of West Broadway and Grand Street. The architects transformed the former 19th century chocolate factory into a collection of 22 expansive LEED-certified condominium residences.

Echoing the transformation of SoHo from the industrial backbone of Manhattan to a world-renowned residential and retail neighborhood, the project features expansive and highly-detailed residences on the former site of a chocolate factory. XOCO 325 is a ground-up residential building over ground-floor retail. Its cast-aluminum façade is a modern reinterpretation of the district's historic cast-iron loft buildings. The top three floors step back from the street wall in a slate-clad manifestation of the endemic mansard roof to provide panoramic views of the Manhattan skyline.

The impressive design extends beyond the façade into the lobby, where residents are greeted with an elevated design experience. The lobby is outfitted with a bluestone floor and a custom chandelier. Sculptural walls are richly textured with board-formed concrete and complement in situ cast-concrete furnishings.

Natural light floods interior spaces from full-height window walls at east and west. The project offers 21 residences over 10 stories. Each of the one-to-four-bedroom residences offers impressive detailing such as custom sculptural plaster coves, medallions, and soffit edges. In an effort to create a smooth transition between the building's bold exterior architecture and warm inviting interiors, the residences offer ceiling heights starting from 10 feet (3 meters) in primary living areas, private terraces and balconies for most units, 7.5-inch-wide (2.3-meter-wide) Austrian white oak plank floors, custom millwork and hydronic radiant heated floors, and open layouts that accentuate a luxury lifestyle.

A truly unique feature at XOCO 325 is a private courtyard garden that flaunts a naturally-lit, sculptural concrete fitness studio. In addition to a private garden, the building offers additional amenities, including a 24/7 doorman, a bike room, and private storage.

01

01- Front façade of the building

RETAIL
SPACE
RETAIL
SPACE

02 03 | 05 06
04 | 07

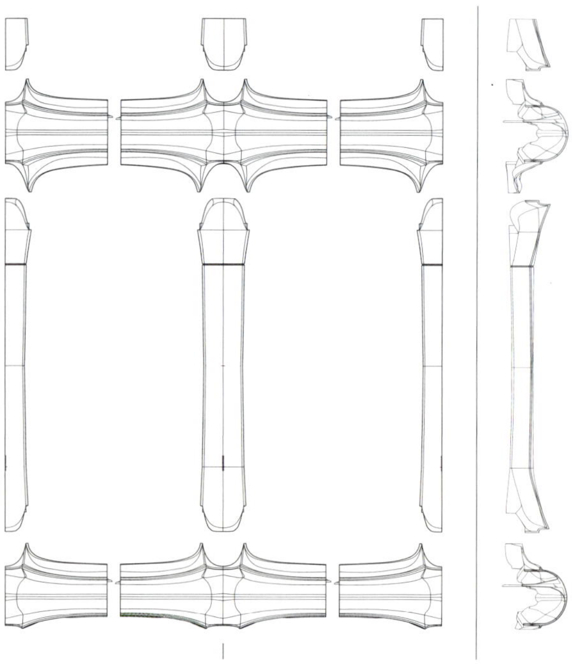

Aluminum façade drawing

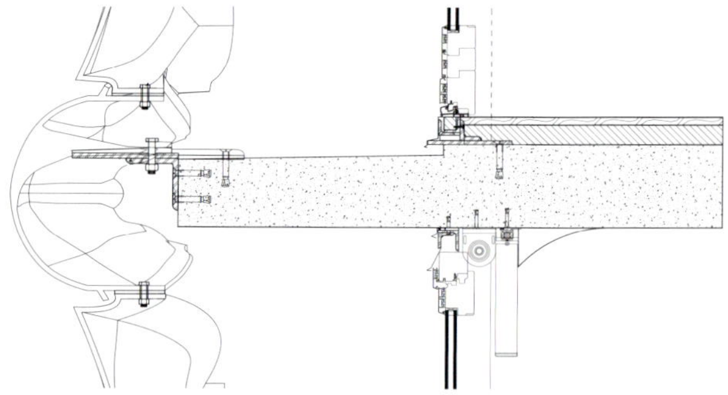

Aluminum façade detailed section

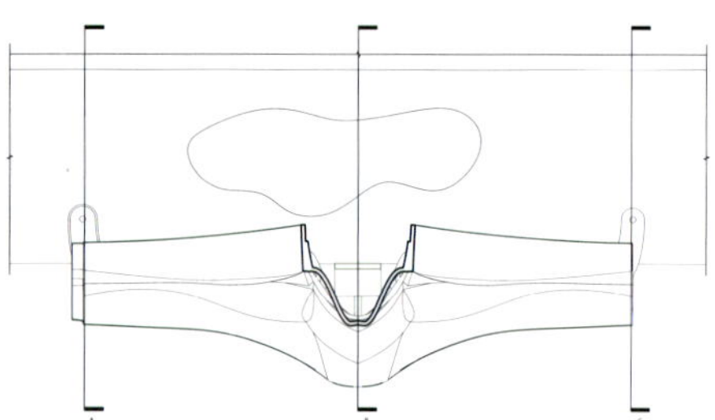

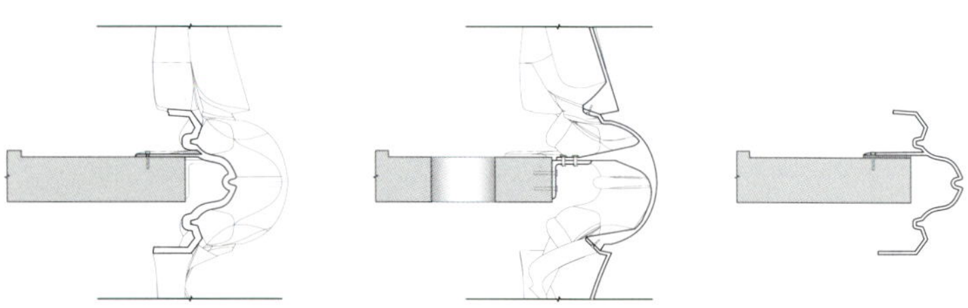

Aluminum façade section drawing

02, 03- Existing structure
04, 05- Details of the façade
06- Penthouse west terrace
07- Northwestern view from the penthouse

08- West great room of the penthouse
09- West master bedroom of the penthouse
10- West dining room of the penthouse
11- West kitchen of the penthouse
12- West master bath of the penthouse

- 01 Private terrace
- 02 Dining room
- 03 Kitchen
- 04 Media room
- 05 Balcony
- 06 Bedroom
- 07 Utility room
- 08 Master bath
- 09 Service
- 10 Pantry
- 11 Elevator
- 12 Private gallery
- 13 Great room
- 14 Refuse
- 15 Master bedroom
- 16 Dressing room

West floor plan of the penthouse

A distinctively sculpted cast-aluminum framework, reminiscent of SoHo's older cast-iron loft buildings, is suspended in front of this apartment building's glass façade; it provides a sense of privacy and shading, while also creating a unique pattern that makes it instantly recognizable.

08 09 10 11 12

Ding Hui Yuan Zen and Tea Chamber

An elongated industrial box

Location-Beijing, China
Principal architect-He Wei
Architects-He Wei Studio / 3andwich design
Area-4844 square feet (450 square meters)
Completion-2016
Photography-Zou Bin, He Wei
Client-Better Lift Art Club Co., Ltd

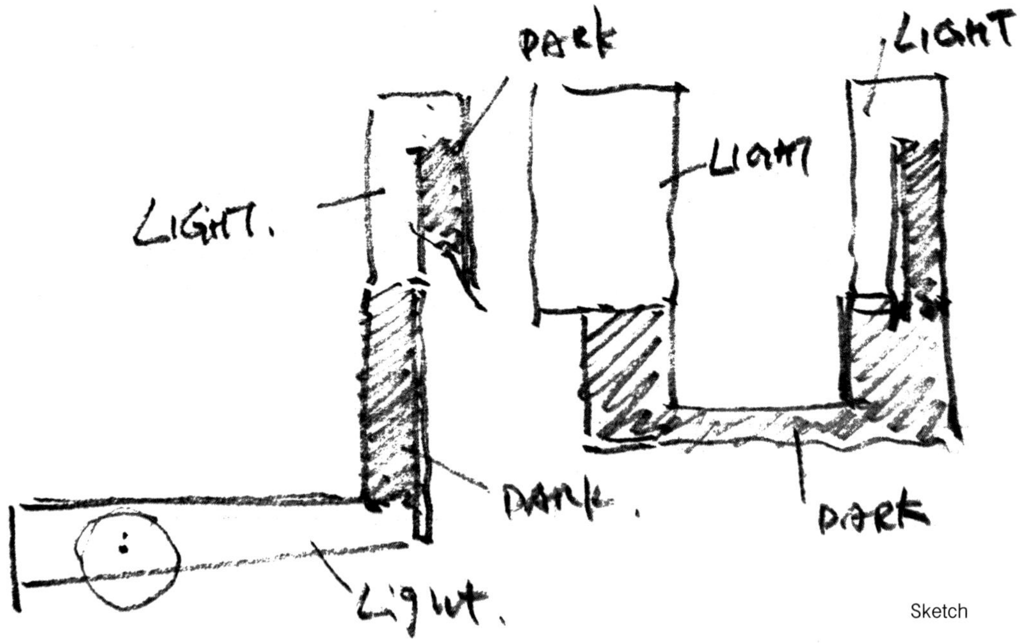

Sketch

This is a factory renovation project. Rebuilt into an office in its latest renovation, the old factory experienced several rounds of renovation after its construction in 1970s. Unlike other factories with large spaces, this factory doesn't have a large span—rather, it is exceptionally high—nor does it have any special features, apart from a backyard of 1076 square feet (100 square meters), which is quite impressive. Based on the owner's requirement, the designers had to reconstruct it into a Zen chamber.

As a Zen chamber, it should be imbued with the spirit of the East and a sense of history, which should not be achieved through a simple display of traditional symbols. The design should convey the essence of the Chinese private gardens, which is 'seeing a bigger picture from small matters' and 'the path winding through high peaks.'

The core of the design was restructuring the circulation of the space. Designers eliminated the simple layout of the existing circulation route with hanging stairs directly attached to its entrance and, rather, created a longer circulation for people to calm down when entering the main space, in the philosophy of Zen tea.

Taking advantage of the 'L' shaped layout and the backyard court, an extra-long, zigzag path was created: people can enter the building from the western side after passing through a newly-added long and narrow semi-outdoor corridor; they will enter the backyard after turning to the north and walking through the entire Zen chamber. The architect added a folded staircase in this area, located between the long ramp and parallel stairs. People will see the inner courtyard and a big tearoom through the grating racks while stepping up the stairs. Then, they can reach the second floor through a long, narrow, and closed space. The second floor serves as the main public space of the building, and includes a Guqin (a representative instrument of traditional Chinese musical culture) room, small tearooms, a meditation room and a large tearoom.

Another staircase to the second floor is positioned at the turn of the 'L' shape layout at the back of the building. The original staircase at the western entrance was demolished, creating more space for the entrance area. The newly-added stairs elongate the spatial experience of the building, assisting visitors to calm down from the noisy outside downtown area and to enter their inner world.

The changing rhythm of the brightness is another key aspect of the renovation. Around the inner court, the newly created space changes its appearance between the natural light and the artificial light arranging the transparent, semi-transparent, and close-up visual effects. After entering the building, people can enjoy the courtyard at different time and from different perspectives, and vice versa, which is also a practice of sampling the Chinese garden.

The entrance façade of the original building was constructed with red brick, showing its industrial identity, but this was no longer suitable for the repurposed function of the building. During the transformation, a new entrance and façade was constructed with an environmentally-friendly bamboo-steel grille. This new façade is semi-transparent, which is a perfect fit for the Zen style of the tea chamber. What is also worth mentioning is that the architects retained the tree on the site. They even included it into the landscape of the entrance hallway by carving a round hole in the bamboo-steel grille façade, adding a sense of nature and fun in the plain artificial building.

01

01- Keeping the trees in the site as an element of the new façade.

Sketch

The backyard court was also an important part of the renovation. The folded stairway at the east of the courtyard forms a stacked abstract figure along with the building, serving as a view to the tea room. The original wall of the courtyard was heightened to protect the introversion of the courtyard from the landscape outside. The red-bricked wall was painted white, so that the industrial flavor is mitigated and a scholar's style was added. The irregular openings of the original building were modified, shaping a more rhythmical façade. Finally, the use of pines, bamboos, stones and ponds animates the yard and echoes well with the Eastern spirit of the whole building.

02, 03, 04, 05- Before renovation
06- White walls, black bricks, tree shadows
07- The courtyard
08- Overlooking the courtyard from the roof terrace

02 03 | 04 05 | 06 | 07 08

Sections

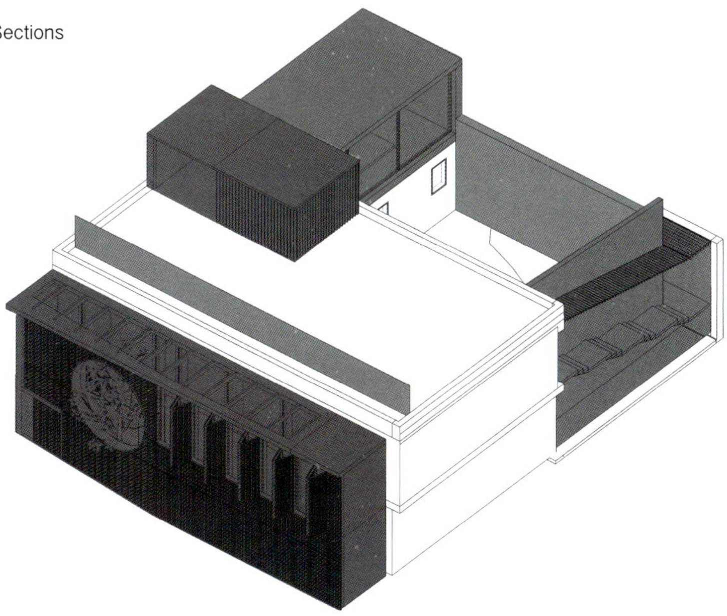

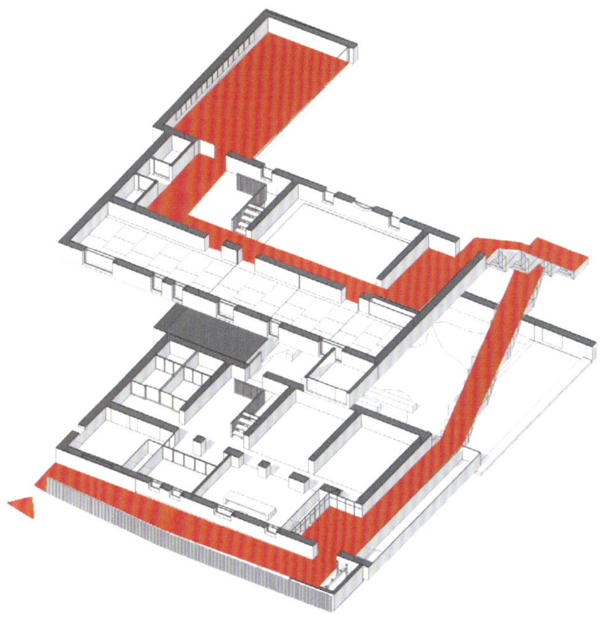

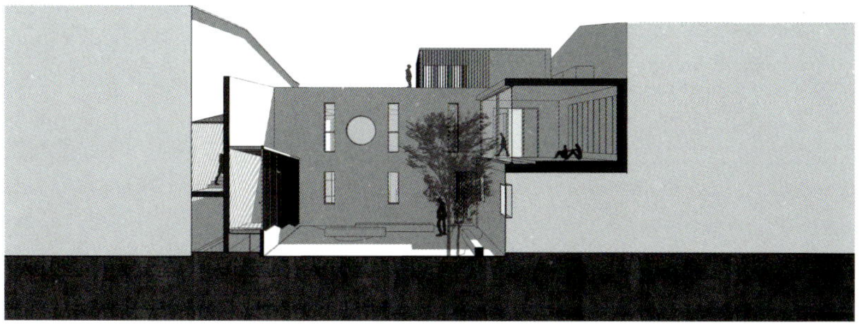

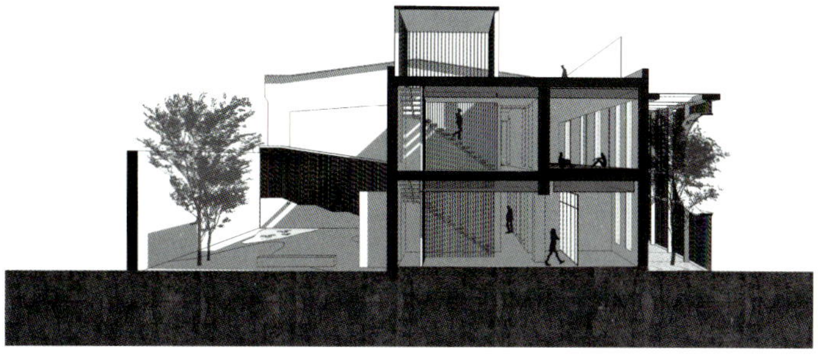

Through the consideration of outside space and the insertion of a new architectural promenade, this building's transformation allows visitors to experience a sense of the calmness inherent to the traditional Chinese garden.

09 10 | 12
11

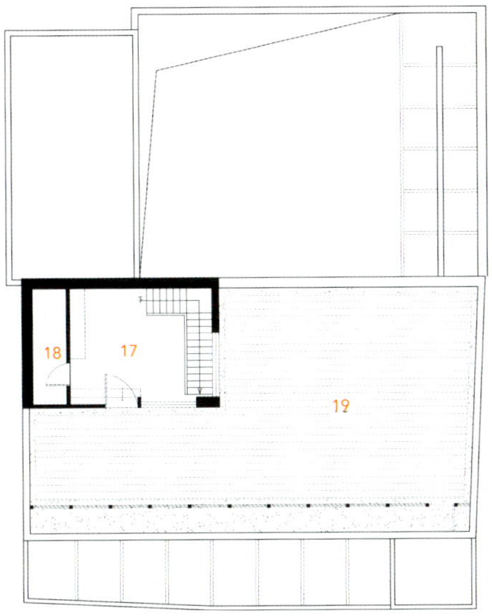

Third floor plan

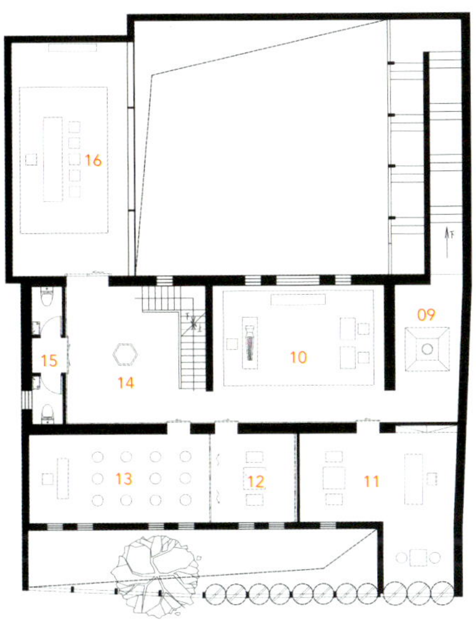

Second floor plan

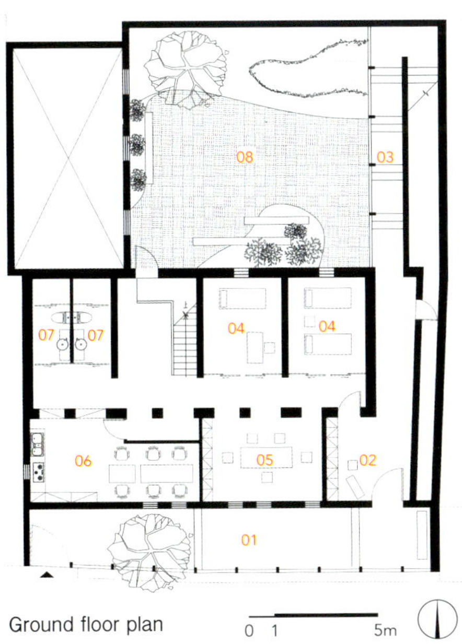

Ground floor plan

01 Front porch
02 Entrance hall
03 Back porch
04 Medical room
05 Tea room
06 Office
07 Restroom
08 Inner courtyard
09 Entrance hall
10 Gathering space
11 Library
12 Scriptorium
13 Meditation room
14 Staircase
15 Restroom
16 Tea room
17 Preparation room
18 Facility room
19 Rooftop

09- Façade detail of the entrance
10- The front porch, a semi-exterior space, guiding people to enter the building
11- Back porch, the traffic space is deliberately stretched
12- Back porch, glass roof and grille form rich light and shade

13 14	16
15	17

13- The gathering space
14- The entrance hall of the second floor
15- Space between the gathering space and large teahouse
16- The large teahouse on the second floor, a bright space to overlook the courtyard
17- Meditation room

Allez Up rock-climbing gym

Conversion of four silos

Location-Montreal, Canada
Architect-Smith Vigeant Architectes Inc.
Area-13,132 square feet (1220 square meters)
Completion-2013
Photography-Stéphane Brügger
Client-Richer de la Plante Family

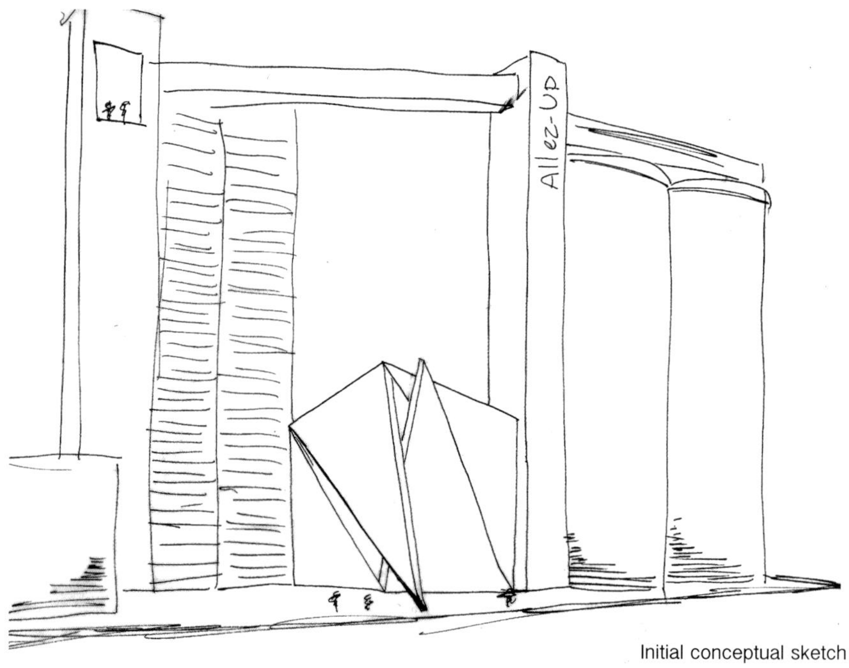

Initial conceptual sketch

Located on the Lachine Canal in Montreal's Southwest borough, rock-climbing gym Allez Up's newest facilities are part of an important urban and social renewal project.

In 1825, the Lachine Canal opened as a solution to allow boats to bypass the upstream rapids of the Saint-Laurent. This new commercial path kick-started the industrial development around the canal and the area of what is now the Southwest borough. By the 1860s, the area was a busy industrial neighborhood. In fact, it was the most diversified concentration of industrial establishments in the country. In 1952, four silos were erected by Redpath Sugar Refinery to serve as storage for the factory.

However, the canal was already in its later days, as it couldn't be expanded to allow for larger ships to pass through. In 1959, the completion of the Saint-Laurent seaway marked the end of the canal's golden age. In 1970, the canal was officially closed, causing companies to relocate and eventually leading to the desolation of the neighborhood. While other industrial buildings in the area were reused and re-purposed, the silos—more difficult to transform because of their unusual shape—were left completely abandoned for nearly 40 years.

Allez-Up's previous gym was located nearby, in a converted industrial site. The client wanted to triple its facilities' capacity and believed that the site and the silos offered amazing potential for a rock-climbing gym. The re-purposing of the abandoned silos was a unique way to exploit the potential of Montreal's neglected industrial heritage. Their transformation into recreational use was the first intervention of its kind in Canada and has significantly added to the recreational and touristic attractiveness on the Lachine Canal.

The cylindrical volumes were connected by a rectangular form, filling most of the site's vacant space. This reconfiguration created new limits within the site while connecting the two sets of abandoned silos.

The concept for the new building extension was shaped by the dynamic movements of the interior climbing walls. Instead of organizing the space in a traditional way and stacking floors on top of each other, the architects wanted to make the most of the vertical spaces by using vertical planes, providing maximal functionality to the climbers.

The main façade of the building extension reads as three solid elements sliced by inclined openings. The windows run full height and fill the interior space with natural light throughout the day. The angularity of the façade provides an interesting dialogue with the verticality and solidity of the silos, while the metallic exterior finish complements the industrial character of the neighborhood.

The silos were carefully integrated in the program. The reception area is located in one of the west silos, and climbing routes are set on the inside and outside walls of the massive concrete structures, taking advantage of their verticality. The silos became a full part of the climbing experience at Allez Up, and they carry with them the historic industrial heritage of the site, informing the visitor of the site's previous function.

The insides of the silos were originally covered with two layers of cedar wood planks running full height in order to protect the stored sugar from humidity. However, some of them had to be removed to allow for the reconversion. As initiated by the client, they were reused as furniture and interior finishes.

01

01- Allez Up's main entrance

allez UP
1555

02 03
04 05
06

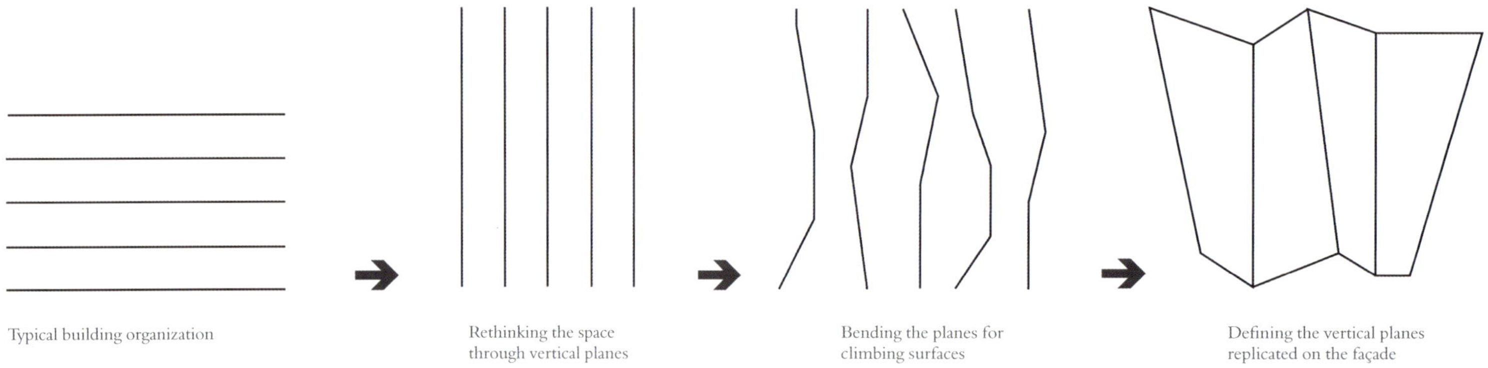

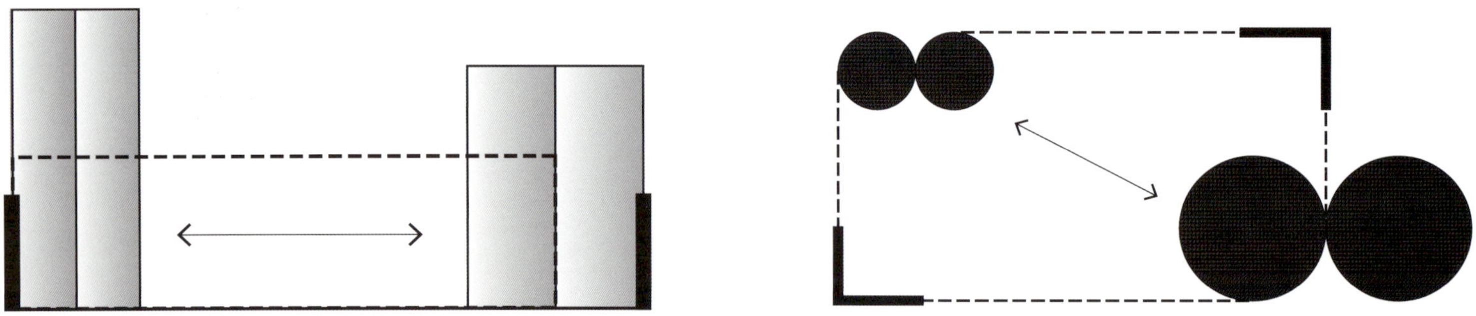

Schematic diagrams

02- Historic aerial view of Lachine Canal
03- The Redpath Silos before the transformation
04- View after the transformation
05- Global view after transformation
06- Climbing the silos

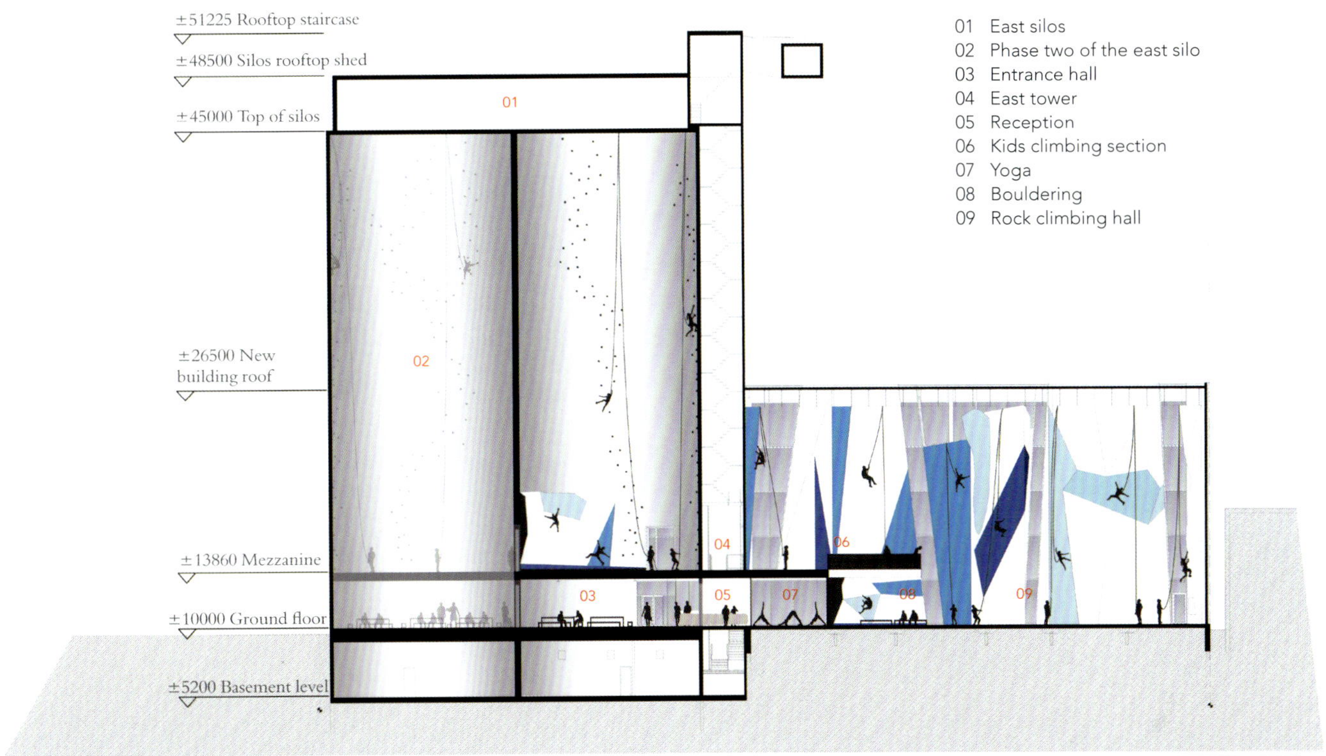

Cross section of Allez Up

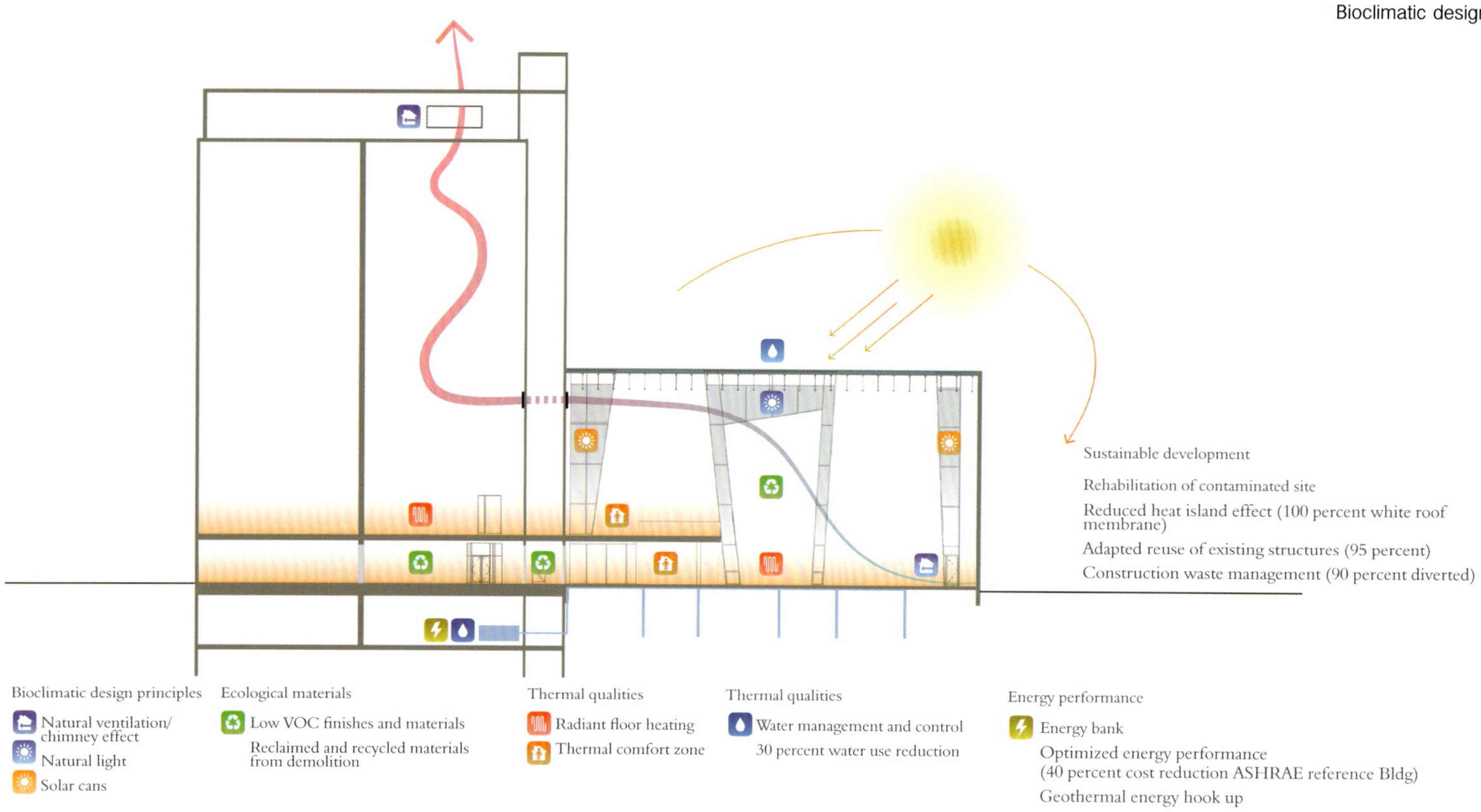
Sustainable development
Rehabilitation of contaminated site
Reduced heat island effect (100 percent white roof membrane)
Adapted reuse of existing structures (95 percent)
Construction waste management (90 percent diverted)
Bioclimatic design principles
Natural ventilation/ chimney effect
Natural light
Solar cans
Ecological materials
Low VOC finishes and materials
Reclaimed and recycled materials from demolition
Thermal qualities
Radiant floor heating
Thermal comfort zone
Thermal qualities
Water management and control
30 percent water use reduction
Energy performance
Energy bank
Optimized energy performance
(40 percent cost reduction ASHRAE reference Bldg)
Geothermal energy hook up

08
07

07- Large angled windows fill the space with natural light
08- Inside the climbing hall, the white walls are reminiscent of the sugar that used to be stored here

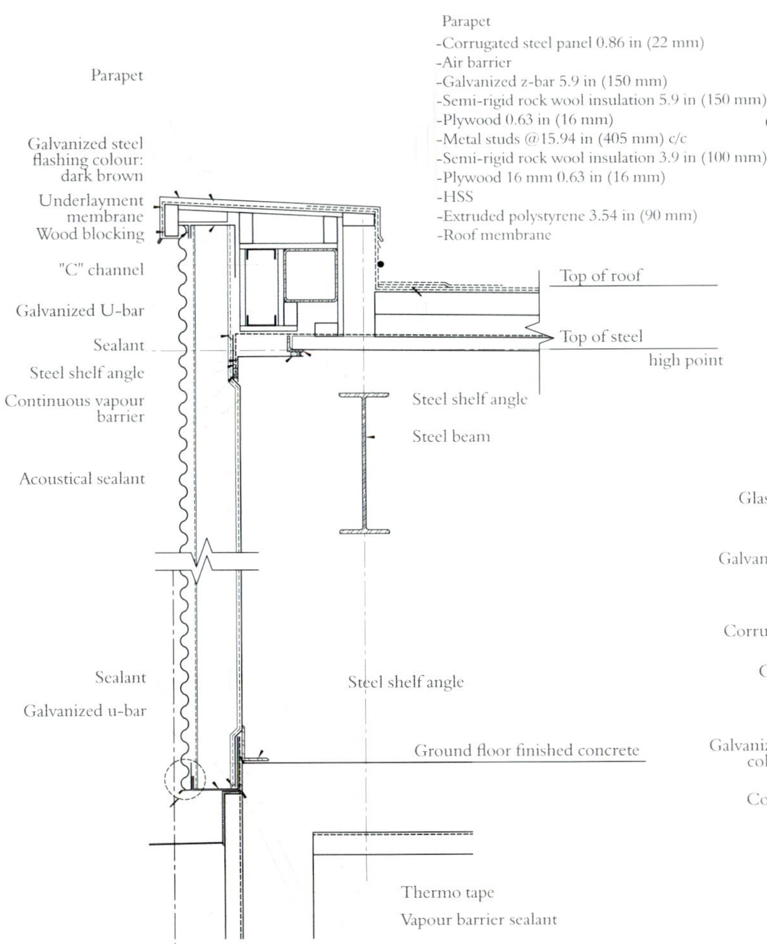

Metal siding wall section

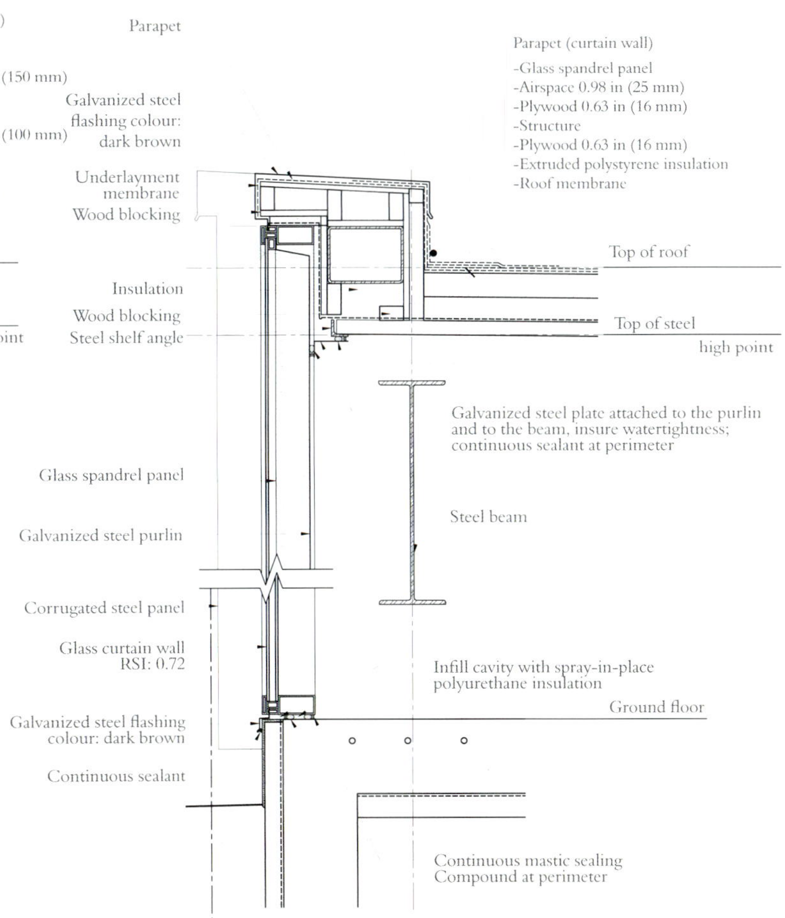

Curtain wall section

Inserting a suitable program helped to preserve and emphasize the verticality of these existing silos, while an original internal timber skin was harvested for use elsewhere in the building. A vibrant speckling of color on the new internal climbing walls makes for an unexpected counterpoint to the grey concrete of the existing structure.

09- Entrance hall—wood decorative elements are scavenged from the cedar planks that used to line the inside of the silos
10- Inside the center, a glimpse of verticality

01 West tower
02 West silos
03 Lead climbing walls
04 Rock climbing hall
05 Administration
06 Bouldering
07 Yoga
08 East tower
09 Main entrance
10 Reception
11 Phase two of the east silo
12 Exierior climbing on silo

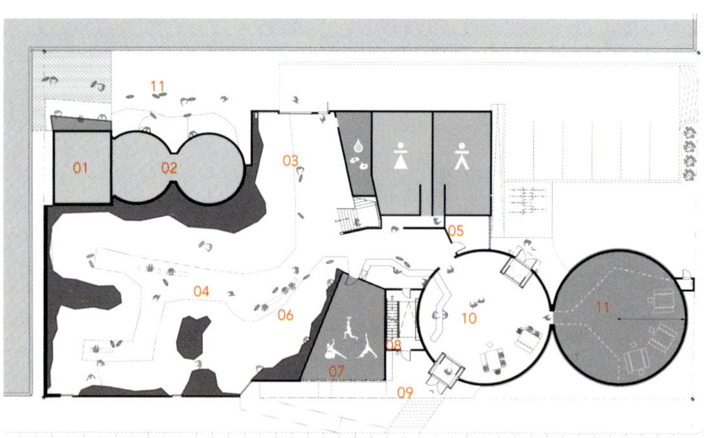

Ground floor plan

01 West tower
02 West silos
03 Bouldering
04 Kids and beginners climbing
05 East tower
06 Lounge and silo climbing
07 Phase two of the east silo

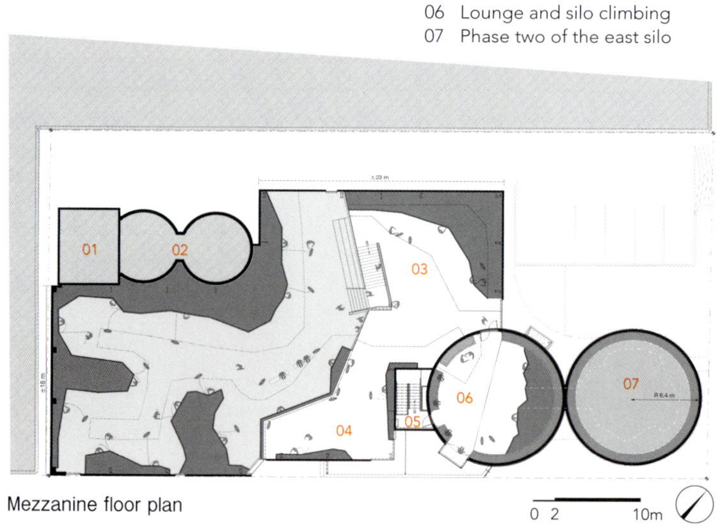

Mezzanine floor plan

09
10

Vivarium Restaurant

Transformation of a tractor warehouse

Location-Bangkok, Thailand
Architect-STU/D/O ARCHITECTS
Interior designer-Hypothesis Design Agency
Area-7018 square feet (652 square meters)
Completion-2015
Photography-PAKKAWAT PAISITTHAWEE, Nunthanut Amornpun
Client-Krung Thai Tractor Company Limited

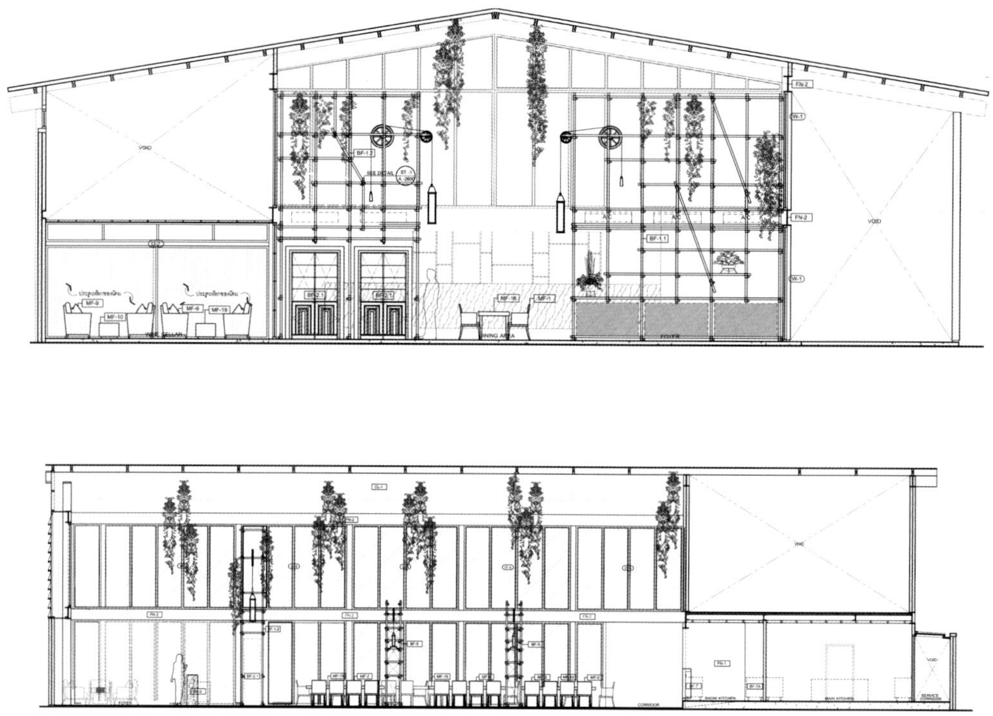

Sections of the restaurant

Vivarium is an Asian-fusion restaurant located in a former tractor warehouse in Bangkok. The adaptive reuse strategy adopted led to the creation of a meaningful dialogue between the old and new elements within the warehouse setting.

In order to highlight the former industrial characteristics of the warehouse, the majority of the existing structure was kept unchanged but delineated from the new addition through the differentiation of vibrant finishing colors—the old parts were kept in their original white color, whereas the new additions were painted with red rust protection primer—accentuating the contrast between the old and the new. Simultaneously, the floor-to-ceiling shelf system acts as partitioning; the tables and seating were arranged beneath the floating plants. To add an industrial essence, the architects employed objects found from around the site—iron doors, steel pipes, dead branches, and tree roots—as decorative interior elements, as well as using scaffolding structures, inspired by the ones that previously existed on the site, as decorative shelves within the restaurant space.

With the aim of injecting life and energy into the warehouse for the new restaurant program, the design team thought of a terrarium as a concept for the interior. A lush green-scape of hanging plants populates the upper volume of the double-height space. Placed around the restaurant are ceramic follies designed by Yarnnakarn Art and Craft Studio, adding to the intricacy and lushness of the interior landscape—counterbalancing the rustic industrial setting. The design theme was then reflected in the name of the restaurant, Vivarium, which means a container of life.

Conceived with a small budget, the tractor warehouse was transformed into a spacious and inviting place, which demonstrates the technique of adaptive reuse as a strategy to preserve a building's contextual history.

01

01- Front façade of the building

VIVARIUM
MINISTRY

02, 03- The existing warehouse during the construction
04- Front entrance into the restaurant
05- Dining area in the main hall
06- Vertical space dominated by the scaffolding shelves and the hanging plants

Varying colors help to differentiate between the existing structure and the new interventions in this restaurant, while the interior space has been filled with found industrial objects and scaffolding. The space is animated by planting that adds a softer layer and contrasts well with the red steel primer of the new interventions.

02 03 05
04 06

07 08 09 10

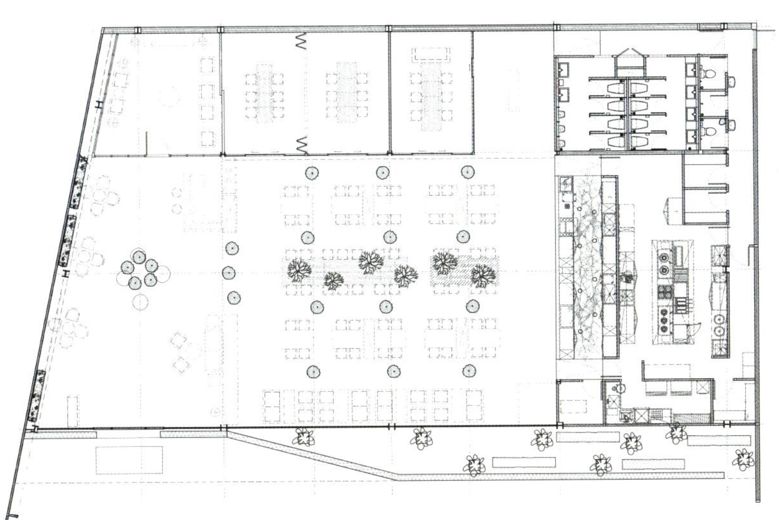

Floor plan

07- Seating area by the windows
08- Entry foyer
09- Main dining area
10- Bar area

The [B] Zone

1882 concept store

Location-Arzignano, Italy
Architect-[A+M]^{2}Architects
Area-12,917 square feet (1200 square meters)
Completion-2016
Photography-Davide Pretto, The Cool Couple
Client-1882 Srl

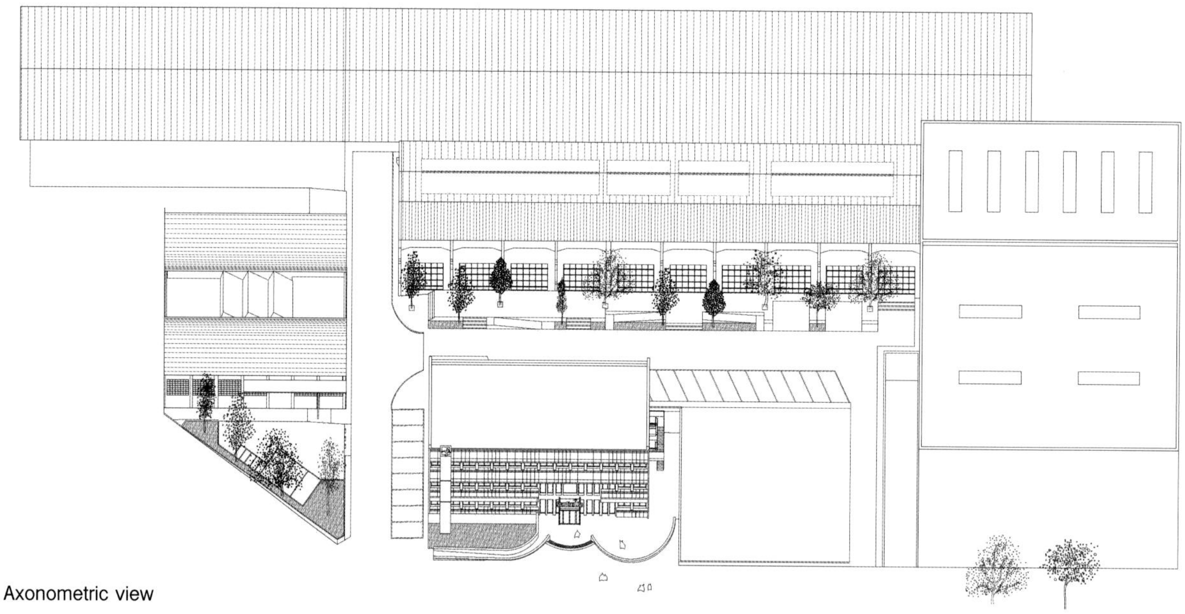

Axonometric view

A former Pellizzari's pump factory, the building was left abandoned, showing the ravages of time, along with the sequence of layers that had been added over the years. Due to the lack of land available for construction, old buildings offer themselves as great opportunities for preservation and are often the only possible way to build under the Italian architectural context.

The [B] Zone project sought to reuse the materials of the site—concrete and steel—to preserve all the distinctive features of the building. The building's façade was painted and some existing windows were enlarged. One more layer was added: the exterior platform in black concrete. This specific tool links two different levels—the inside and the outside—through stairs and ramps. It also gives the shop an extra space outside, which is protected from the road, thanks to this difference in level.

On the inside, an open and neutral space is divided by the archetypical steel frames of the greenhouses that host the 'production' and the new 'product.' Each area is then personalized with the selected and designed furniture. The objects and the materials, derived from the industrial tradition (such as concrete, steel boards, corrugated, or perforated sheets), create an intriguing contrast between the classy atmosphere and the roughness of the industrial case (the existing building). Marble is used as a material connected to the urban context (that is, the Chiampo's Valley). The project dialogues with the natural light thanks to a completely custom-made approach.

The newly-selected uses have a social impact on the surroundings: a multifunctional complex (cafeteria, bakery, bistro, and pizzeria) brings a new centrality into the existing urban settlement and modifies the previous fluxes. An area of 4.9 acres (2 hectares) is now capable of generating a positive 'shock wave' of 14.8 acres (6 hectares).

01

01- Entrance hall of the food court

CAFFÈ
OLIVIERI
PASTICCERIA
BIANCO
OLIVIERI

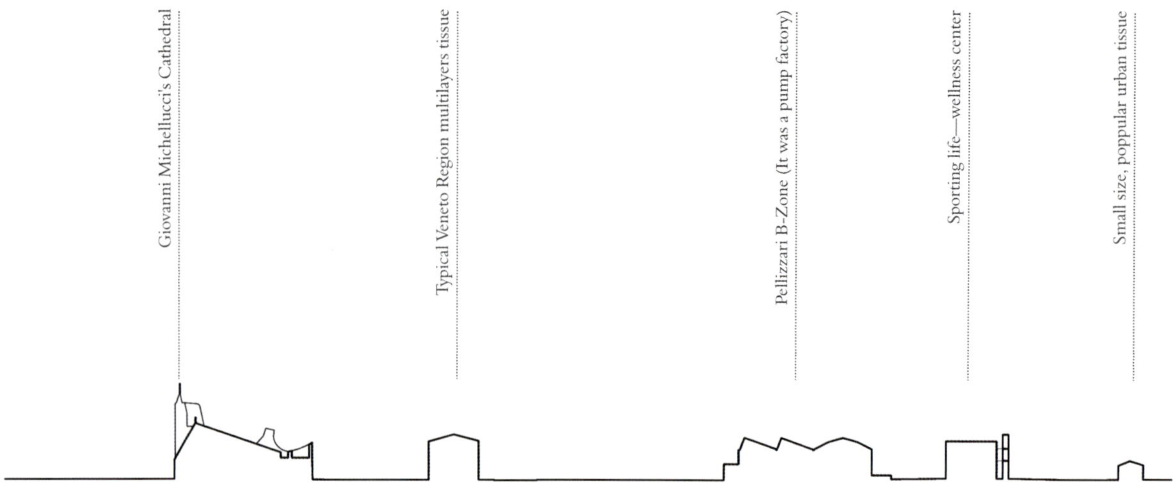

Urban skyline: The [B] Zone and its surroundings.

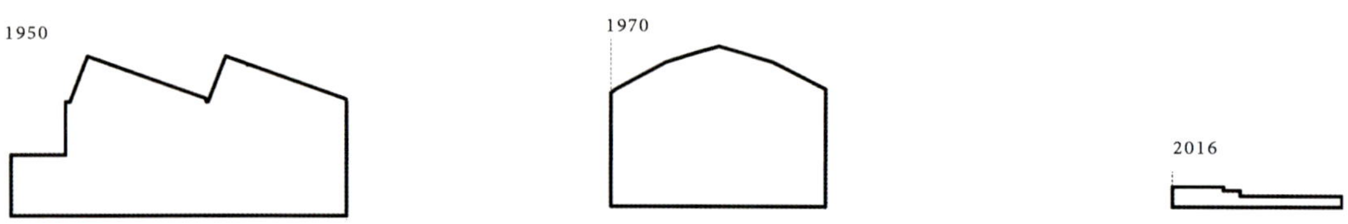

Building's development: the original volume and the later additions

02 03 | 05
04 | 06 07

02- The [B] Zone before the restoration
03- 1882 concept store during the restoration
04- Main entrance from the street (1882 concept store on the left)—the project involved all the other buildings of the site
05- The transparency through the steel frames
06- Entrance hall of the food court
07- The bakery corner

1882 Concept store: schematic floor plan

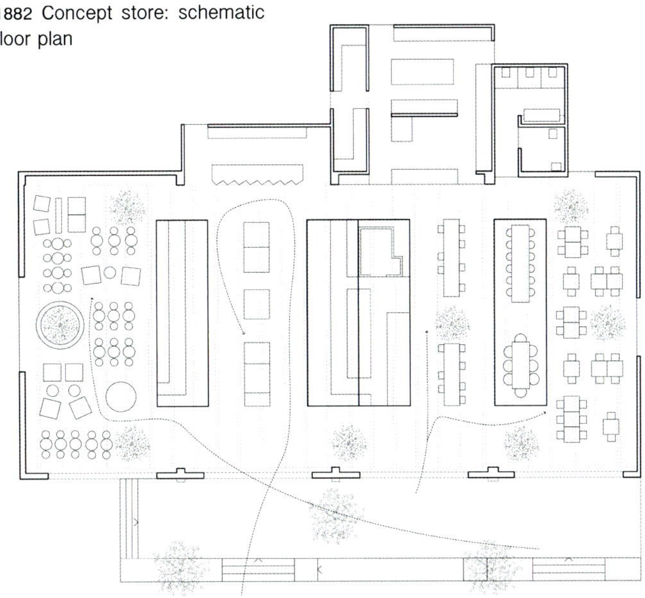

A crisply detailed, luminous white interior elevates this building's robust concrete shell without compromising its industrial nature.

09|10

09- Special tables hosted inside the archetype of a steel greenhouse
10- Selected furniture for the café

Water Tourism Center

Reconstruction of an abandoned Soviet-era pumping station

Location- Rezekne, Latvia
Architect-SAALS Ltd.
Area-5597 square feet (520 square meters)
Completion-2011
Photography-Ingus Bajars, Valts Kleins, SAALS Ltd.
Client-Rezekne Municipality

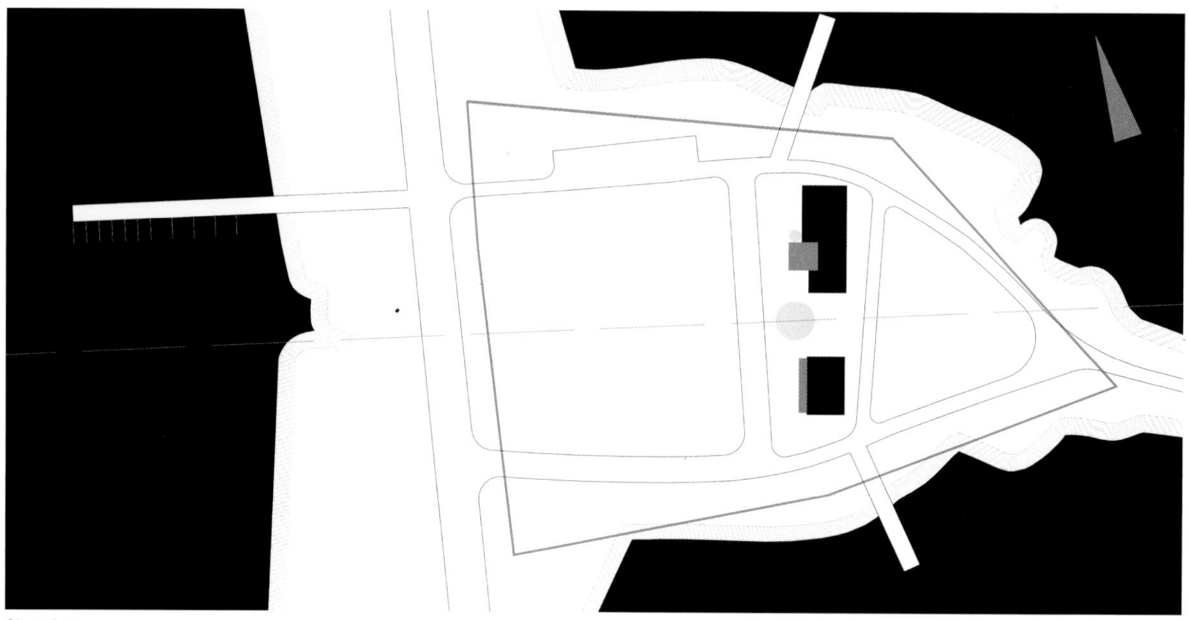

Site plan

The building used to serve as a drainage pump station near the coast in Latvia, but now it's an activity center that promotes water tourism. Before the redevelopment of the Soviet-era drainage pump station and fish farm, the site held a single-story silicate brick building, some old water infrastructure, and a pump. The brief required a new space for the objects of the site to serve the needs of the public near Lubana Lake.

The marshy site had a dilapidated structure, which the architects used as a basis to begin the renovation. The formerly degraded environment was endowed with new functions—a water tourism center consisting of an exhibition hall, a kitchen with leisure room, a sports people's locker rooms, a staff room, a conference room, hotel rooms, and terraces with a roof view. The red building was reconstructed from the ruins of the brick building and modeled in the same fashion. The building's archetypical form, borrowed from ancient traditions, helps one to perceive the environment as a whole and allows for a continuity of heritage while valuing modern building development. The entire third floor is occupied by a glazed terrace, which resembles a light house.

Materials and the color palette used for the building's exterior finish and interior decoration were the same. Floors were covered with wooden boards and tiles in an artificially-rusted material color. On the ceiling, convertible concrete slab panels were exposed. White wall planes serve as background for the play of light and they reflect the changing colors of nature's moods—from morning blush to evening blue. On the same line with the red building, the black wood building nearby is used as a storage space for sports equipment.

The tourism center enjoys great views of the landscape and makes very good use of the natural space for recreational purposes. It also contains a play area for children, a volleyball court, tennis court, grassy lawns, and parking. This project successfully repurposed a former abandoned industrial site into a water tourism destination.

01
02

01- The eastern view
02- The western view

03 04
05
06 07
08

Plans of the spiral staircase and the elevator

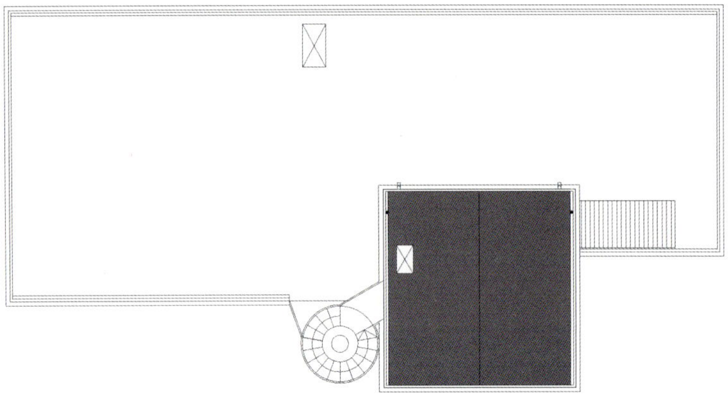

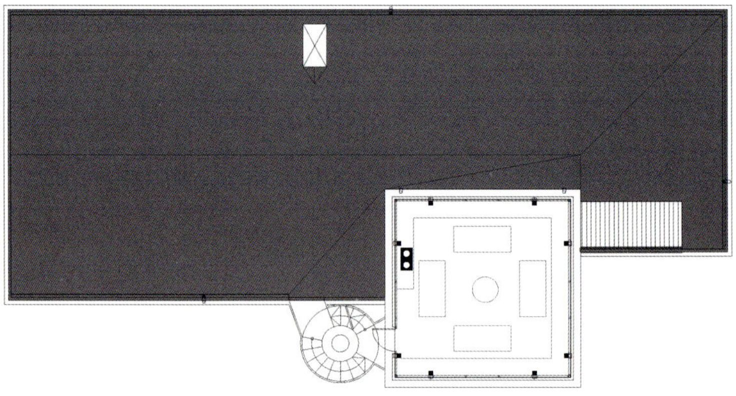

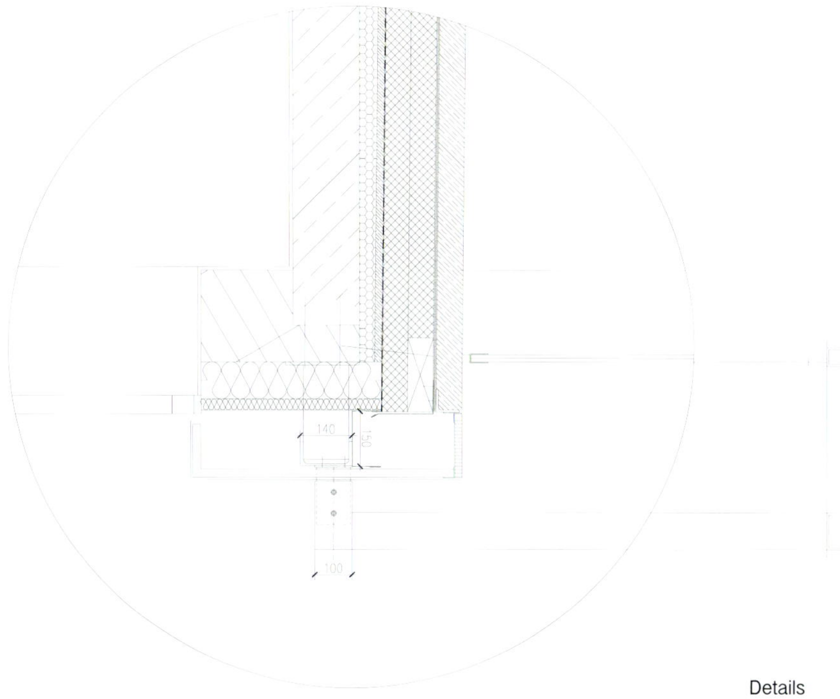

Details

03, 04- Before transformation
05- The building's archetypical form is borrowed from ancient traditions
06- The industrial pump well becomes an attractive sculpture
07- The industrial objects are transformed into an attractive group of leisure objects
08- The signage

09- The leisure room
10- The exhibition hall
11- The guest reception
12- The conference room

09
10 11
12

The newly extruded addition to this existing pump station took cues from the existing ruin's proportions and detailing, and together with a material palette that is both industrial and agricultural, it managed to retain the structure's infrastructural identity while allowing it to sit comfortably within its rural context.

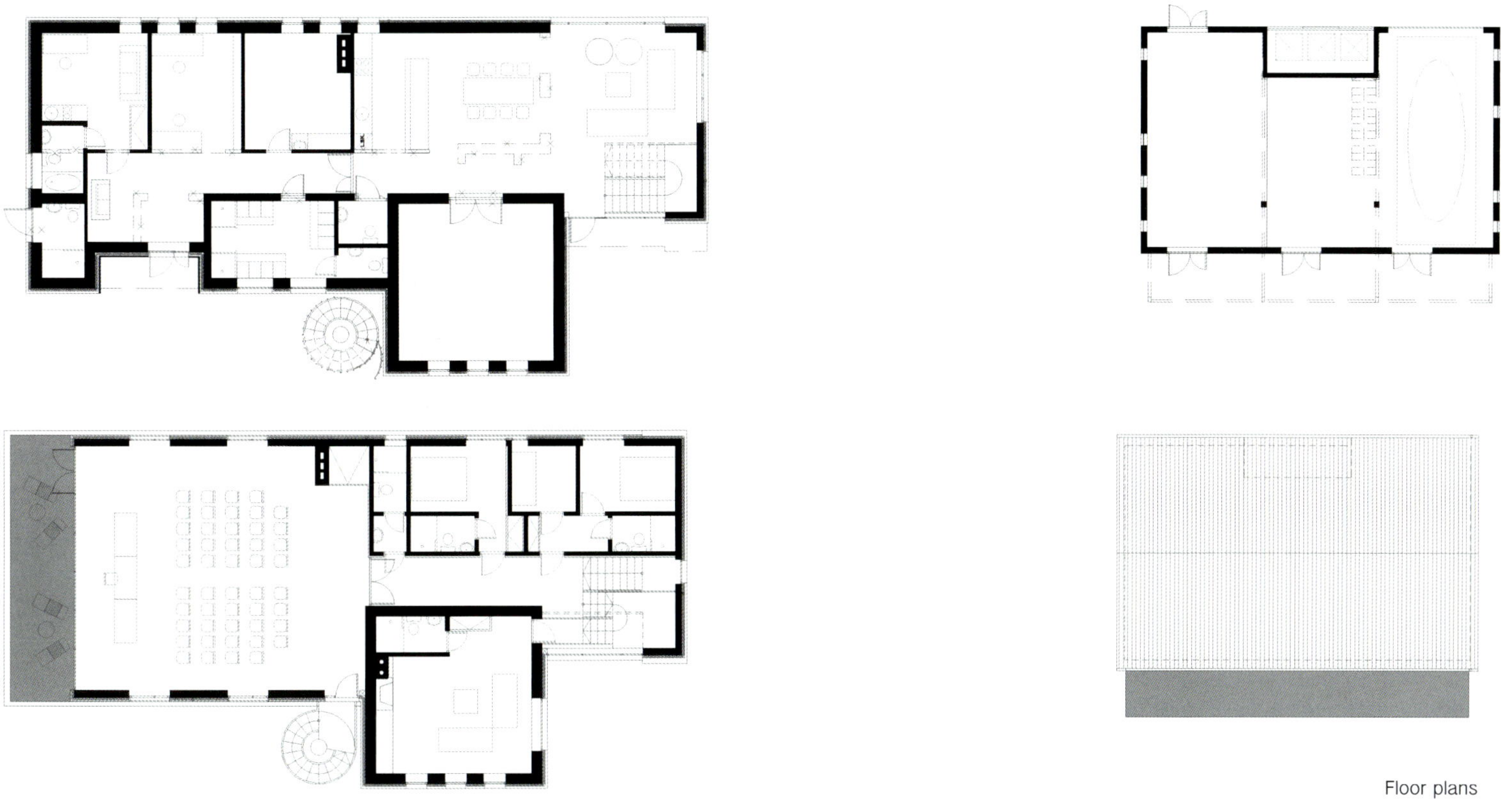

Floor plans

Zhongshan Boda Bund Sales Center

Insight into the old plant

Location-Guangzhou, China
Architect-Inspiration Group
Area-17,836 square feet (1657 square meters)
Completion-2016
Photography-Otto Au
Client-Guangdong Boda Investment Co.,Ltd.

Analysis diagram: The influence of community spreads to the surrounding area

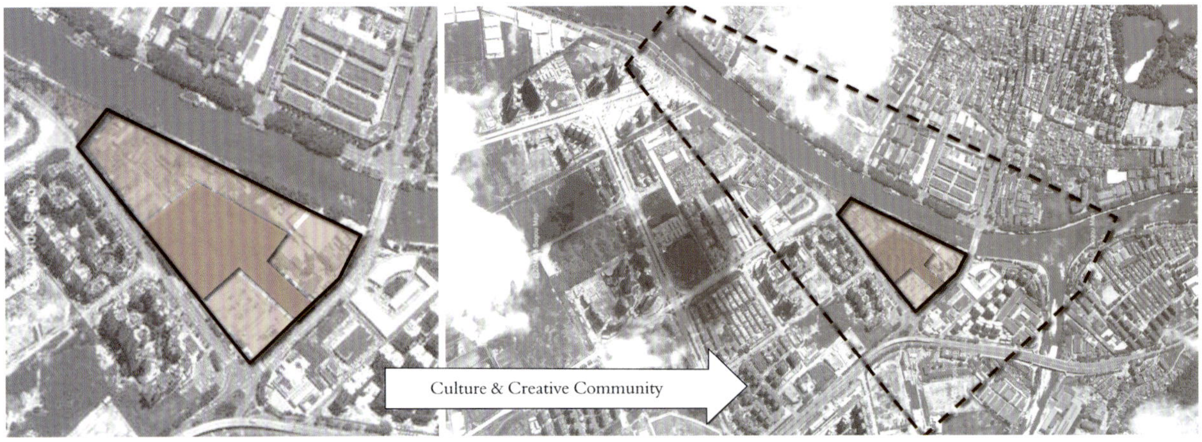

The people of this area have become accustomed to the state of neglect of many old buildings. As such, this project was based on modifying an old plant into a sales center while retaining its historical importance.

With the design concept of 'publicity, openness, and interestingness,' the design team retained the internal spatial structure and brick-wall texture of the original plant and employed the old boiler hole as the window into the whole space. This design approach not only paid respect to the industrial history of the old plant, but enabled the owner to create new significance for the site and to establish a peaceful communication between the past and the present.

The new building is characterized by a visual coherence of space. The old boiler holes were kept to connect the upper and lower spaces while informing people about the building's industrial history. The vertical iron supports in the holes were covered by flourish cirrus plants, endowing the new space with a distinctive identity. Some of the old walls were retained without treatment, while some parts were covered with rusted boarding, and the materials react and reflect with each other. The intrinsic beauty of the volumes and the textures enable people to experience the passage of time through the changing surfaces.

On the ground floor, a big bookcase cantilevering and crossing two floors and the huge transparent glass wall enable the sun to radiate into the whole room and make the cold wall and wooden bookcase warmer. 'The book wall of business negotiation' forms a large artistic backdrop composed of hundreds of books. The orderly book arrangement provides reasonable balance to the romantic book space.

The whole space demonstrates a sense of openness: the transparency brought about by vertical continuity and the huge glass wall, the endless vertical feeling and the huge glass wall. Within the parallel space-time of review and reconstruction, people can also enjoy the slow and slight passing of time. The designer hoped that it can be more than a temporary site for making transactions, but that it can also be a starting point for public community life in the future.

01

01- Stairs lead to the second floor

DECOR ALL-AMERICAN FLAIR
WESTERN TAI CHI CHUAN
Expo Express Furniture
DECOR ALL-AMERICAN FLAIR

02
03 04 | 06
05 | 07

02- It was a soy sauce factory in the past
03, 04- Some old boiler holes on the floor
05- The appearance of the sales center
06- The visual coherence of the space
07- The book wall in the business negotiation area

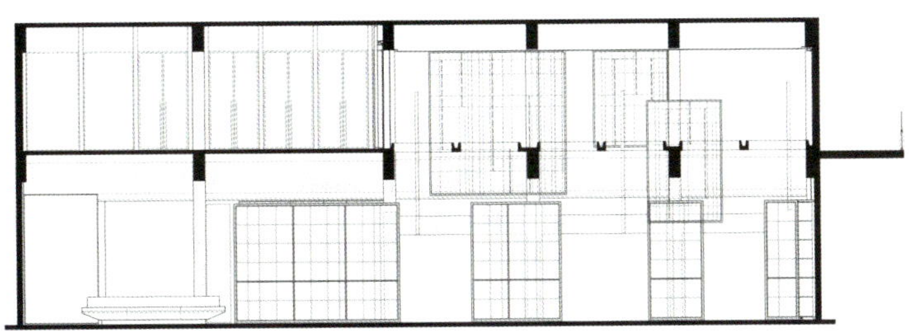

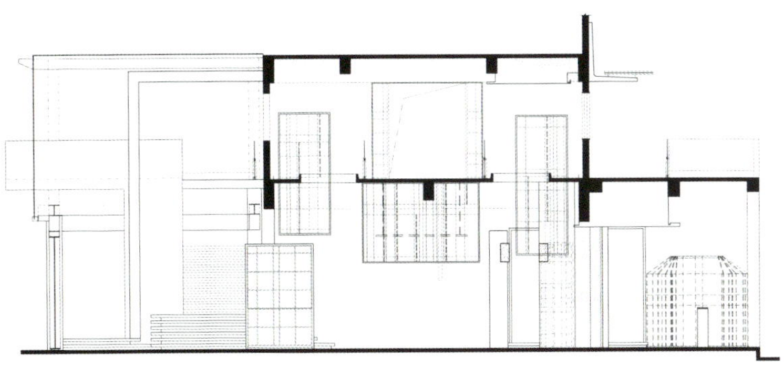

Sections

08- The semi-open contracting room
09, 10, 11- The transparent glass wall creates a broad view

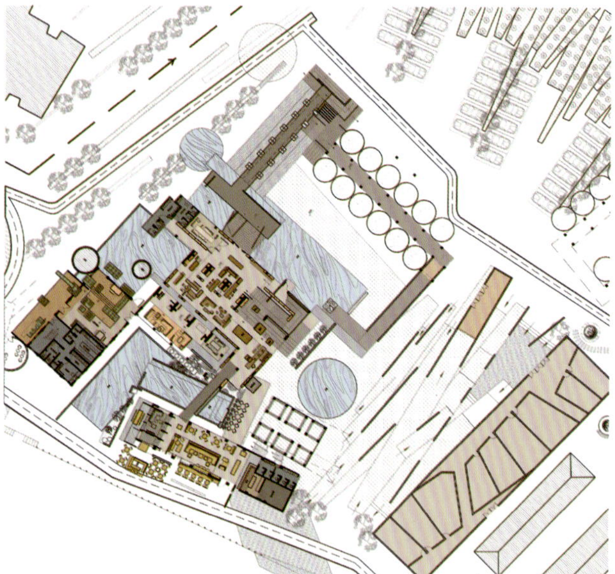

First floor plan

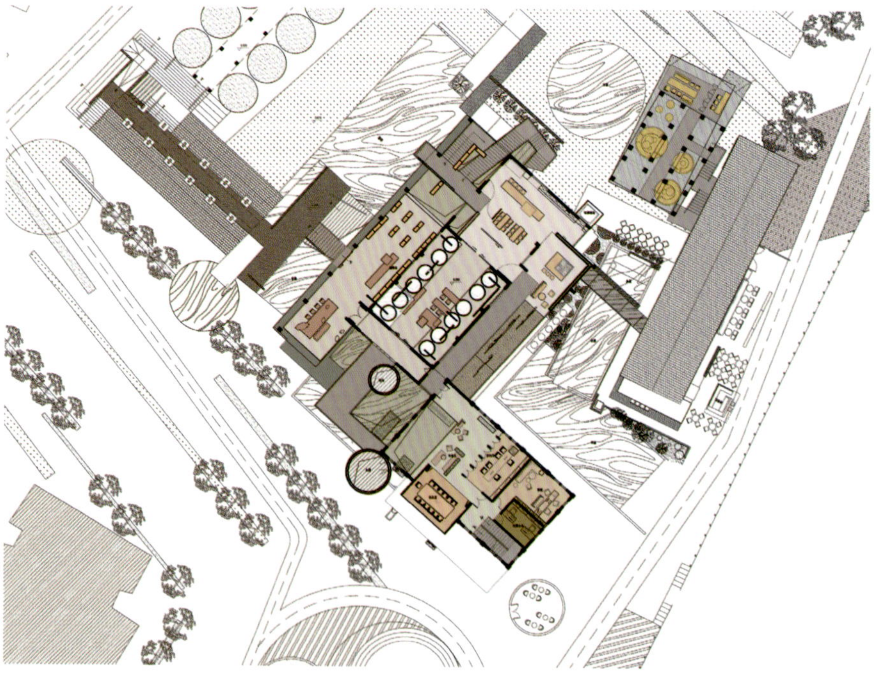

Second floor plan

A series of parallel boiler holes that are intersected by steel elements and bright strips of planting provide a sense of verticality in this space, which is further augmented by the existing structural grid and a number of tall bookcases.

08 09
10 11

12
—14
13

12- The open communal kitchen is located on the second floor
13- Wondering through the art gallery
14- The vertical iron stand is covered by the flourish cirrus

Public library and music school in Almonte

Warehouse rehabilitation

Location-Huelva, Spain
Architect-Donaire Arquitectos
Area-18,568 square feet (1725 square meters)
Completion-2010
Photography-Fernando Alda
Client-Almonte Town Hallk

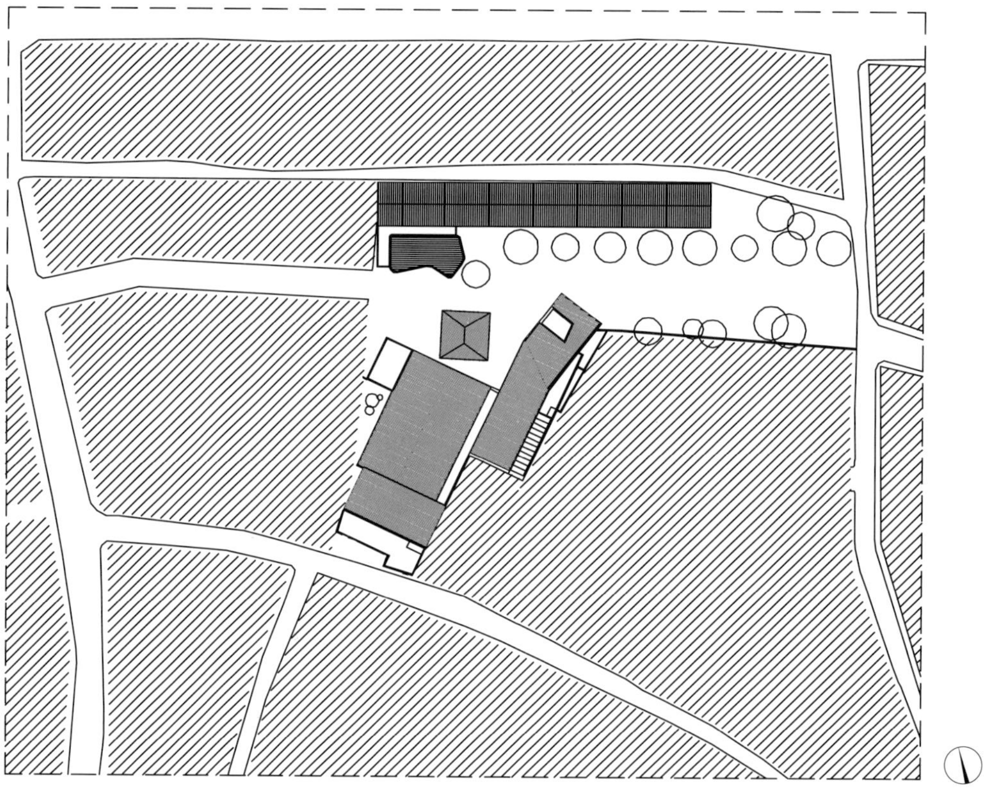

Site plan

Situated in the Culture City of Almonte, Huelva, Spain, next to the town's theater and enclosed within a public square, the warehouse building was registered as being of cultural interest. The rehabilitation of the Los Reales de Almonte warehouse was aimed at adapting it to a public library and a school of arts (music, dance, and art).

Specifically, the library is located in a former wine cellar, a typical structure of the local area. Open on three sides, the building is 256 feet (78 meters) long and 36 feet (11 meters) wide, with a total area of 821 square meters. The work included the construction of a gallery with a new structure and foundations without altering the original structure of the building to maintain and incorporate the original features. The library occupies 14 of the 17 modules, while the three remaining modules in the East Wing house the school of arts.

The main entrance is in the south-east of the building, situated in such a way that gives it a spacious feel. Book control, loaning, and administration are the first area encountered, which has a controlled height. This is followed by a press and reading room using the full height of the warehouse. The last section is the children's area, lit by large and diffuse light sources, with a small storage area and a second flight of stairs. In the upper floor, there is a reading room and audio-visual center.

The project accentuated the original features of the building as a warehouse, creating different spaces, each adapted to its new use. The interior design and furniture formed a fundamental part of the work, with simple designs easily repeatable within the different needs and varied program of the library and public services offered in this space.

01

01- The new structure adds a fresh feeling to the old structure without destroying the original feature

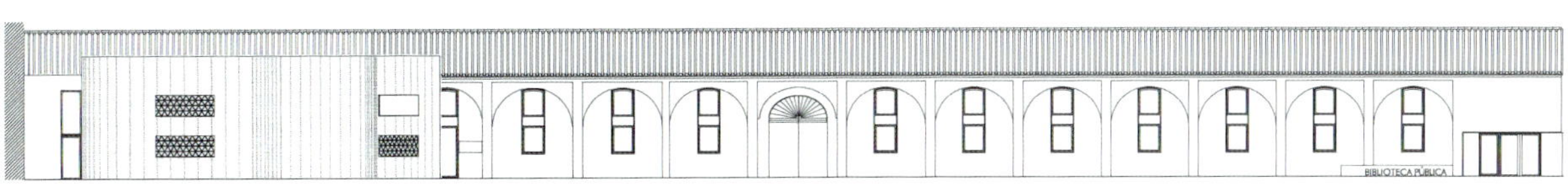

South elevation

Longitudinal section 1

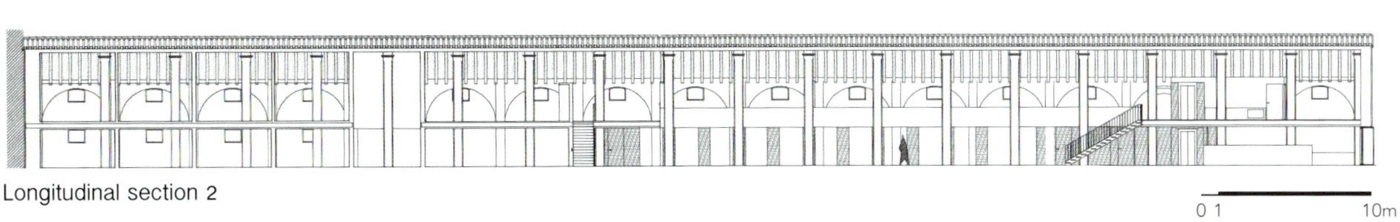

Longitudinal section 2

02 03 04

05 06

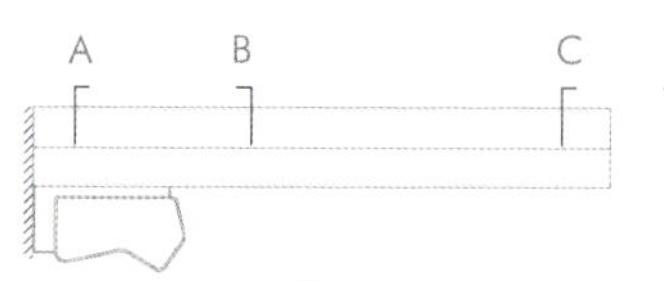

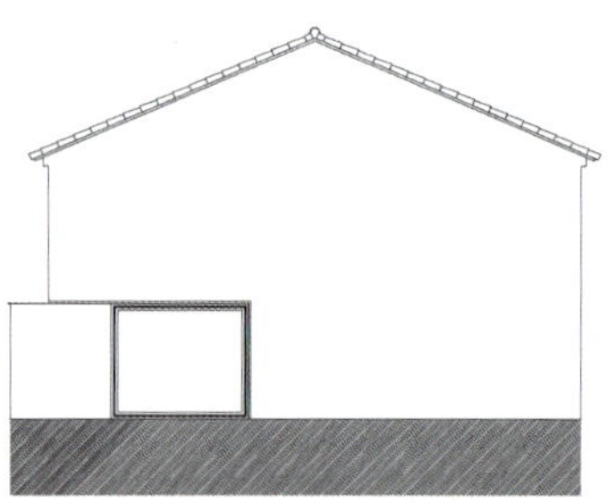

Elevation

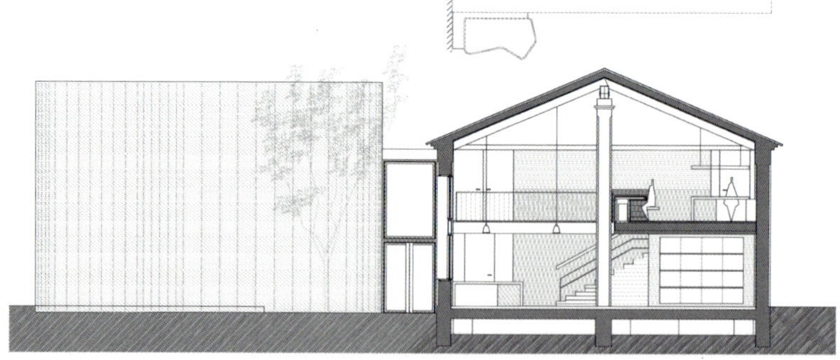

Transverse section B

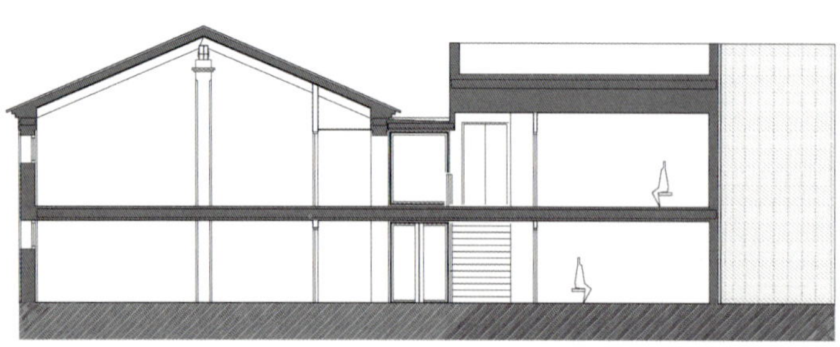

Transverse section A

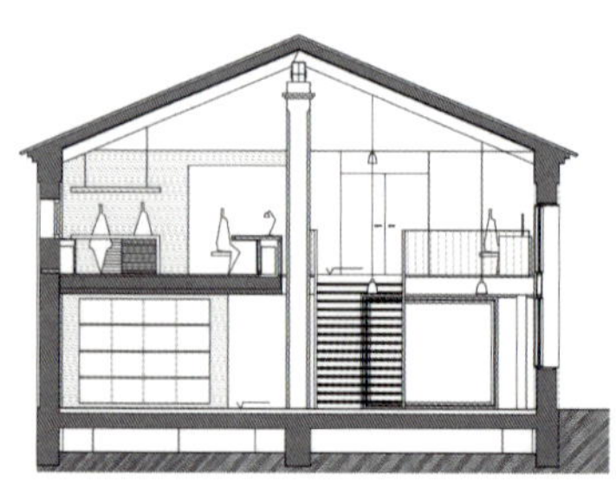

Transverse section C

02, 03- Before transformation
04- The main entrance
05- Night view of the south façade
06- Night view of the courtyard

First floor plan

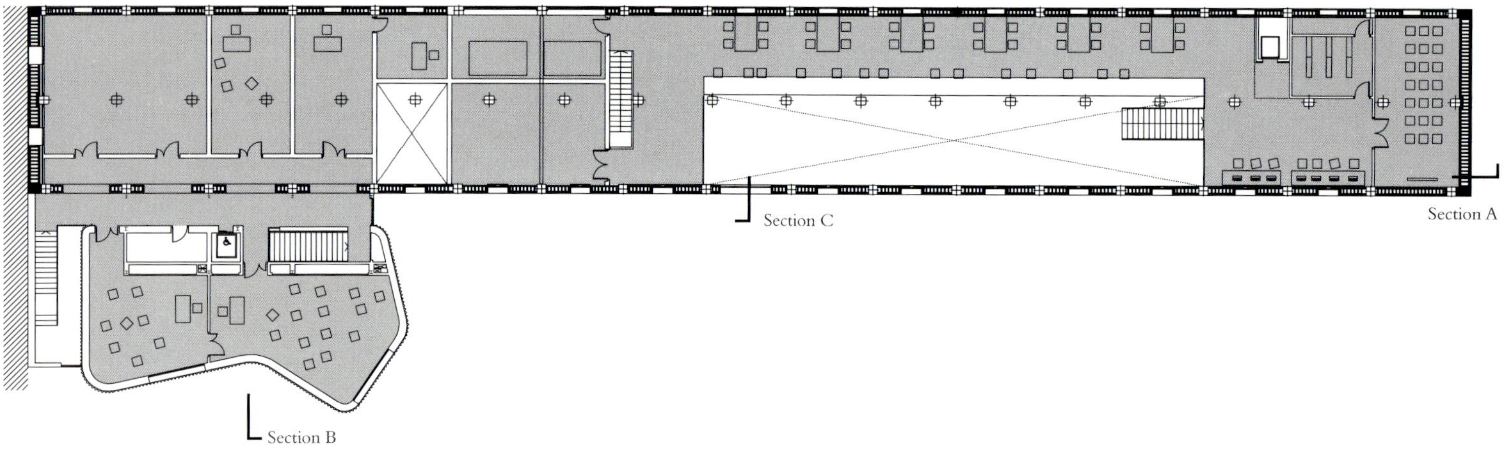

Ground floor plan

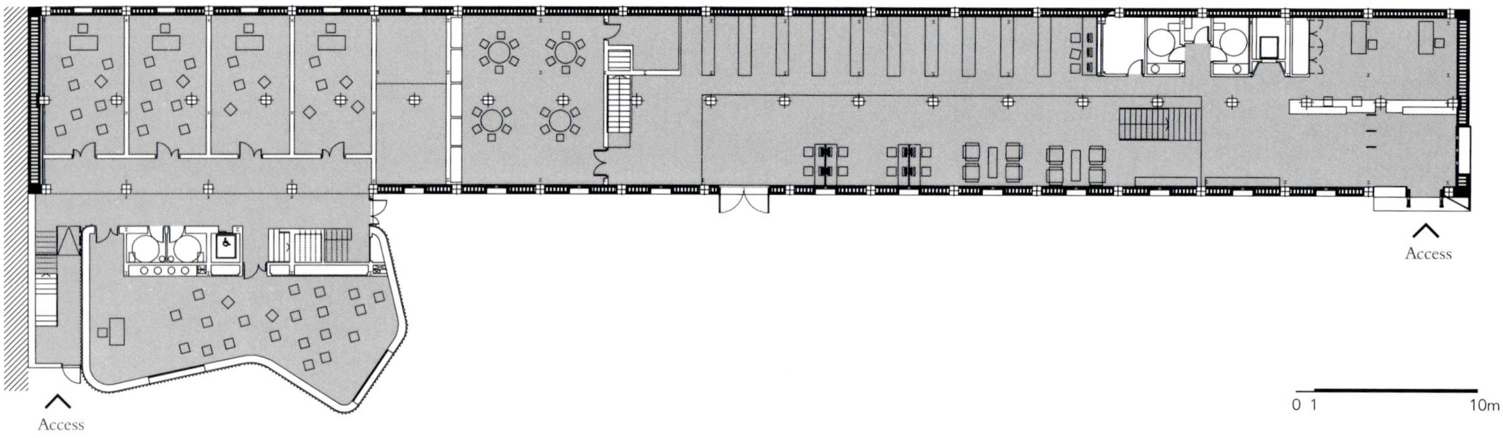

07- Book-loaning section
08- The stairs to the second floor

09 | 11 12
10 | 13

A new amorphous form with openings that mimic the ventilation grilles found in the old wine cellar is offset against the calm rectilinear shape of the existing building. Crisp detailing and a sense of restraint allow the older fabric to retain its own character.

09- Book-loaning section
10- The second-floor reading room
11- Children's area
12- A simple interior design maintains the original flavor
13- The gallery housed in the new structure

Charles Malis City Hall

The new life of a cigarette factory

Location-Brussels, Belgium
Architect-LD2 Architecture, Stéphanie Willocx Architecte, MAMOUT Architectes
Area-10,656 square feet (990 square meters)
Completion-2016
Photography-Studio Fifty Fifty
Client-Municipality of Molenbeek-Saint-Jean

Longitudinal section

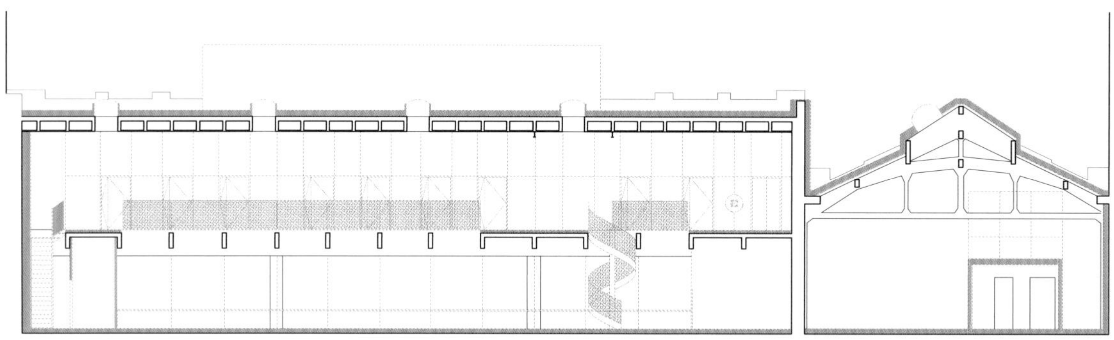

The building is located in Molenbeek-Saint-Jean, a multicultural and dense municipality situated in the northern part of Brussels, Belgium. Molenbeek-Saint-Jean has a living industrial history. Called 'Little Manchester,' the municipality used to host many manufacturers of tobacco and cigarettes. The cigarette factory on Charles Malis Street is one of those remaining buildings, erected around 1930.

After the factory closed in 2001, the building was then divided into three plots. The first plot was turned into social housing; the second was demolished and reserved for a kindergarten; while the third plot was turned into the administration center. The building is a perfect example of an early concrete industrial building. Along the street, the frontage offers a beautiful ornamented brick façade, hiding the rest of the factory. It has a clear ornamental function, while the rest of the building is entirely made of in situ cast concrete. The contrast between this neat and ornamented façade and the rough aspect of the indoor structure was of great heritage value and was therefore an excellent reason for not demolishing the building.

However, the existing structure appeared to be very flexible. The client's brief fit very well into the existing building's composition. The brief for the architectural competition was to transform an industrial site into a local city-hall branch including a waiting room, 12 counters and administration offices. The proposal took advantage of the existing situation by inserting the program in a fluid and logical way into the structure, without degrading it. The shed-shaped volume logically becomes the new public entrance, making its public function evident from the street, while the horizontal volume accommodates the counters and the offices on two levels.

To enhance the accessible nature of this public service, the waiting room is designed as an extension of the street—an in-between space that can be experienced as a part of the city. The counters are organized in a repetitive way, aligned with the concrete beams. They offer room and storage for an effective treatment of the citizens' requests. The offices, situated on the upper level, are linked with the counters by a large circulation area, designed for informal meetings with visual connections in order to create an efficient yet convivial way of working.

Although the existing structure remained untouched, the façades and techniques of the building were greatly improved to achieve a high level of energy-efficiency and wellbeing for visitors and employees. The materials used for the renovation contributed to the structure's sustainability: the existing concrete was renovated with high-quality coating, which regenerates the concrete and the reinforcing bars. The floor of the waiting room is paved with recycled pavers from the streets of Brussels. The light fittings are also made from reused material—from the collective rotor—while the new partitions were cladded with natural birch plywood.

01
02

01- View from the street—public entrance
02- View from the street—employee entrance

03 04 05 07
06 08

03, 04, 05- Before renovation
06- View from the waiting room with the benches
07- Visual relation between the two floors
08- The counters are built with steel and birch plywood

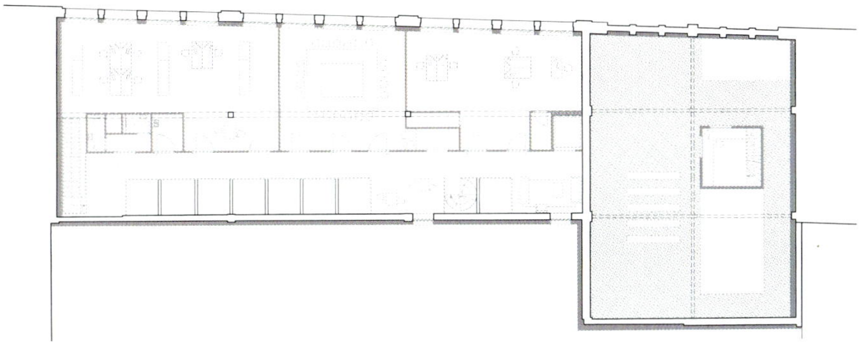

First floor plan

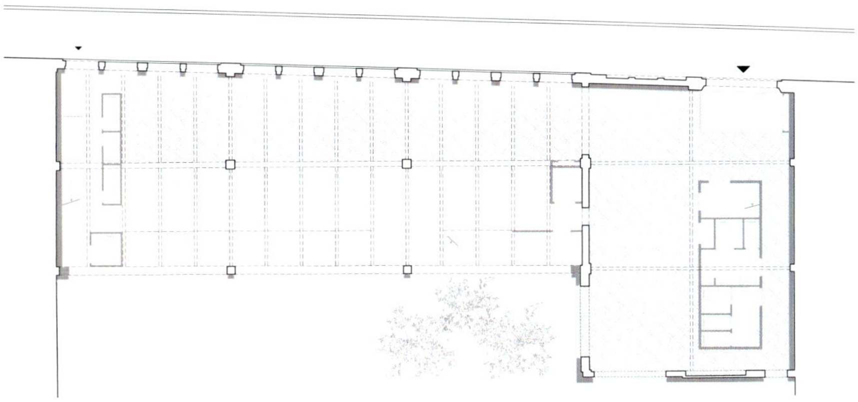

Ground floor plan

The relationship between a carefully crafted existing brick façade and a concrete frame was seen as a valued asset in this building and they were suitably refurbished, while recycled street pavers reinforce this new municipal facility's character as an extension of the public realm.

09|11
10|12

09- The corridor designed as an informal meeting place
10- In between the counter and the staircase
11- The waiting bench in front of the counter
12- View from an administration office

10

OostCampus

City hall and Civic Center, upcycling a former Coca-Cola factory

Location-Oostkamp, Belgium
Architect-Carlos Arroyo Architects
Area-9.9 acres (4 hectares)
Completion-2012
Photography-Miguel de Guzmán
Client-Autonoom Gemeetebedrijf Oostkamp

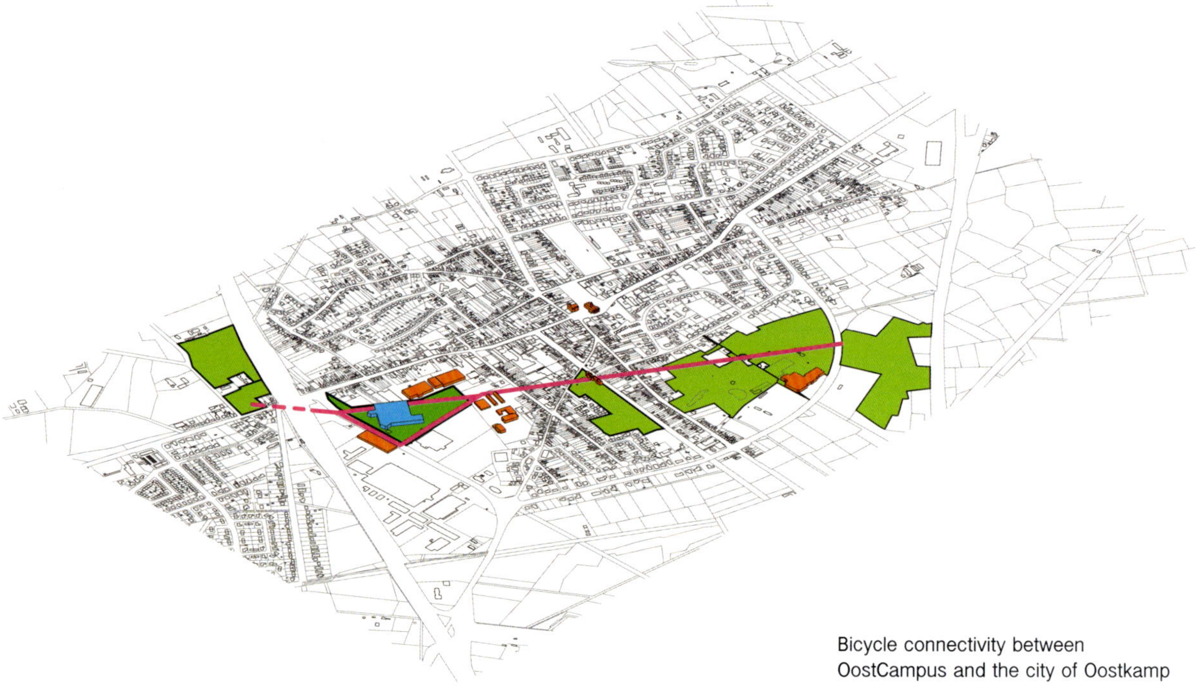

Bicycle connectivity between OostCampus and the city of Oostkamp

The city of Oostkamp acquired the former Coca-Cola factory, a 9.9-acre (4-hectare) plot with a 2.7-acre (1.1-hectare) industrial shed built in 1991. The competition brief required a building complex that could gather most of the public service buildings of the city on this central and well-connected plot in an arrangement to be called OostCampus.

The starting point for this project was an uncompromising in situ recycling of the existing industrial building, including foundations, bearing structure, outer skin, waterproofing, services installations and equipment, electric power station, heating plant, water ducts, fire hoses, drainage and even parking space, fencing, and accesses.

To transform the vast industrial hall—with minimal footprint but maximum spatial result, the architect designed a sheltered interior public space, wrapped in a 'luminous landscape of white clouds.' Thin shells of GRG (Glass Reinforced Gypsum) span the large space like huge soap bubbles. They are only 0.28 inches (7 millimeters) thick. The GRG is cast on bubble-shaped molds onsite, just like plaster and bandage around a broken arm; instead of cotton bandage, it is a glass fiber mesh.

Within this landscape, a set of modular clusters provides the administrative services and spaces, designed to facilitate the relationship between citizens and administration. The clusters of city services are arranged according to a topogram—a graphic depiction of the work-flow in relation to space—developed through workshops with the city employees and the citizens. The chamber hall is in full sight in the middle of public space. Citizens can see what is going on in their town hall. The 170 workers of the city, from clerks to cleaning people, participated in workshops to discuss the project, from spatial arrangement to the maintenance of materials.

The architects chose basic materials, either recycled from waste, or very light and simple materials, or plain raw materials with only basic production procedures to follow the sustainability criterion.

In this airy bubble-space of transparency and democracy, the city services are clustered in a dendrite structure, like a crystallization of a new relationship between citizens and administration. The architects turned an enormous, ugly factory into a wonderful experience, within a tight budget.

01

02

01- Main access to the building
02- Open patio bringing natural light to the inner spaces

03, 04, 05, 06- Main access to the building
07- Bicycle lane along northwest façade; window shape result of the intersection of bubble and perimeter walls
08- Info-point for one of the administrative clusters

03 04
05 06
07 08

Sections before and after the refurbishment

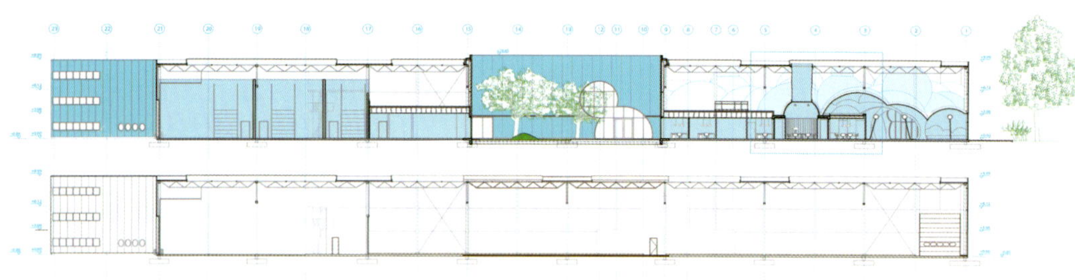

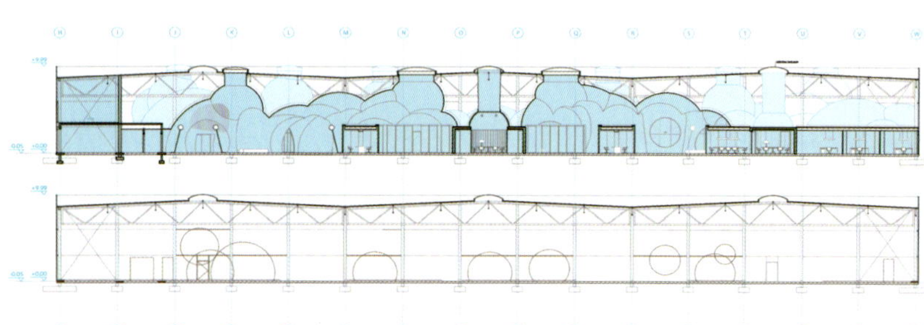

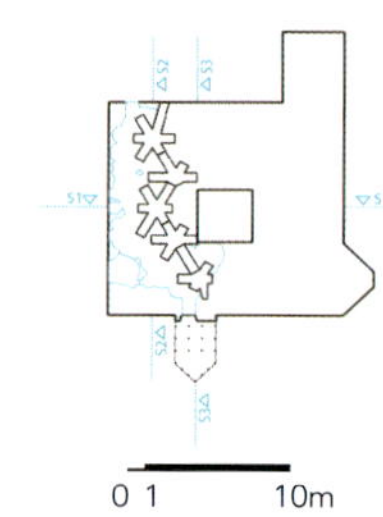

Diagram of OostCampus Park, designed for energy production and water harvesting

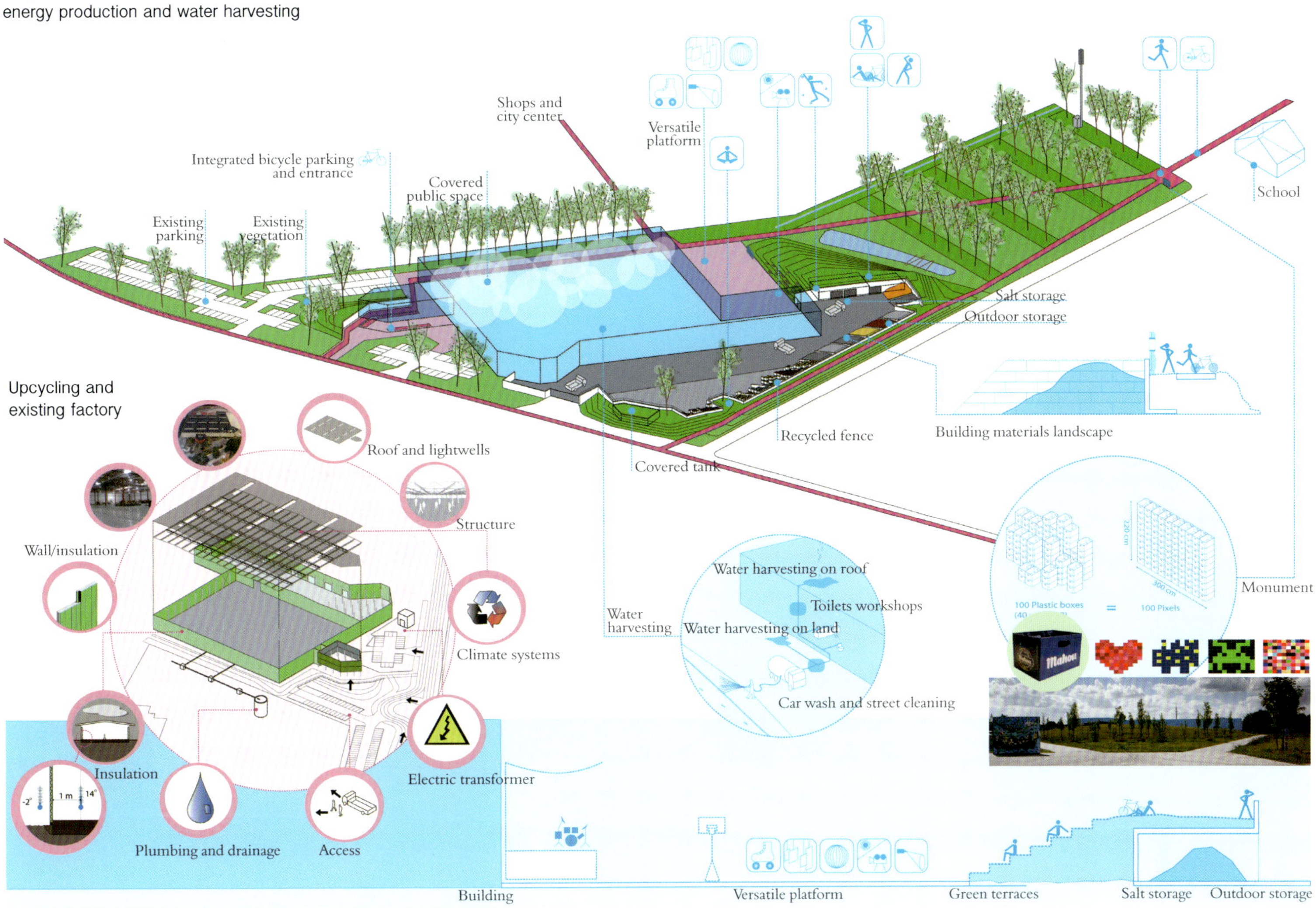

09- Public space within the white cloud landscape: a grand place with permanent mild weather
10- While addressing the issue of embedded energy, the architect propose a fun way to do things—this has been defined by critics as Sustainable Exuberance

Building material strategy: upcycling, recycling and reusing

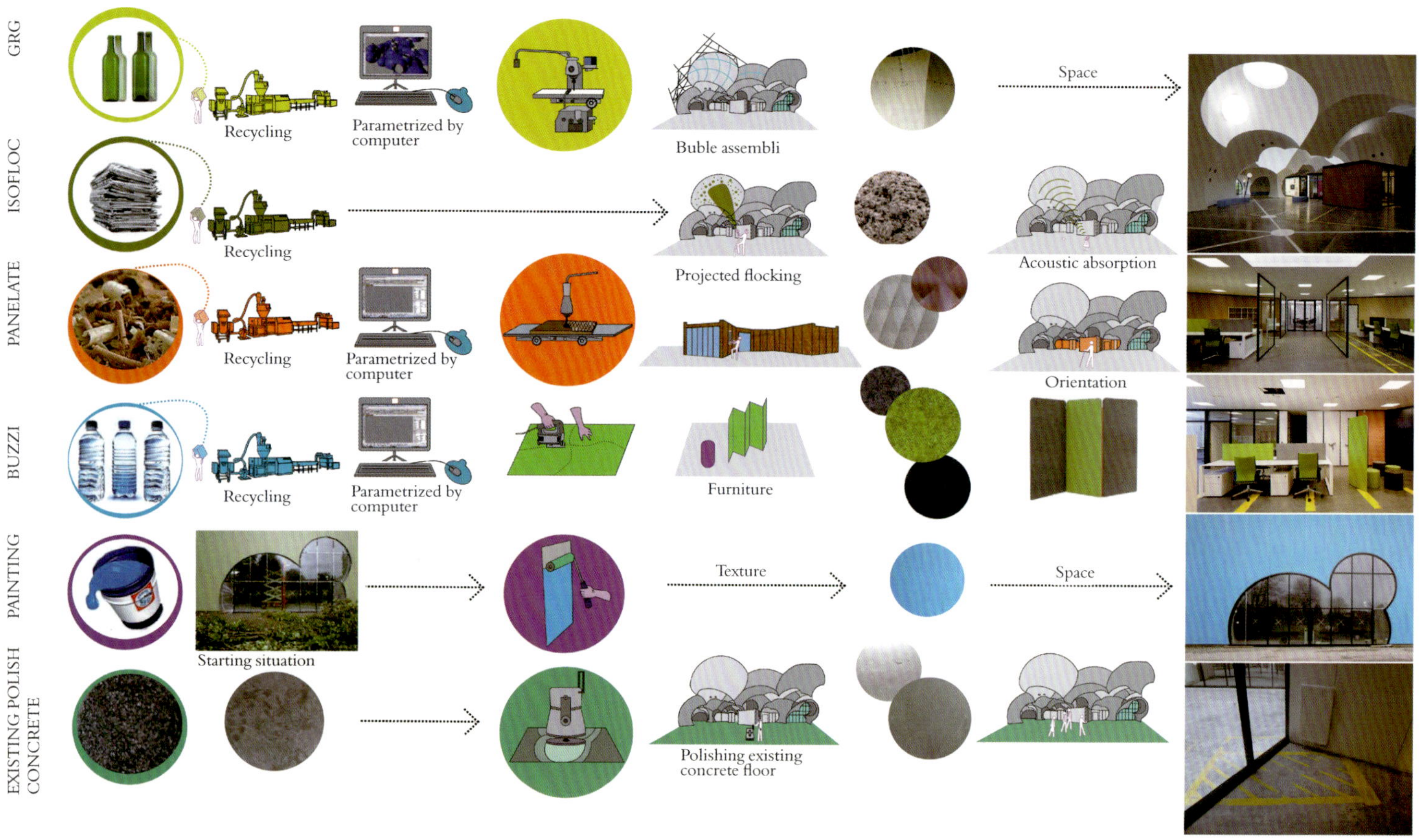

10
09

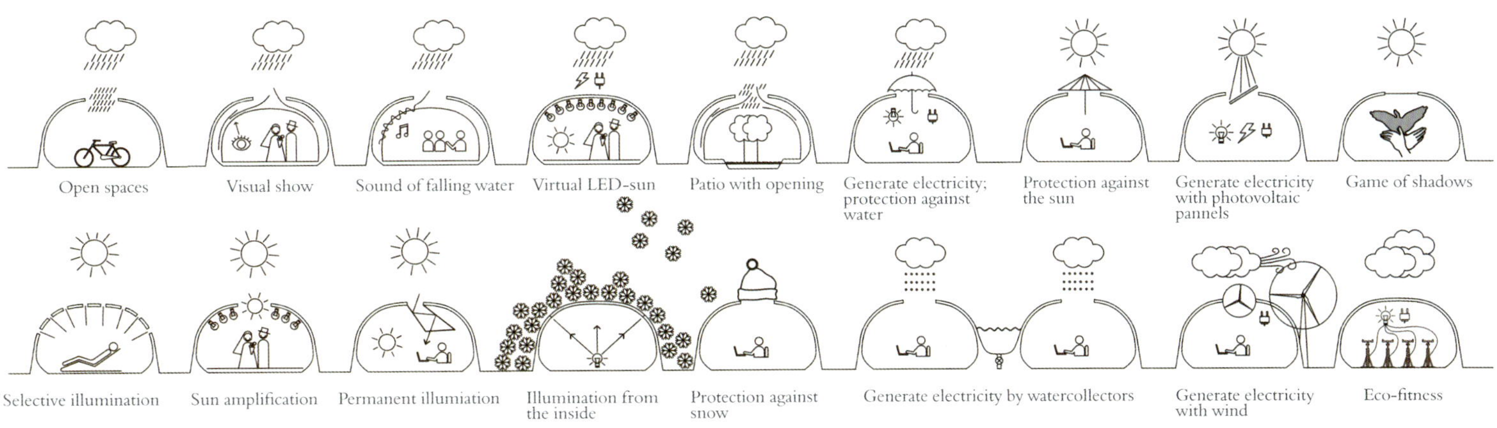

The openings among the clouds are equipped with simple devices that transform all kinds of weather conditions into wonderful events. An LED sun shines over people leaving the registrar at a wedding.

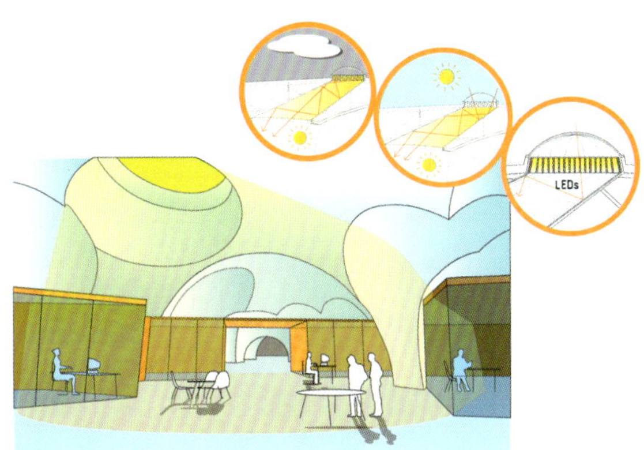

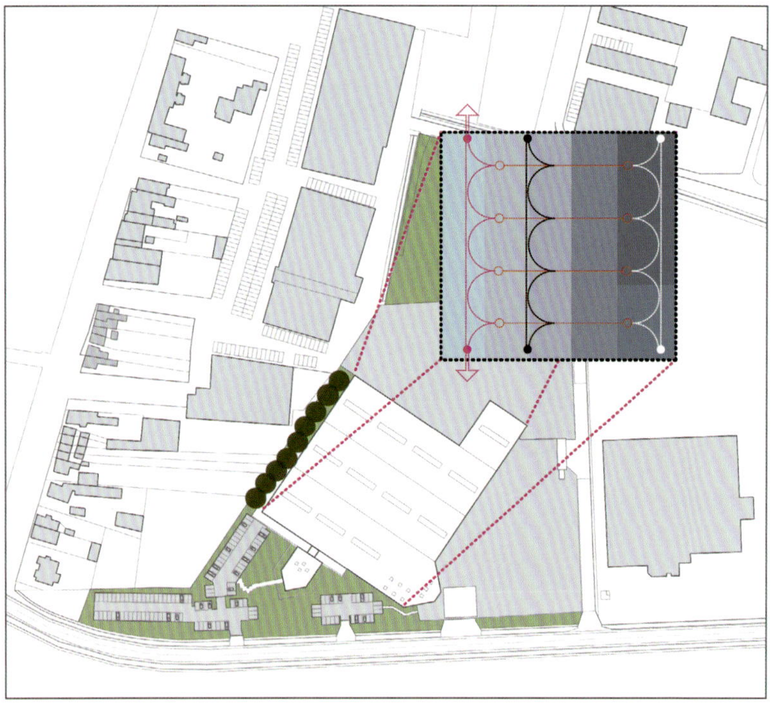

Circulation

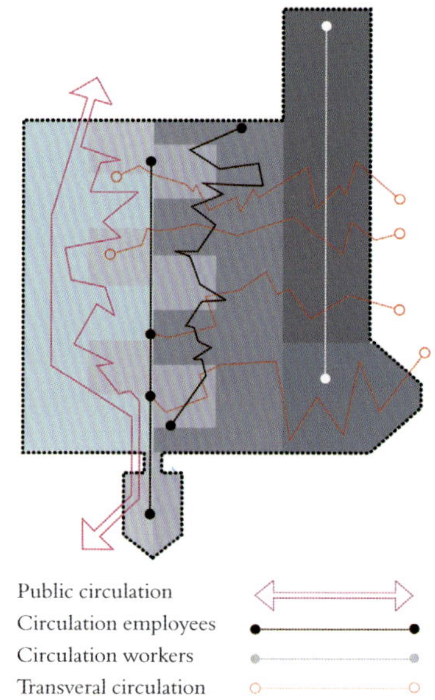

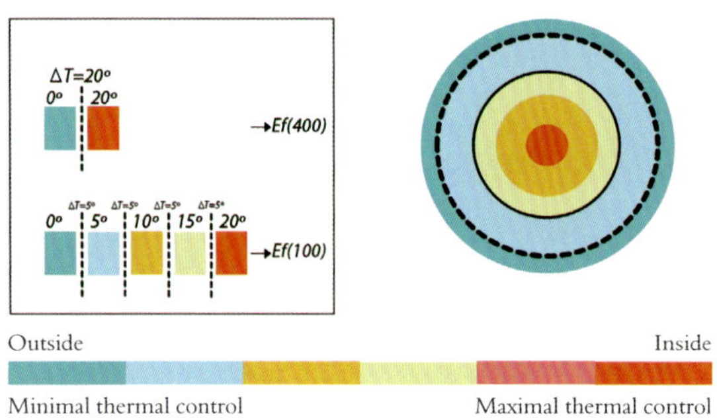

Thermal diagram

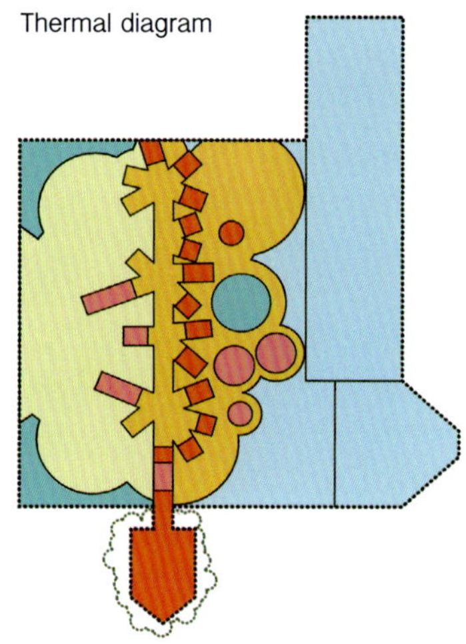

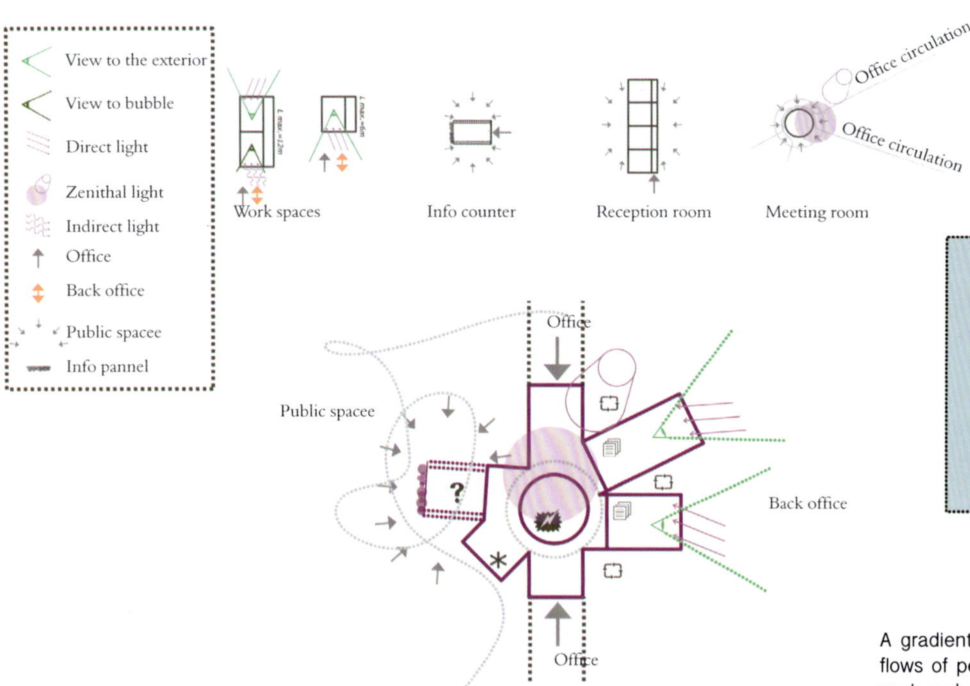

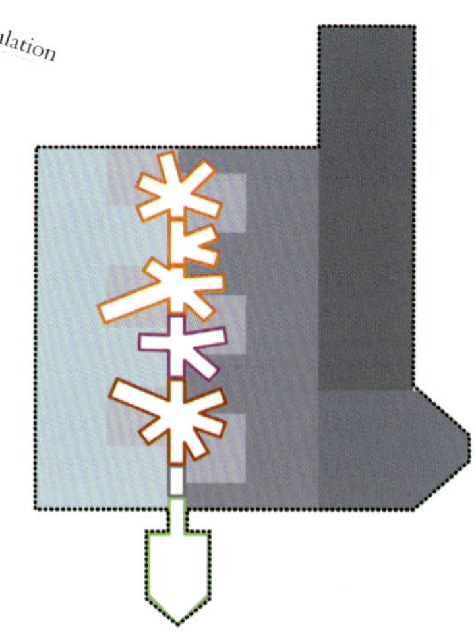

A gradient from 'soft' to 'hard' elements of program, to control flows of people and materials, energy loss, noise and dust, daily work and celebration

A playful bubble-like interior made from Glass-Reinforced Gypsum (GRG) belies the complex process of transforming this former Coca-Cola factory into a building dedicated to public service.

11, 12- A playful bubble-like interior made from Glass-Reinforced Gypsum (GRG)— the key for the complex process of transforming this former Coca-Cola factory into a building dedicated to public service

11
12

13

14 15

13- The city chamber surrounded by public space—citizens can see what is going on in their town hall
14- The back offices are also accessible to the public
15- Canteen as a meeting place

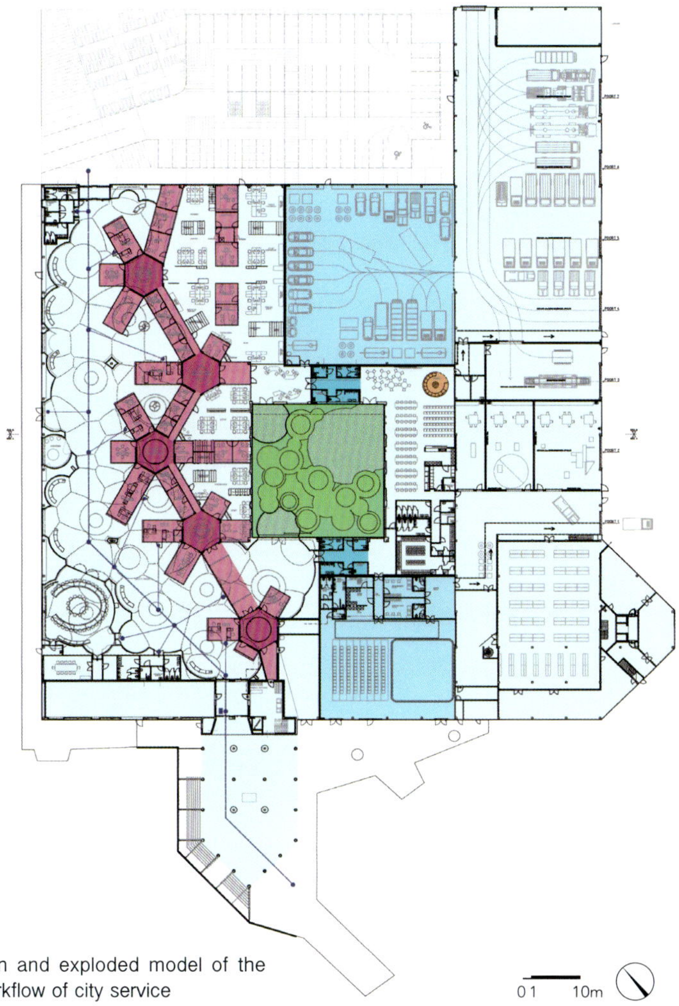

Plan and exploded model of the workflow of city service

Opificio Golinelli—Citadel for Knowledge and Culture

Renovation of an industrial complex

Location-Bologna, Italy
Architect-Diverserighestudio
Area-48,438 square feet (4500 square meters)
Completion-2015
Photography-Giovanni Bortolani
Client-Fondazione Golinelli

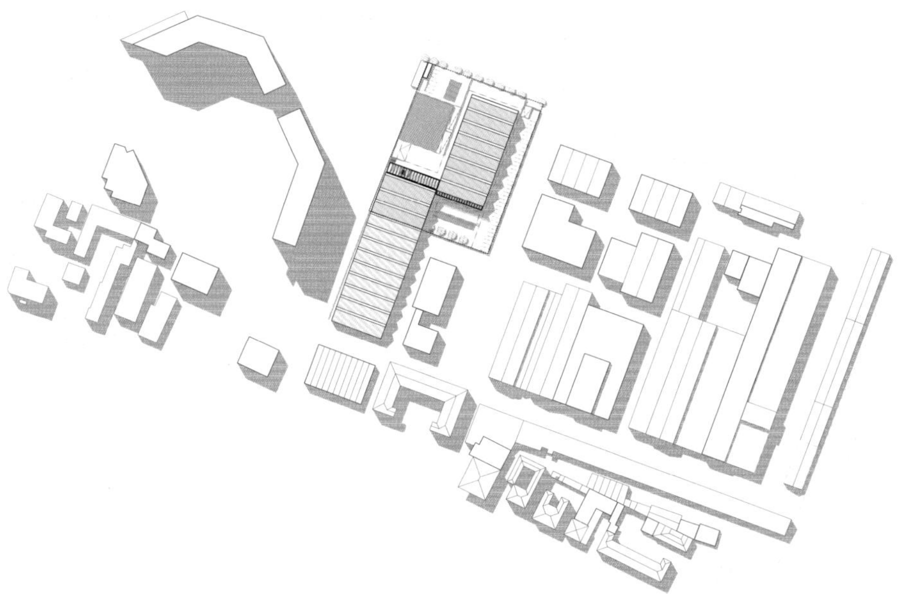

Urban setting—general plan

The site is located on the western outskirts of Bologna, in the industrial complex of the former Fonderie Sabiem next to the former Prati di Caprara barracks. The character of this portion of the city is determined by a number of old industrial facilities, some in a complete state of abandon. In 2013, Fondazione Golinelli decided to purchase part of the zone—an area of 96,875 square feet (9000 square meters)—containing an industrial building dating back to the 1960s, with the aim of renovating it and moving the Foundation's cultural and educational activities for people from aged 3 to 99 years old into the new facility.

The goal of the project was clear: education on the scientific aspects of art and the artistic intuitions of science, bringing out the affinities of the two fields in a perspective of implementation of creative thinking. It hoped to create a public space suitable to contain different activities and sustain social interaction, where shared services and spaces were organized.

This character of openness led to the design of a space with a local exterior, refurbishing an existing industrial building, and a global interior, interconnected with the world through open work modes. The space was divided into pavilions and independent structures linked one to another by a system of walkways, gardens, and squares in a way similar to how the city's public spaces are arranged. All this happens inside the existing industrial building, below the characteristic saw-tooth profile of the reticular roof structure, whose light underlines the public, open dimension of the internal space. The outdoor spaces were also renewed and connected to the mobility system and the existing public parking areas.

The project is an example of a regenerated industrial setting, a fertile place of scientific experimentation and social innovation. Observing these places inside urban development means foreseeing major themes of research on the complex city, redefining the meaning of 'state of abandon' and permitting an inclusive reinterpretation of such spaces; from a negative signified to a design signifier, a social and cultural catalyst, the pretext metamorphoses of uses and spaces, which having been rethought return to life, reutilizing what already exists. The process leading to the completion of the work has been shared with the City of Bologna, which, with a resolution of the City Council in 2013, has recognized the civic benefits of the project.

01
02

01- Panning shot
02- Night view

Axonometric views

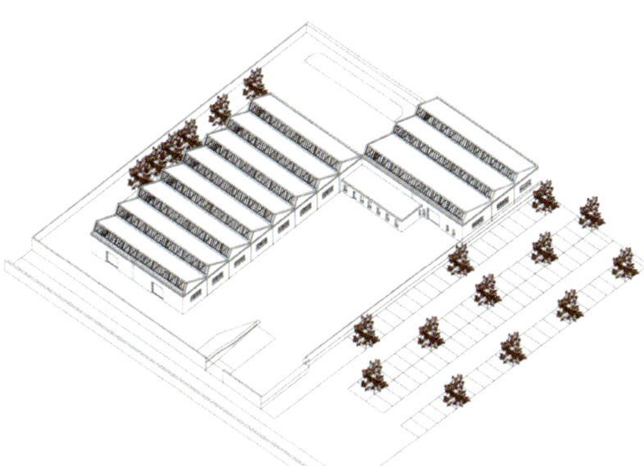

The existing building

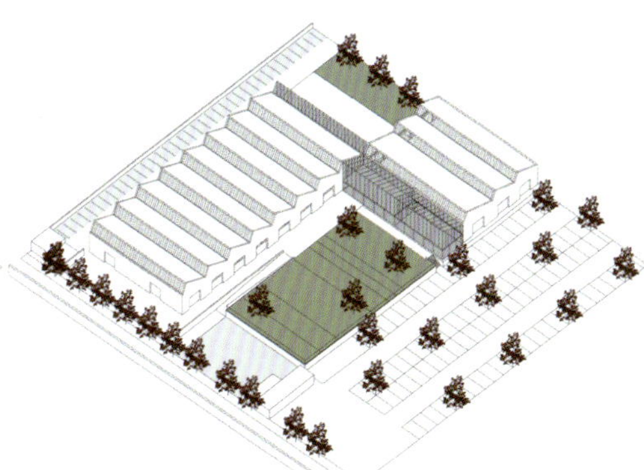

Entrances and open spaces

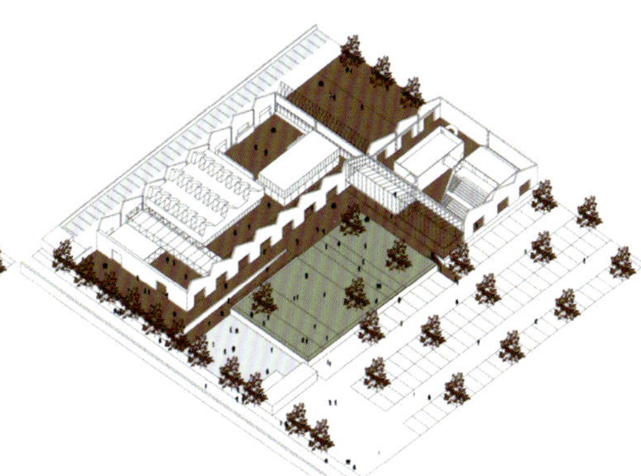

Public spaces / indoor and outdoor

03 | 07 08
04 05 06

General axonometries

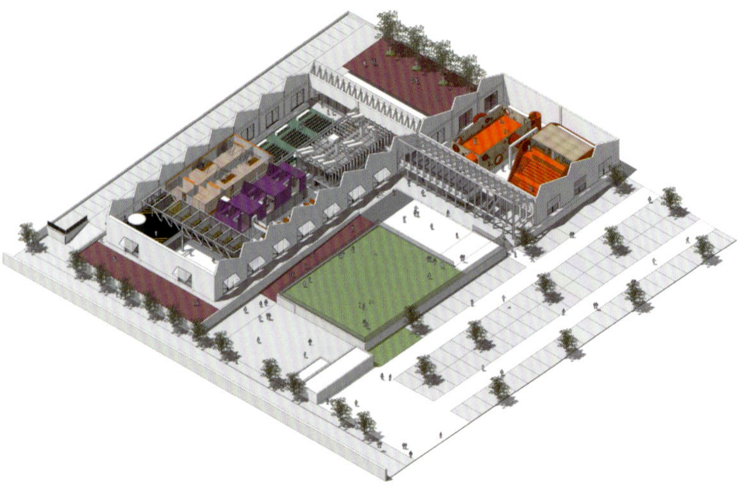

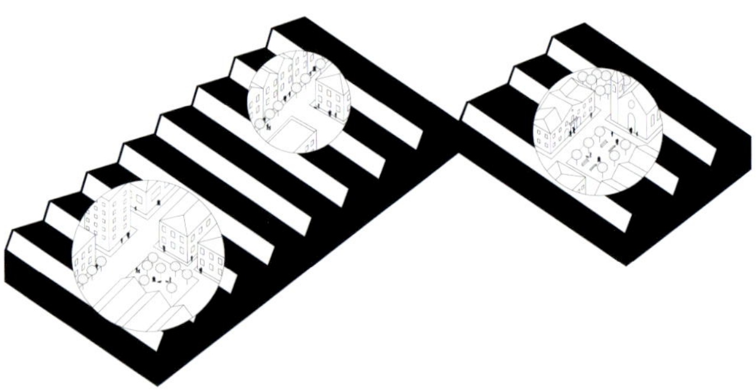

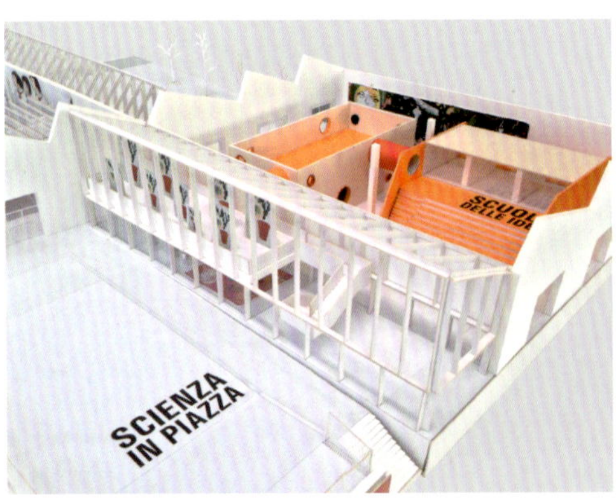

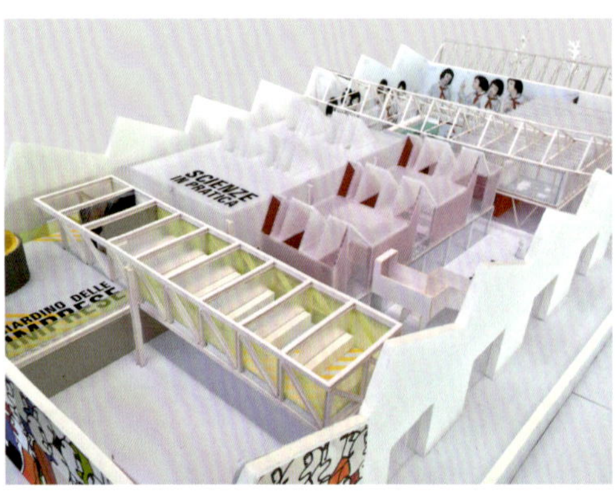

03- Existing building internal view
04, 05, 06- Model views
07- Multipurpose space
08- Public area

Activities diagrams and positioning

Infrastructure

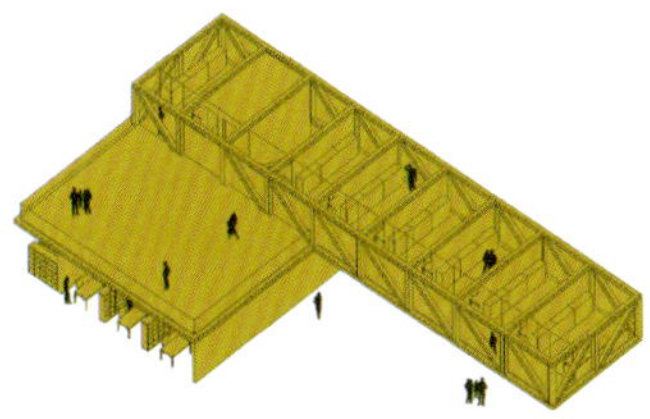

Giardino delle imprese
Objective: to bring out the creativity and talents of young people, helping them to approach enterpreneurial culture

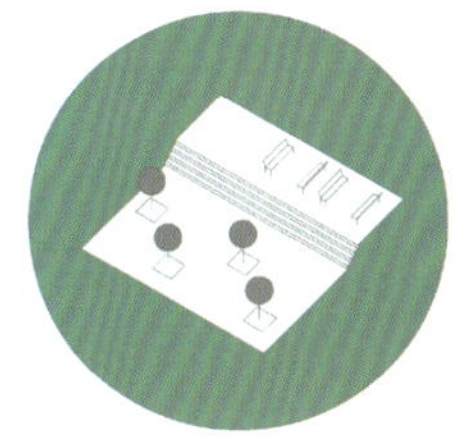

Gardens and squares

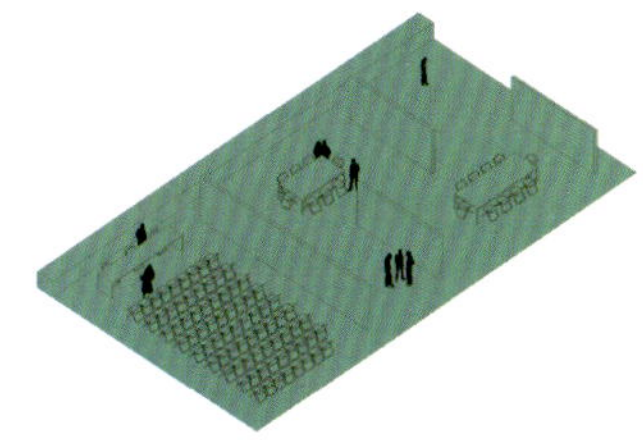

Educare a educare
Objective: to train educators in an interactive, participatory method, especially in the field of the sciences to develop innovation and research in the field of pedagogy

Institution

The foundation
Foudazione golinelli was established in bologna in 1988 with the goal of promoting education and training, spreading culture, and encouraging the intellectual and ethical growth of yound people, the citizens of tomorrow

Institution

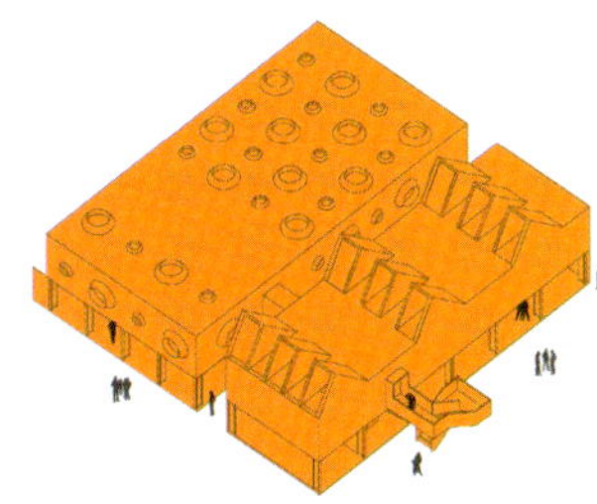

High schools
Scienze in Pratica
Objective: to ignite the interest of teenagers in the sciences and technology, through concrete laboratory experimentation
Adience: Young people between the ages of 14 and 19

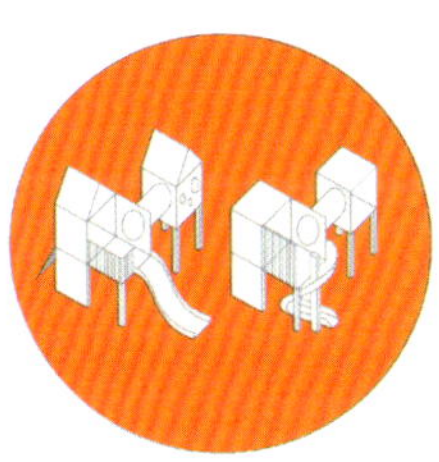

Kindergartens and child care spaces

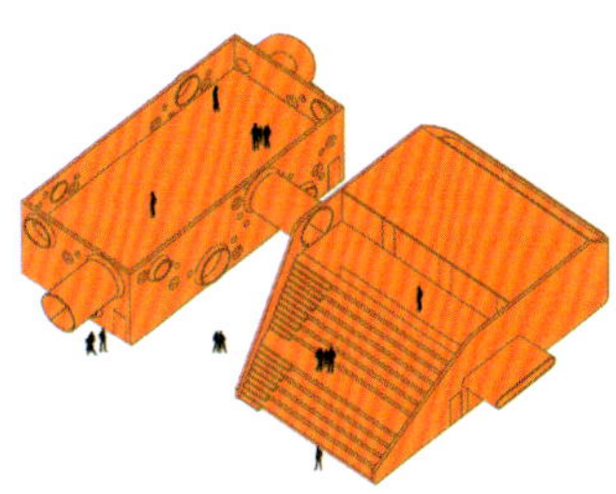

Scuola delle idee
Objective: to promote creativity starting from early childhood, and to help to develop it through all the phases of education, thanks to an approach of informal learning

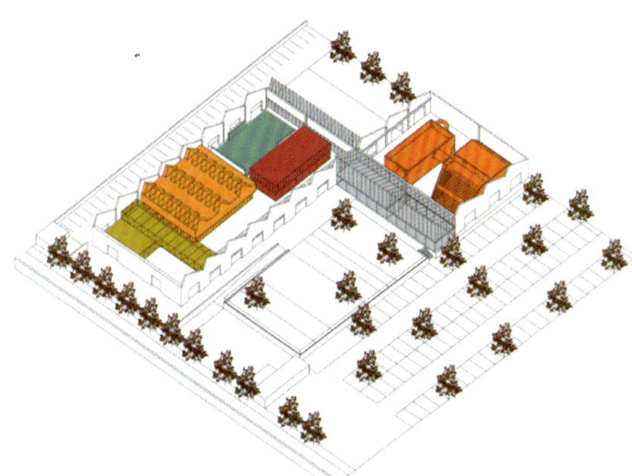

09- Internal view of Giardino delle Imprese
10- Public spaces
11- Scienze in Pratica laboratories
12- General view of Scuola delle Idee
13- Detail view of Scuola delle Idee
14- Detail view of the connection to the terrace

09 | 12
10 11 | 13 14

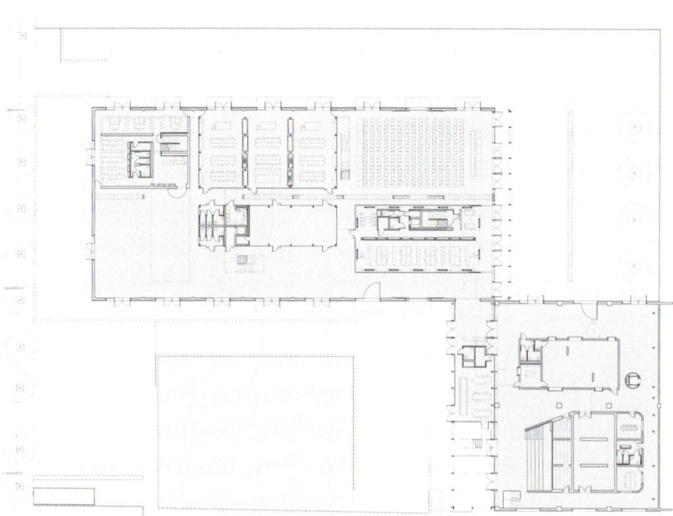

Ground floor plan

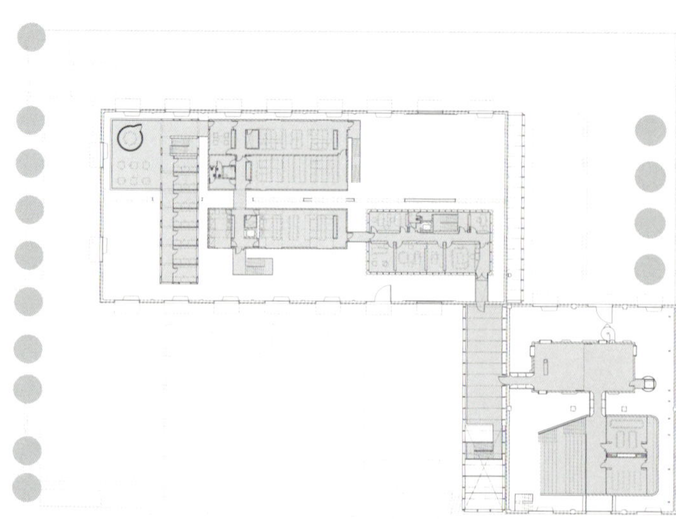

First floor plan

Bright splashes of color stand out against a luminous white background, creating an appropriate metaphor of the union between art and science, which is the key to this foundation. The freestanding and interconnected modules within the space are a reversible intervention that makes the most of the natural lighting provided by an archetypal saw-tooth structure while allowing it to retain its own integrity.

Can Ribas Factory renovation

A rich public space

Location-Palma de Mallorca, Spain
Architect-Jaime J. Ferrer Forés Architects
Area-56,586 square feet (5257 square meters) of urban spaces; 3089 square feet (287 square meters) of industrial heritage restoration
Completion-2012
Photography-José Hevia
Client-Ajuntament de Palma, Consorci Riba, Patronat Municipal de l'Habitatge

Site plan

Neighborhood revitalization and preservation of the industrial heritage were the aims of this urban project in the La Soledat area of Palma, Majorca. Dedicated to the production of wool blankets, Can Ribas Factory was built in 1851 outside the city. In the 1970s, after several extensions and transformations, the factory became obsolete and fell into disuse. At the same time, important changes occurred in the surroundings: a large social housing development was built and the power station of Son Molines went up in 1965, creating a new barrier that further increased the quarter's physical isolation.

The later attempts to redevelop the area were unsuccessful in halting the process of decay, so in 2003, a special plan for the whole waterfront was approved. Since it was organized as an enclosed precinct, the factory of Can Ribas had become a barrier dividing La Soledat into two. This special plan to restructure La Soledat seeks to open the industrial area to the neighborhood.

The first phase established a public area around the main factory building and the chimney, connecting two empty spaces and eliminating traffic along Ferriol Street. Furthermore, it inverted the main access to the civic center in the building, placing it in the new plaza. The factory and the chimney were listed elements, so they were protected. The buildings affected by the plan for the new street were partially demolished. In developing the project, however, the most valuable heritage elements were recovered and integrated into the urban surroundings.

The creation of an urban porch in the remaining part of the main building, the steam pavilion, and the façade of the warehouses emphasize the value of this industrial complex that comprised several pavilions for the different stages of the textile manufacturing process. A system of open public spaces is thus structured by a concrete foundation, which serves to create a visual and physical connection between the new Brotad Street and the historic elements of the Can Ribas factory, generating a richer, more complex public space.

01

01- The creation on an urban porch in the remaining part of the industrial building

Plan and sections

01 New housing block
02 Main pavilion; civic center
03 Industrial passage
04 Façade of the remaining part of the pavilion
05 Steam boiler pavilion
06 Urban porch
07 Can Ribas square
08 Chimney
09 New Brotad Street

An architectural inversion, where former interiors become framed outside public space, has successfully transformed a former factory into a series of interconnected walkways and squares. A clear differentiation of old and new is achieved, where the warmth and rusticity of existing walls is complemented by crisp new geometries.

02|04
03|05

02- General view of Can Ribas factory complex before intervention
03- Can Ribas public plaza
04, 05- Can Ribas new urban space—recovered sandstone from demolished buildings were used to complete pilasters of pergola on the northeast

01 New housing block
02 Main pavillion; civic center
03 Chimney
04 Steam boiler pavilion
05 Urban porch
06 New Brotad Street

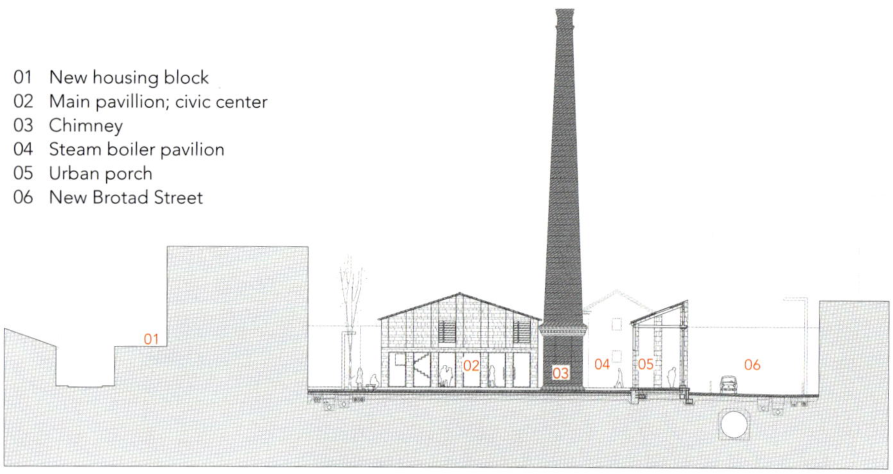

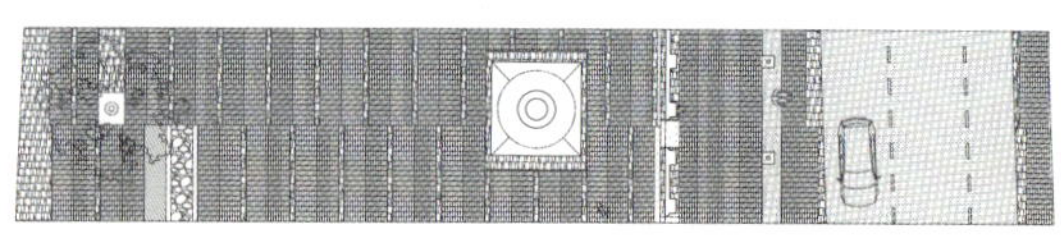

Section through the new public plaza

01 New housing block
02 Main pavilion; civic center
03 Industrial passage
04 Façade of the remaining part of the pavilion
05 New Brotad Street

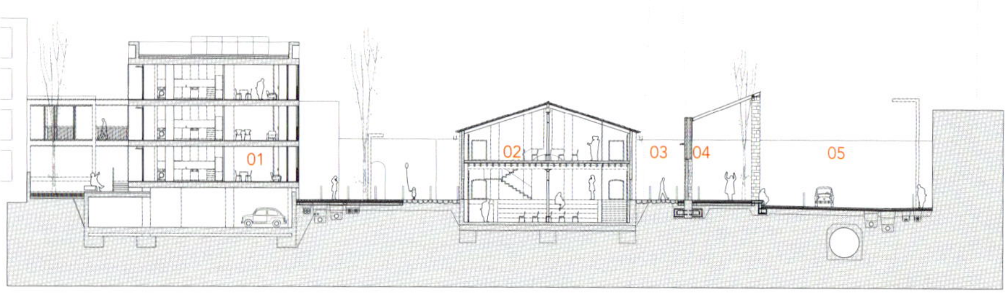

Sections through the new housing block and the refurbishment of the main factory 1

01 New housing block
02 Main pavilion; civic center
03 Industrial passage
04 Steam boiler pavilion
05 Industrial boiler premises
06 New Brotad Street

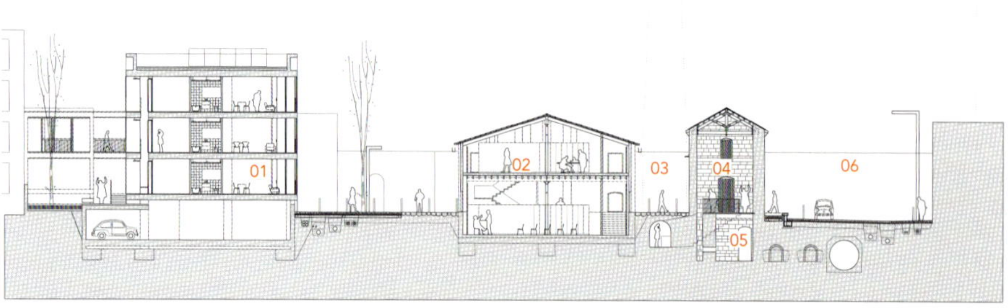

Sections through the new housing block and the refurbishment of the main factory 2

Axonometric drawings

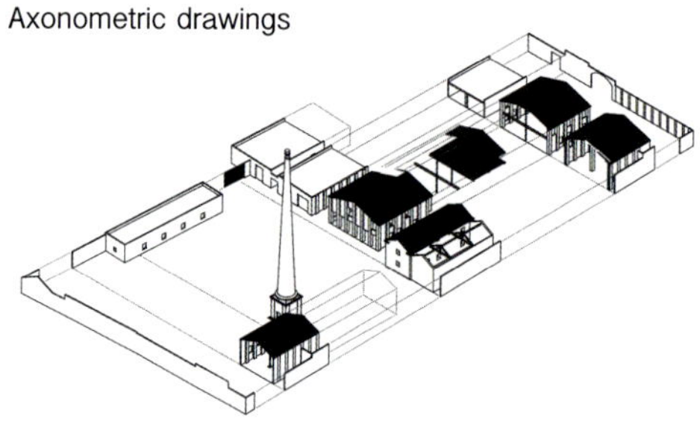

Condition prior to the intervention

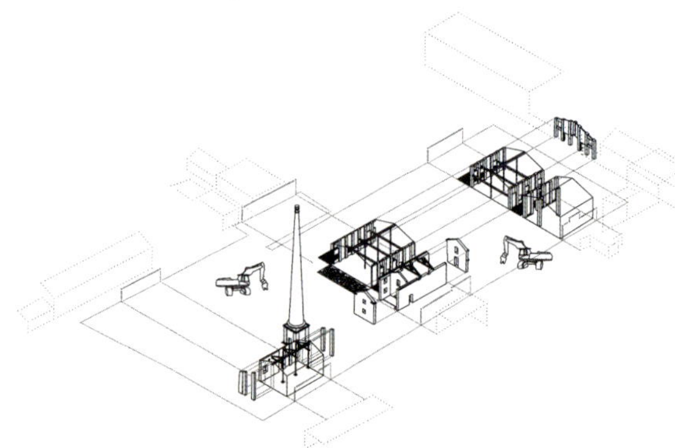

Demolition of some of the existing building

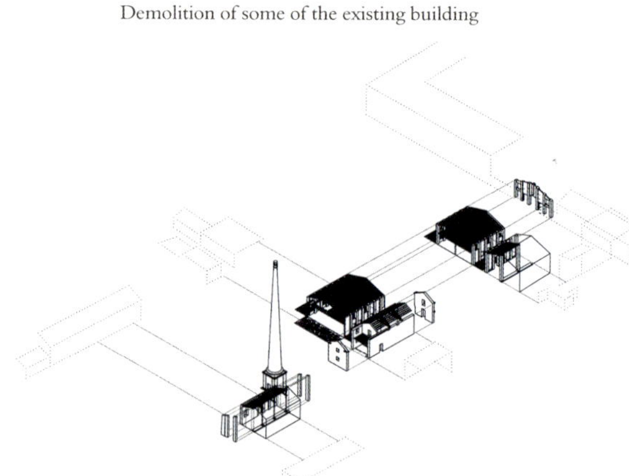

Consolidation of preserved buildings

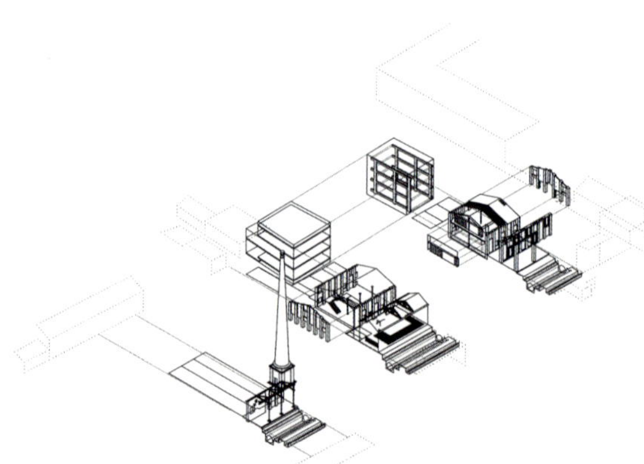

After completion of refurbishment and new construction

Public spaces

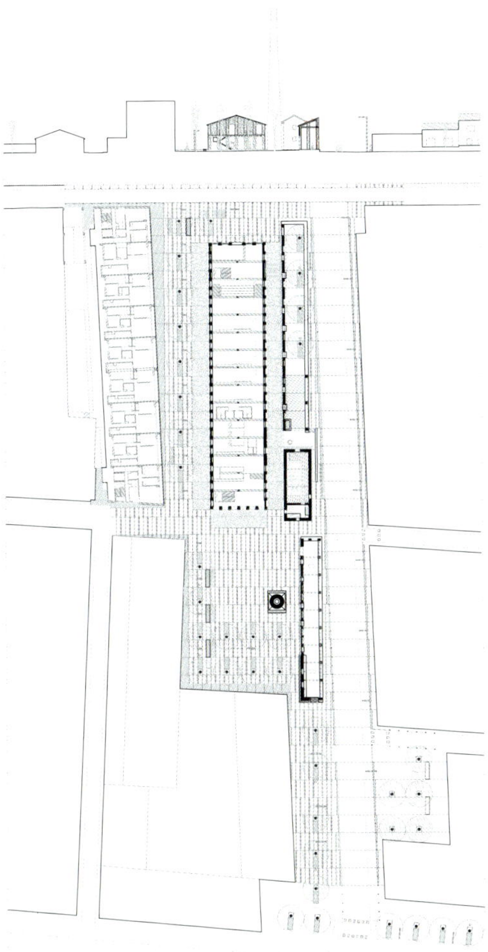

Infrastructure and mobility

Urban services

06

07, 08- The industrial buildings affected by the new street have been partially demolished and selectively preserved
09- The urban pergola
10- The steam pavilion

07|09 10
08|

Plan and sections of the urban porch and the steam pavilion

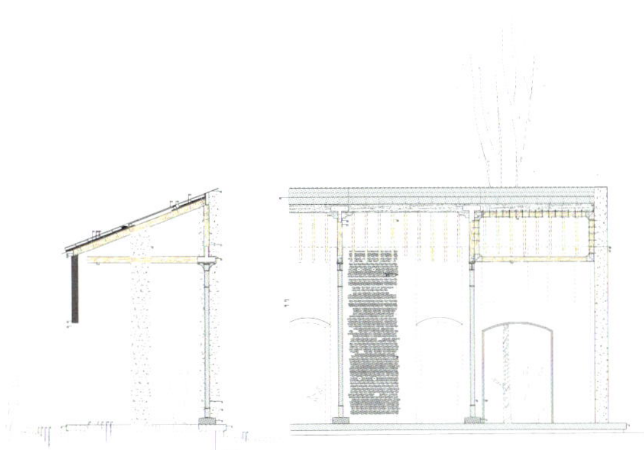

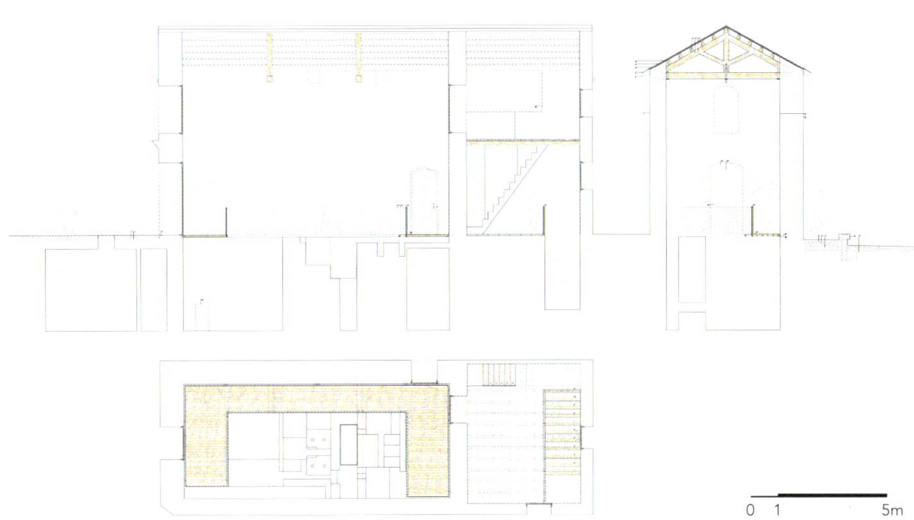

Rotermann Grain Elevator

Offices, dancing studios, and commercial spaces

Location-Tallinn, Estonia
Architect-KOKO architects
Area-60,277 square feet (5600 square meters)
Completion-2016
Photography-Tonu Tunnel
Client-Rotermann City OÜ

Site plan

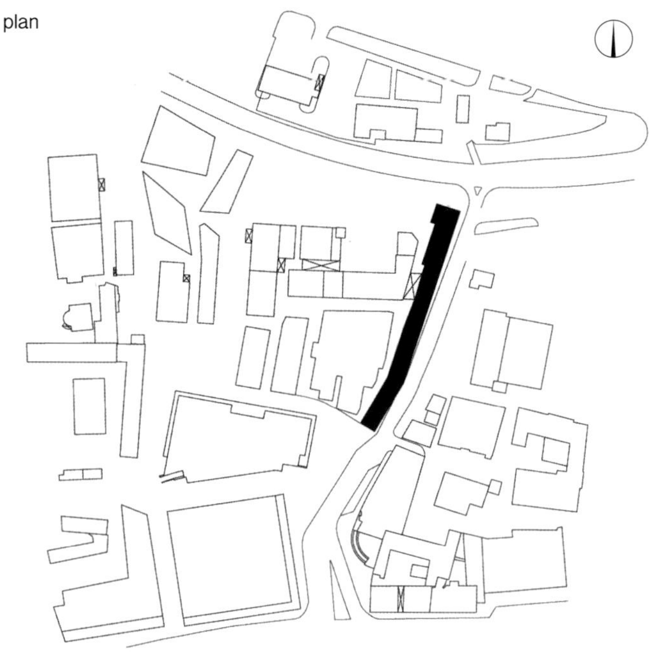

The Rotermann Quarter is in a historically important location in the heart of Tallinn—between the Old Town, the harbor, and Viru Square. The roads to Tartu, Narva, and Pärnu already intersected on Viru Square in the 19th century, making it Tallinn's official central point. The Rotermann Quarter is packed with historical buildings almost as densely as the Old Town.

Christian Abraham Rotermann, the owner of the enterprise Rotermann Factories, which was established in 1829, initiated the development of the compact industrial district. Industry and trade in the quarter has seen both good times and bad. The Soviet years wrecked the buildings, and during the uncertain years that followed, the buildings became dilapidated so that repairs seemed impossible. In 1979, the decaying district became the set for Andrei Tarkovsky's world famous movie *Stalker*. The National Heritage Board designated the Rotermann quarter historically valuable in 2001, and so the old industrial buildings that have found a new function should coexist peacefully with high-quality contemporary architecture.

When the developer approached the architects with this project, the first assignment was to find a suitable function for this remarkable, but very particular building. As the building is about 361 feet (110 meters) long and about 33 feet (10 meters) wide and does not have any windows on its façade, it was a difficult task to find a suitable function. Different ideas from art galleries to bowling alleys, spas and parking garages were tried. The final solution was a combination of offices throughout the fourth and fifth floor where additional light would be provided after restoration, and dance studios on the second and third floor where there was no natural daylight needed, and commercial and public areas on the ground floor where there had originally already been openings on the inner side that allowed enough daylight to access.

The original building was conserved and as little as possible was changed with the existing façade. The main changes were done on the fifth floor where additional roof windows and dormers with terraces in between were added on the inner side of the building to give additional light for the offices that are situated throughout the fourth and fifth floors. These skylights also provide offices with views across the district and the Old Town. The glass tower on top of the building follows its historical measures and gives the building a unique and modern feel. Another big change was to add inner floors as the grain elevator's original function was to house grain shafts that extended vertically throughout the entire building. Smaller details like rainwater pipes and other metal details were reconstructed according to the original details.

Since the inner street side has openings that have been walled shut at various periods, the ground floor of the building houses business premises. The interiors of these rooms have preserved the old grain hoppers hanging from the ceilings. An arcade that crosses the middle part of the building on the ground floor divides the space and creates an entrance to the inner street leading towards the center of the district.

The historic supervisory building in front of the grain elevator houses a restaurant. The biggest changes made to it were to first reconstruct its roof, as it had been destroyed, and also to raise the roof by 3.2 feet (1 meter) in order to be able to let natural light enter, and make it possible to use the second floor. This reconstruction project of Rotermann Grain Elevator was awarded as exemplary heritage restoration by the 2016 National Heritage Board of Estonia.

01

01- View to the east façade covered in anchor plates of metal straps that historically held the walls intact when grain expanded

viru
keskus

This project grappled with the tension between existing enclosure and the need for natural lighting and functions were carefully selected to respond to the building's different conditions.

02- View from south to the west façade, added roof windows and dormers on the fifth floor to allow natural daylight to enter
03- View to the east façade of the grain elevator and the historic control building in front of it
04- View to the east façade with the added arcade leading towards the center of the district.
05- View from the north to the limestone tower that historically housed the machinery

02 03
04 05

Section

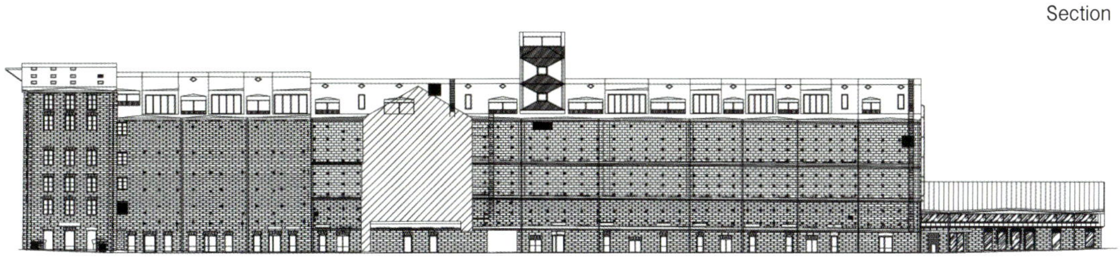

06- View from the south to the control building that now houses a restaurant
07- Night view to the east façade
08- Glass tower on top of the grain elevator that follows the historic volume and now houses a unique office
09- The Stalker passage—an inner street with cafés and shops that runs along the grain elevator building

Cross section

07
06
08 09

Floor plans

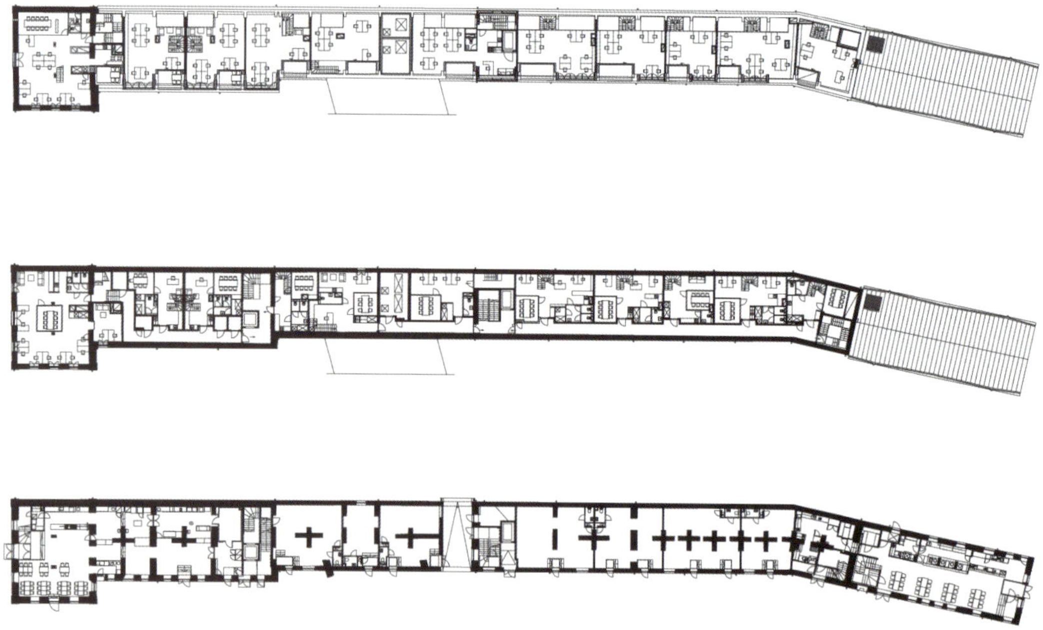

10- View to the ground floor that houses cafés and shops—the historic limestone constructions and grain hoppers have been preserved
11- View to the minimalist interior design of the lift
12- View to the office space situated throughout the fourth and fifth floor
13- View to the inner staircase of an office space
14- View to the staircase integrated inside an historic grain garner

10 | 11 12 / 13 14

Xintai Warehouse architectural renovation

Industrial heritage in a new light

Location-Shanghai, China
Architect-Kokaistudios
Area-64,583 square feet (6000 square meters)
Completion-2016
Photography-Dirk Weiblen
Client-Lonsen Group

The front elevation

The project is located in Shanghai on the north bank of the Suzhou Creek. The area, once the vibrating industrial engine of colonial Shanghai, is today undergoing an unprecedented and controversial process of transformation, where consistent portions of the original urban fabric—'carpets' of Shikumen intertwined with warehouses and industrial artifacts—are being erased, together with the memory they represent, and replaced by high-rise residential and office towers.

The warehouse, an early 20th century British facility for the production and stockpiling of textiles, is among the few testimonies of the industrial history of the city still standing in the area. Its unconventionally large scale, 64,583 square feet (6000 square meters) in total, and its remarkable state of conservation had it listed as a protected industrial heritage. In order to survive, the building had to be repurposed to house new functions, and had to be technologically upgraded and transformed into flexible commercial and office spaces, and readapted to a context radically transformed and different from the one it originally belonged to.

The architectural renovation project was devised as a careful mix of rigorous conservation and innovative solutions. The first phase included the design of all common areas and part of the future tenants' interiors.

The original textures of the building were resurfaced through a careful process of surveying, cleaning, removal of non-original additions, and reconstruction of damaged or lost parts. The restoration was always based on the principles of being 'reversible' and 'distinguishable from the original.'

The internal circulation was redesigned around the main atrium, covered by a shimmering glass roof. The light steel-structure balcony and the spirals around the void, cantilevering from the old brick façade, connect the entrance to the upper floors. A sculptural surface of glass encloses the atrium, resolving roofing and façade with a unifying gesture and terminating in a wood-clad canopy under which the new main access to the building is located. Under these two glazed atriums, past and present come together, both claiming their rights to expression. The two languages complement each other in a coherent and balanced whole.

01

01- Atrium and glass ceiling after renovation

02, 03, 04- Façade before renovation
05- The front façade
06- The back façade
07, 08- The atrium

Sections

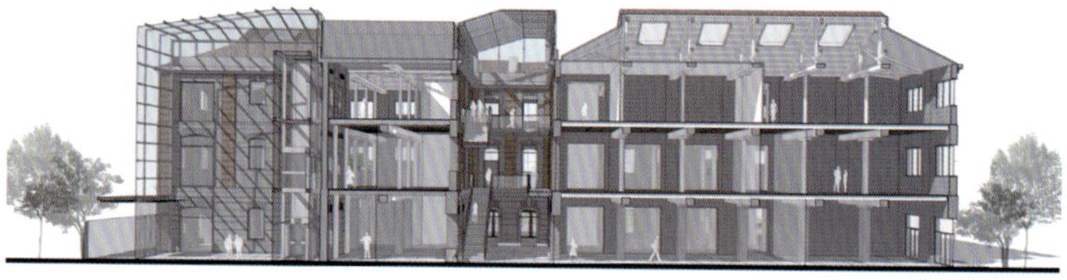

02 03 04 | 06
05 | 07 08

Technological upgrading and designing for flexibility in a well-preserved warehouse is ensuring its continuous survival in an area that is subjected to drastic transformation. Its adaptive reuse is helping to prevent the complete erasure of a former industrial precinct and its associated memories.

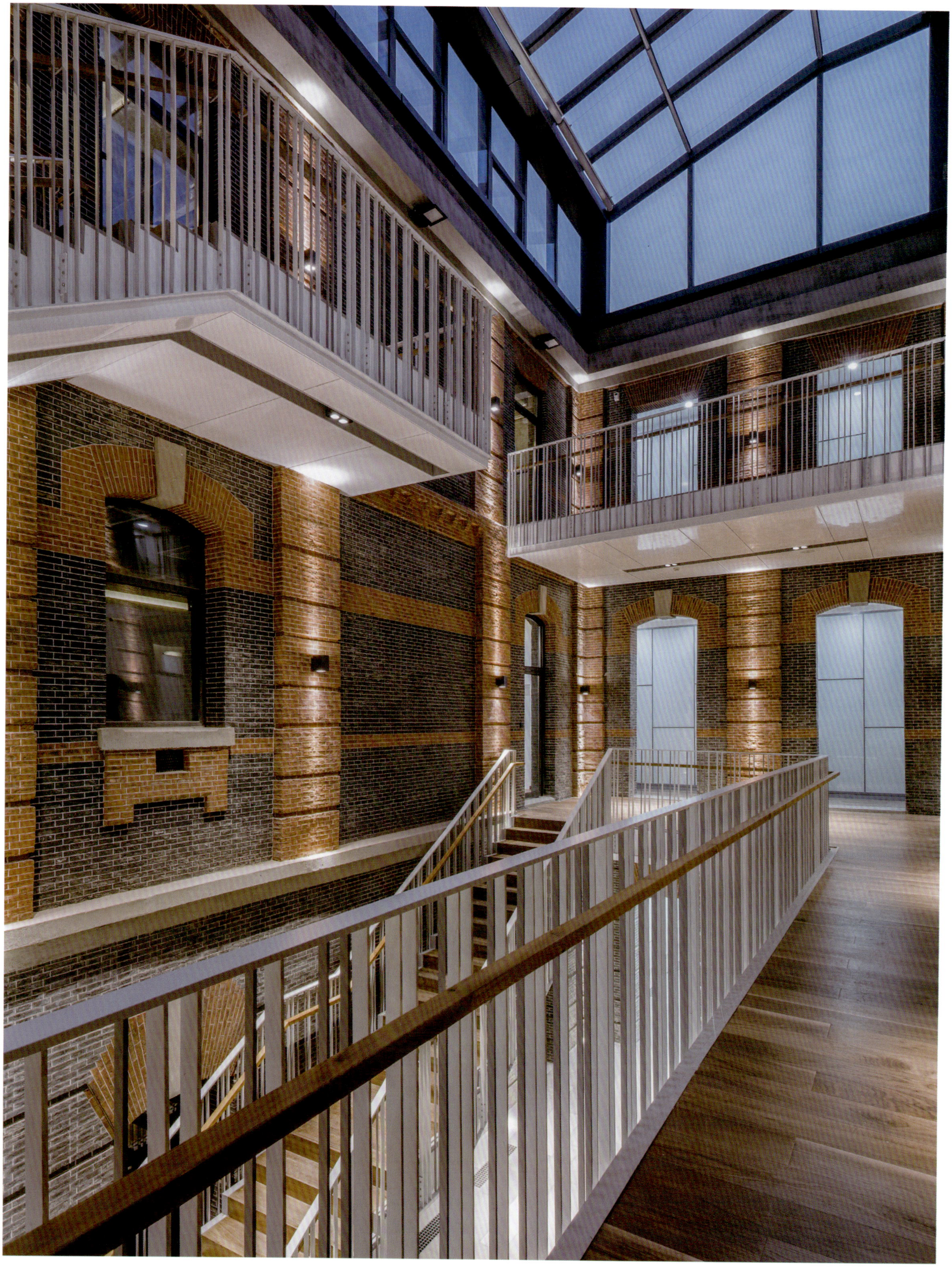

09 | 10 11 | 12

09- The staircase and handrail
10, 11, 12- Primary interiors after renovation

Recovery of Ex-Furnace Riccione

A secondary school, a theater, and an office building

Location-Riccione, Italy
Architect-Pietro Carlo Pellegrini Architetto
Area-36,597 square feet (3400 square meters)
Completion-2014
Photography-Mario Ciampi Fotografo
Client-Municipality of Riccione

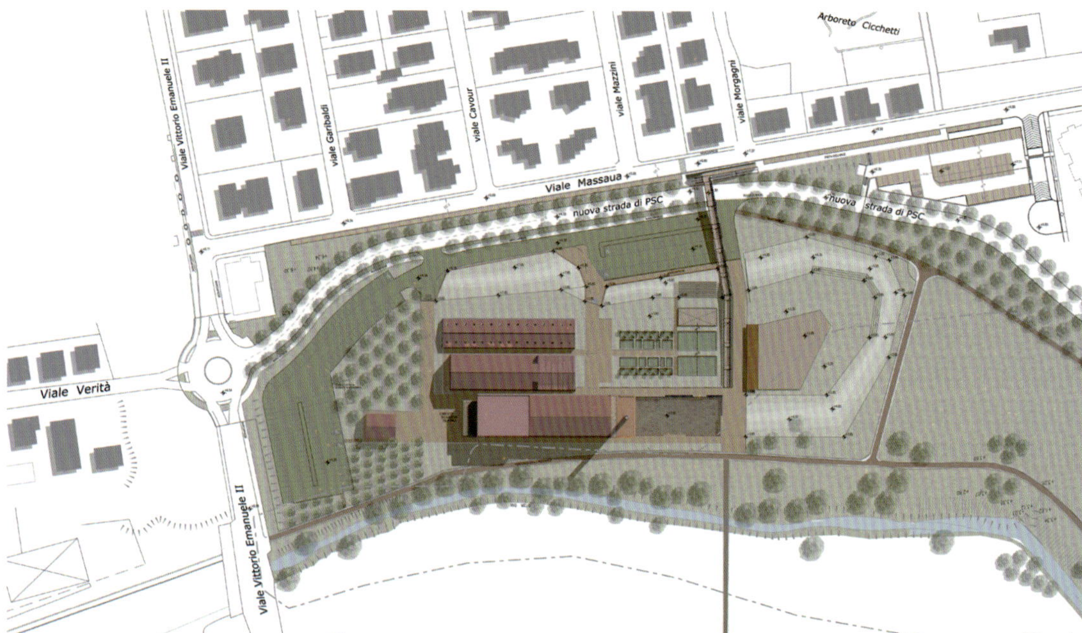

Site plan

This project involved the recovery of the Ex-Furnace Riccione, an industrial complex for the production of bricks, built in 1908 and decommissioned in 1970. The total site area was 9.9 acres (4 hectares), while the covered surface was 36,597 square feet (3400 square meters).

The old structures gave way to the new ones, exploiting the existing spatial possibilities, while maintaining the shapes of the old factory as a historical memory of the place. In the buildings, a middle school of 18 classes, a 650-seat multi-purpose theater, and a building office are located. The project aimed to reduce the environmental impact, replacing the old buildings with new ones characterized by high energy efficiency, without adding more surfaces.

The design hoped to create simple and easily-recognizable architectural volumes. Through standardizing forms, materials, and colors, the project reinterpreted the historical aspects of pre-existing archaeological sites in a contemporary way. As the buildings had been restored and extended several times in the past, the architects aspired to follow this continuity with history, which was not just in terms of stylistic concerns. They tried to adapt the old buildings to accommodate new functions, while maintaining the original identity. Additionally, an energy-saving strategy was adopted through using materials that were easily found nearby the site.

The middle school consists of a one-floor building and a two-floor building that are connected. It is characterized, on the one hand, by the restoration and enhancement of the existing brick masonry elements, and on the other hand, by differentiating the new elements from the existing to maintain a compositional coherence throughout the intervention.

Externally along the perimeter, an insulating red-brick-color glass wool flows to the pillars, while the infill of the walls is entrusted with brick blocks filled with insulating material in the cavities. Inside the building, a layer of plaster serves as the finish. The roof adopts a metal trusses structure and an imbricate system of double planking, insulating layer, and a flat tile layer.

The exterior finish of the walls is a system of brise soleil ('shutter brick') using a traditional material in an innovative form. The terracotta-colored bricks protect the red insulation panels behind them from direct sunlight. They also create a micro-ventilation façade that contributes to the insulation value of the wall. The whole system of heating, air-conditioning, and production of hot water is achieved through the use of electrical heat pumps fed by a photovoltaic system integrated into the building envelope, which is further supported by radiant floor heating.

01

01- Pre-existing perimeter wall with trefoil segmental arc windows and the cladding of façade with brise-soleil

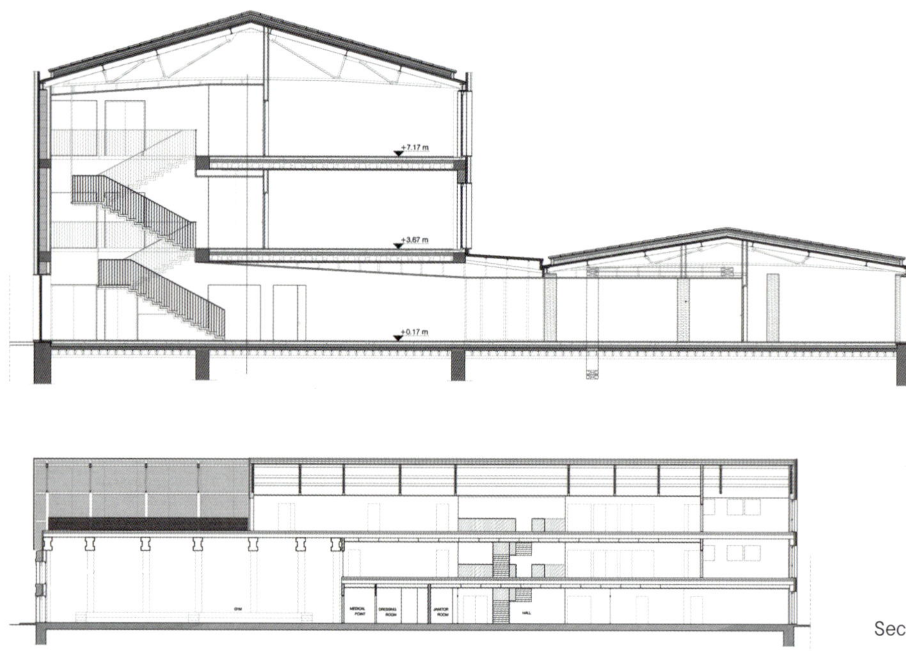

Sections

02 03 | 05
04 | 06 07

A layering of materials acknowledges the building's different identities over time, while the sensitive color palette creates a sense of continuity between old and new. A focus on energy-efficiency was used as a driver for experimentation in terms of the façade design.

02, 03- Before renovation
04- Overview of building that highlights the relationship between the volumes and the materials with their chromatic scale
05- The relationship between the different volumes of the buildings
06- Outside walkway that connects the one-story building and the two-story building
07- Detail of the connection between the new element and the building recovered

08
09 10

08- View of the intercommunication staircase
09- Indoor spaces that highlight the intercommunication staircase's use of materials whose colors reminding brick
10- Detail of a perforated wall to protect a glass wall

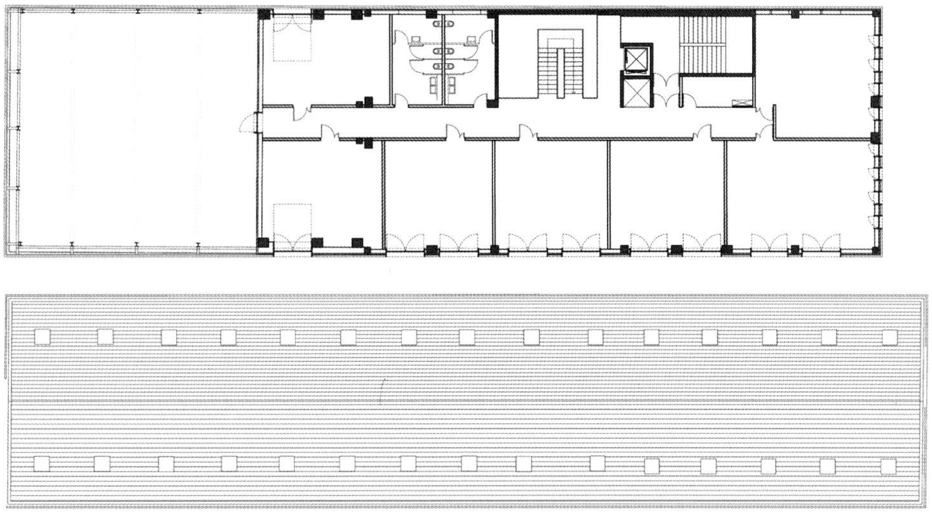

Second floor plan

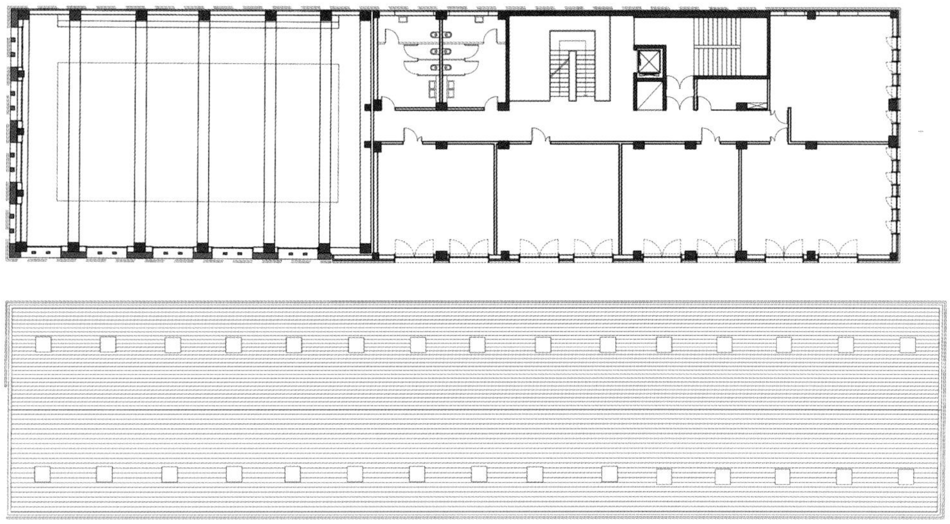

First floor plan

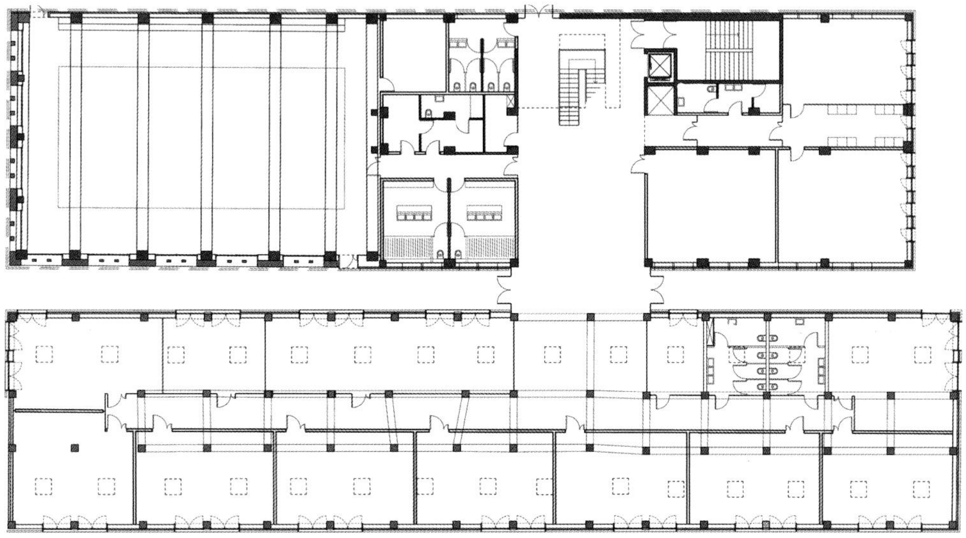

Ground floor plan

Imagine Studio at The Trees

Repurposing a large industrial campus

Location-Mumbai, India
Architect-Studio Lotus, GPL Design Studio
Area-10,764 square feet (1000 square meters)
Completion-2015
Photography-Studio Lotus, GPL Design Studio, Edmund Sumner, Dilip Bhatia
Client-Godrej Properties Ltd.

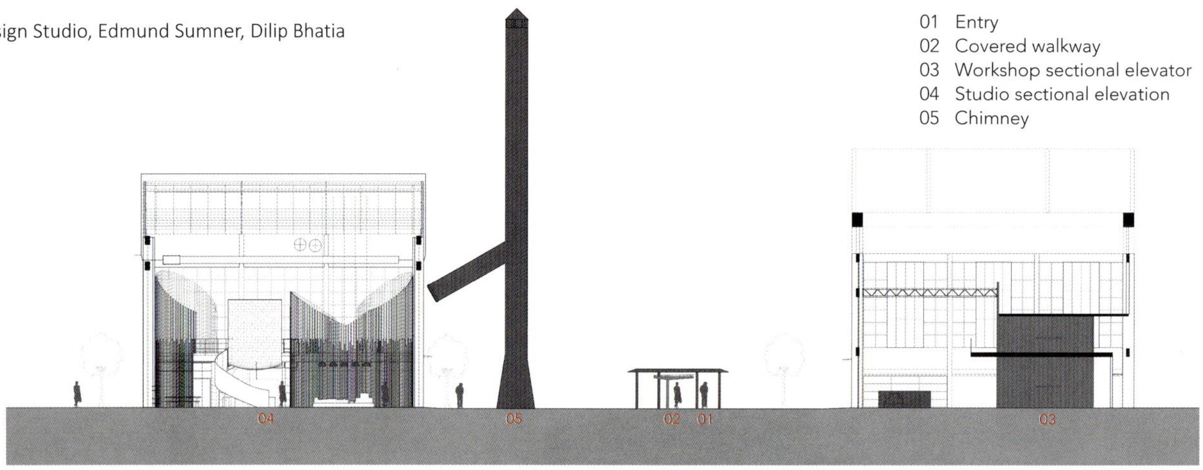

Key section

Unfolding as an adaptive re-use project in Mumbai, the Imagine Studio wove nature, heritage, and urbanism through a compelling narrative of evolving contexts. The scheme, which was initiated as a design for a marketing office, shaped into an exercise for place-making in 'The Trees,' a flagship development for the client.

Set in a 1-acre (0.4-hectare) site, the Imagine Studio complex spans 10,763 square feet (1000 square meters) in area. The project replaced a large industrial campus in Vikhroli. Designed as the Experience Center for 'The Trees,' the intent was to illustrate an invigorated public realm as a microcosm of the masterplan while preserving the essence of the site's industrial heritage. Existing buildings and their elements were recycled, not only to underline their relevance in bygone eras but also to add meaning as important design punctuations in the narrative. The design teams presented the Imagine Studio complex through an attempt to re-envision the customer journey for 'The Trees.' The storyline for this experiential journey was grounded in authenticity and a larger vision for the city germinated with timeless values.

Programmatically, the buildings of the Imagine Studio adapted into a marketing office, with sample showcase flats, meeting spaces, a small café, as well as several outdoor spaces to market upcoming residential and commercial development properties. Two former power co-generation plants and a boiler were repurposed to accommodate new functions as a studio, workshop, and café, respectively. A tall chimney redolent of bygone industrial aesthetic was treated as a graphic memorial. The old louvers of the primary plant, now the Studio, were reinterpreted in corten steel and perforated with patterns. The design simulates the filtering of light from the leafy canopy of rain trees at the site—changing as the day progresses and connecting the spaces to key memories and identities. The timeless architectural forms derived from the current industrial sheds and the materiality of concrete, corten steel, brass and timber work on the principle of 'Wabi-Sabi,' which would allow the buildings to age beautifully across time.

The newly-designed interiors derived inspiration from the 'memory' of the metal silos—cylindrical units that occupy the site. The silhouette of these forms offers contrast to the rigid geometry of the building and hence shows up as a sculptural insert. The silo and chimney suspended within the space root it as a recall of the industrial process and are used internally as a cycloramic projection for the marketing team.

Creating the gateway to the entire development with the Studio, the second co-generator plant was transformed into the workshop. A multi-functional space, it houses sample apartments, a meeting area, and a multi-purpose gallery for cultural events such as art shows, talks, and performances. The interiors connect seamlessly with the outdoors, thus expanding the areas of the activities and driving the dynamism of the landscape and the public domain.

The existing Boiler Plant was converted into an all-day café by retaining the structural framework and a boiler tank as a memory of its original intent. The Boiler Café, Workshop, and Studio together create the edges of a vibrant public space that demonstrates the core philosophies of 'The Trees.'

The landscape design strategically re-purposed the heritage environment in a more urban, community-centric setting. Amalgamating industrial scrap and integrating them with the plants, it used them as a storytelling device.

The buildings of Imagine Studio are redefined as the memories of an industrial past; its contemporary form ready to shape new thoughts within its body. These sit sculpturally into a landscape, which, with its places for public engagement and participation, will go on to evolve new ideas for the future.

01

01- The existing boiler plant, repurposed as an all-day café retains the structural framework and a boiler tank as a memory

02 03 | 04 05

06

02- The site was a large industrial campus integral to the client's history
03- The boiler café in construction
04- Co-Generator Plant 1 exterior as it was
05- An existing silo cluster at site
06- Imagine Studio transforms a small cluster of industrial buildings and its surrounding landscape into an experiential journey of commemorative identities

07
08

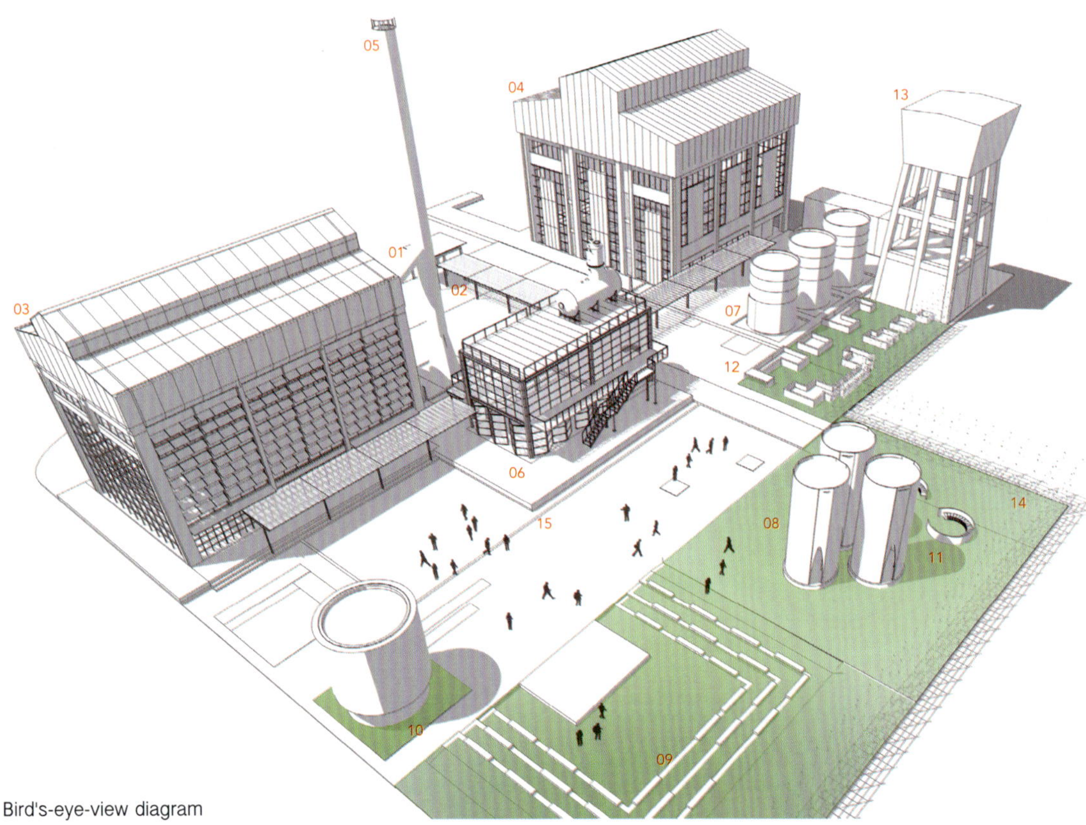

01 Entry plaza
02 Covered walkway
03 Studio
04 Workshop
05 Chimney
06 Boiler café
07 Market silos
08 Legacy silos
09 Amphitheater
10 Beacon silo
11 Silo benches
12 Urban farm
13 Water tank
14 Scaffolding
15 Corten strip

0 1 10m

Bird's-eye-view diagram

This large industrial structure has been carefully dissected to leave well-preserved remnants that help to retain the memory of its former life. Repurposed corten louvers shade generous openings while rusted industrial elements are placed like curated pieces of sculpture in a landscaped garden.

07- The boiler café, the walkways, the chimney, and the studio
08- View of the studio, boiler café, and the workshop with the beacon silo and legacy silos in the foreground

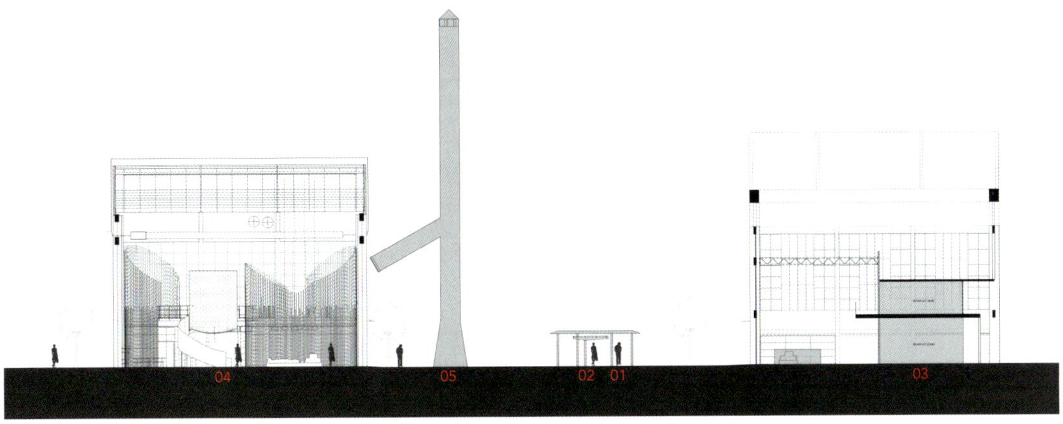

01 Entry
02 Workshop sectional elevator
03 Covered walkway
04 Studio Sectional elevation

01 Covered walkway
02 Studio
03 Amphitheater
04 Beacon silo
05 Scaffolding

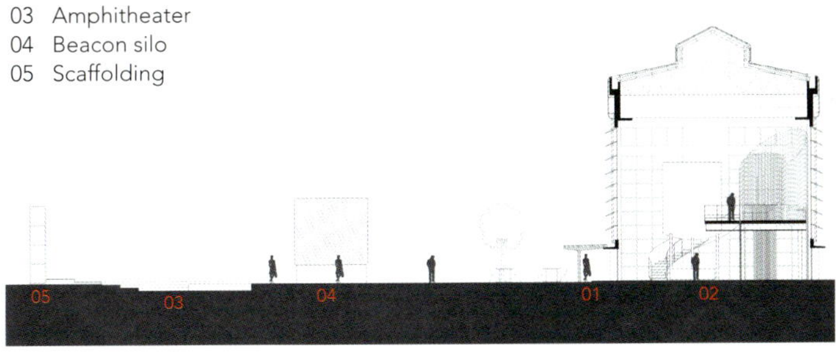

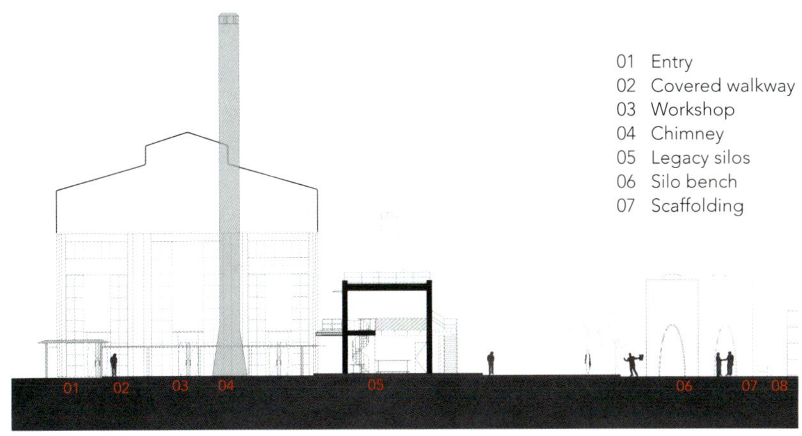

01 Entry
02 Covered walkway
03 Workshop
04 Chimney
05 Legacy silos
06 Silo bench
07 Scaffolding

Sections

01 10m

Site plan

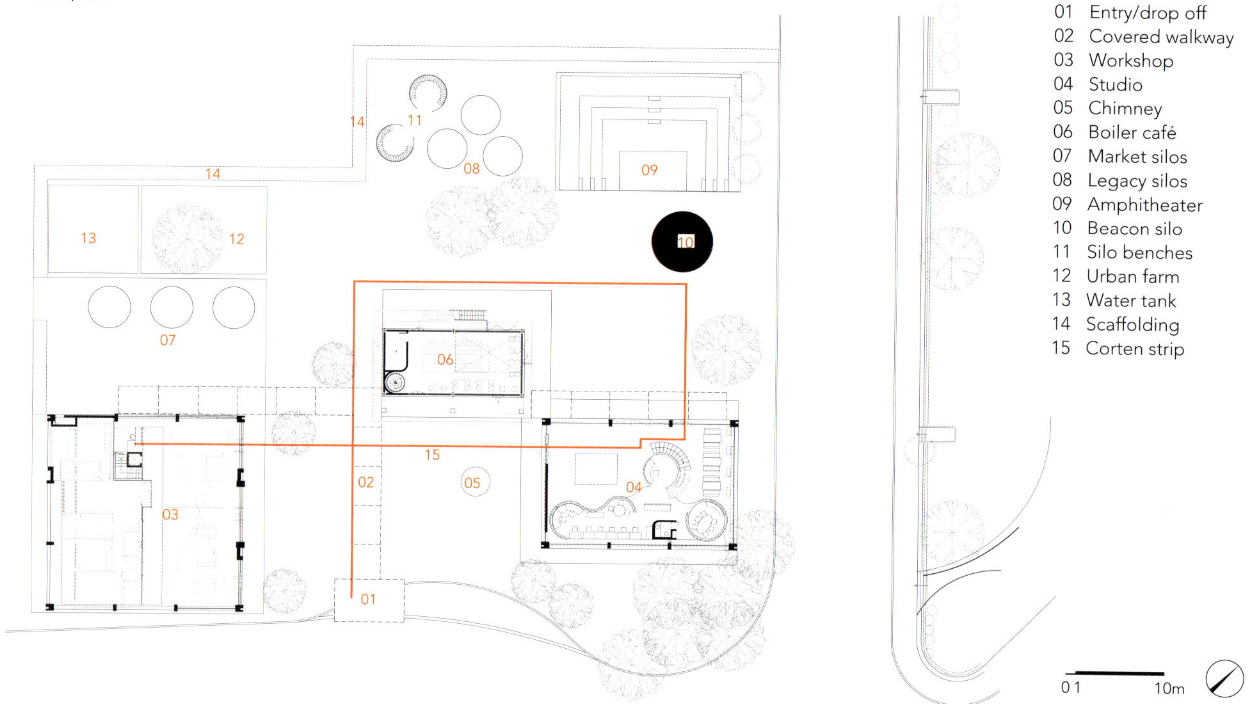
01 Entry/drop off
02 Covered walkway
03 Workshop
04 Studio
05 Chimney
06 Boiler café
07 Market silos
08 Legacy silos
09 Amphitheater
10 Beacon silo
11 Silo benches
12 Urban farm
13 Water tank
14 Scaffolding
15 Corten strip
0 1 10m

IMAGINE LIFE IN THE TREES

09- The cluster of legacy silos show the brand history and vision
10- The photo wall tells the'memory' of the metal silos
11- The corten steel strip guides the experiential narrative
12- The studio interiors showing corten steel, brass and timber detailing (Image Credit: GPL Design Studio)
13- The workshop interiors

12
13
09 10
11

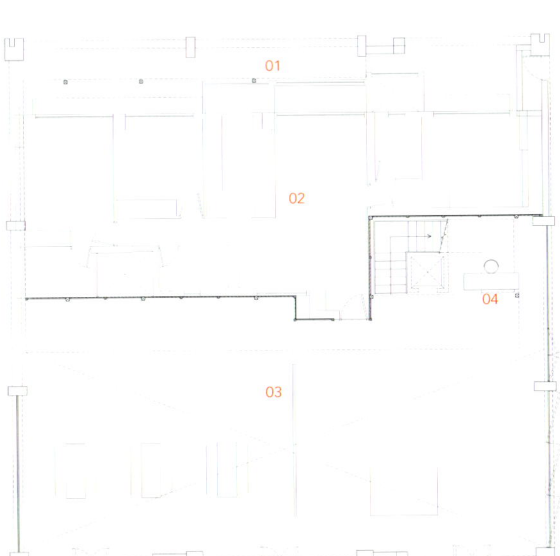

01 Outside
02 Sample showflat
03 Double height multipurpose space
04 Reception area

Ground floor plan

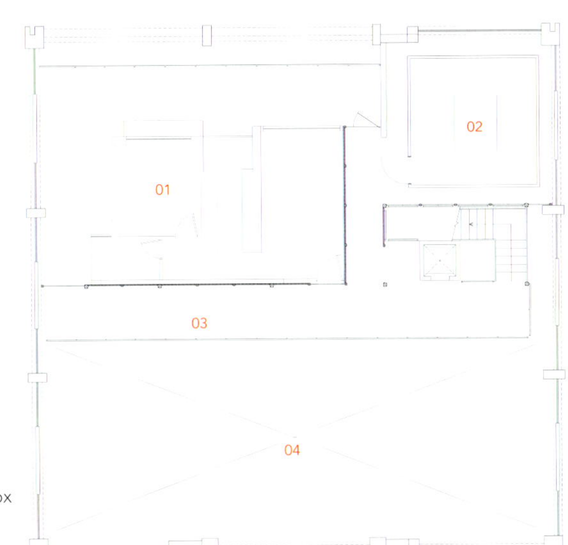

01 Sample showflat
02 Model room/black box
03 Mezzanine deck
04 Double height area

Mezzanine floor plan

01 10m

Transformation of the Smederij at the NDSM

A hotel and working place in a national monument

Location-Amsterdam, the Netherlands
Architect-GROUP A: The Netherlands
Area-90,546 square feet (8412 square meters)
Completion-2014
Photography-Digidaan and Marcel van der Burg
Client-Mediawharf Monumenten bv

Site plan

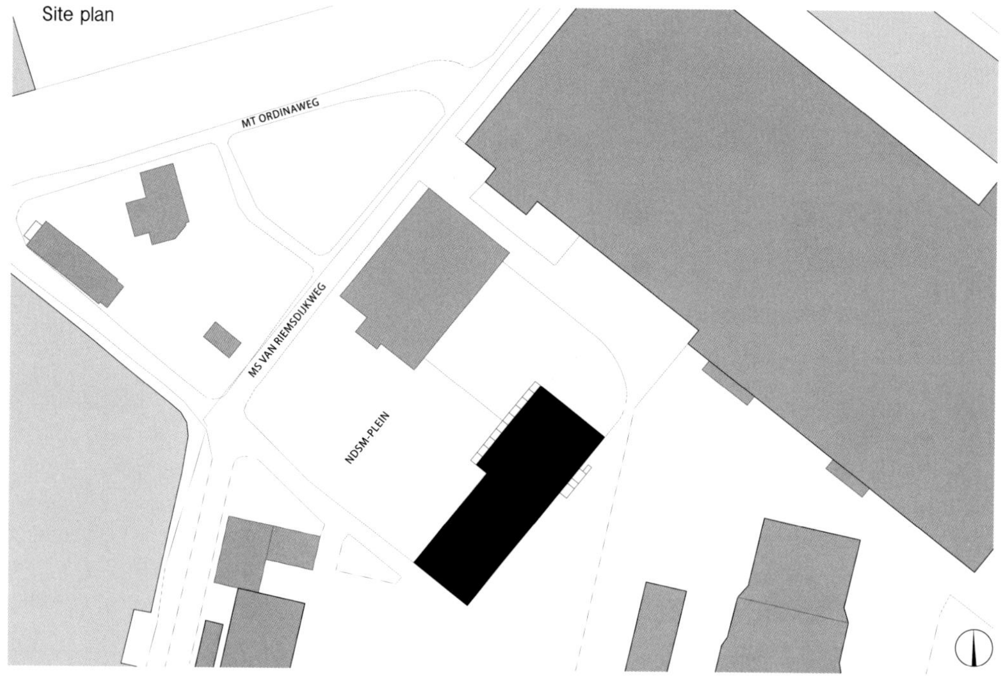

The NDSM Wharf is the historic remnant of Amsterdam's once-great shipbuilding industry. Today, a creative city is developing out of the industrial landscape on the north bank of the River IJ. The Smederij is a national monument that consisted of five smaller workshops and a main forge. The 118-by-148 feet (36-by-45 meter) forge was built in 1909. The client hoped to transform the complex into a hotel and a work environment for a variety of companies.

The most authentic part of the complex is the former forge. Inside the forge, the architects have retained the building's industrial character by maintaining the monumental steel structure. The columns and trusses were only sandblasted and received no further treatment, which gave them a striking contrast to the clean, white elements added to the new structure.

A large wooden stairway and a 46-foot-high (14-meter-high) atrium form the heart of the forge. The original crane bridge used during the wharf's days as a shipbuilding center still hangs here. The floors were returned to their original height, and the gigantic windows run from floor to ceiling, so that daylight can reach the ground floor from the shed roofs.

The ground floor comprises office space and a public restaurant with a terrace facing the square. An industrial stairway is located outside on the first floor with a view over the ramps and the River IJ, which is used as an extra balcony by Greenpeace Netherlands, one of the tenants of the forge. The outer brickwork was cleaned and left intact, so that the rough exterior remains visible. Where bricks were missing, the hole was filled with bricks from other sections of the wall. Glass wall sections were installed where necessary for the building's new function.

The hotel tower was built on the site of the last pitched roofed workshop left standing adjacent to the Smederij. By lifting the roof up 98 feet (30 meters), the architects created a tall, slim tower that serves as a beacon on the NDSM Wharf. The top of the hotel offers visitors a spectacular view of the Amsterdam skyline. From an urban planning perspective, this project demanded a 360-degree design with a raised element, in order to create more of a visual connection between the city and the wharf.

The workshops were in such poor condition that the developers decided to demolish them and start over, using the steel roof spans for the new building. This allowed them to re-build the structures in their original form, with their familiar industrial contours. By adding characteristic high sliding doors in the same shade of blue used elsewhere at the NDSM Wharf, these buildings complement their surroundings.

The transformation has breathed new life into the Smederij, restoring the soul of the original complex. The combination of old and new turns the Smederij into an inspiring new place to work and relax in Amsterdam. Its flexible layout and ceiling heights of up to 15 feet (4.5 meters) make the spaces ideal for a wide range of business concepts. The finished product is a model of Dutch industrial heritage, repackaged for contemporary office spaces and a hotel.

01

01- The hotel building after transformation

BROOKLYN HOTEL
R4
Rb
R5

02- The Smederij, a national monument that consisted of a main forge and five smaller workshops, before refurbishment
03- Entrance side Smederij and Double Tree by Hilton Hotel
04- Smederij with staircase and terrace

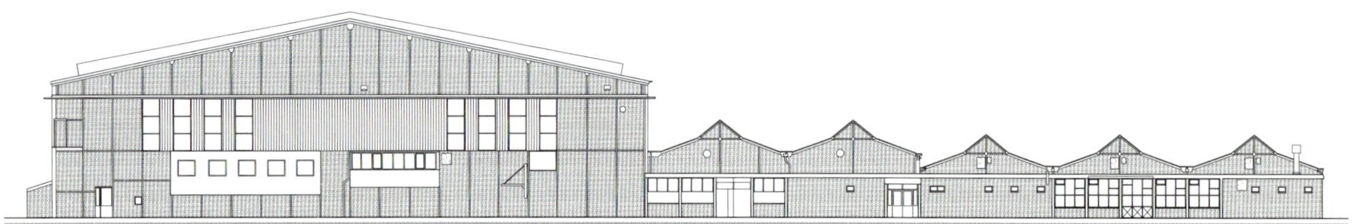

Elevation of the existing building before transformation

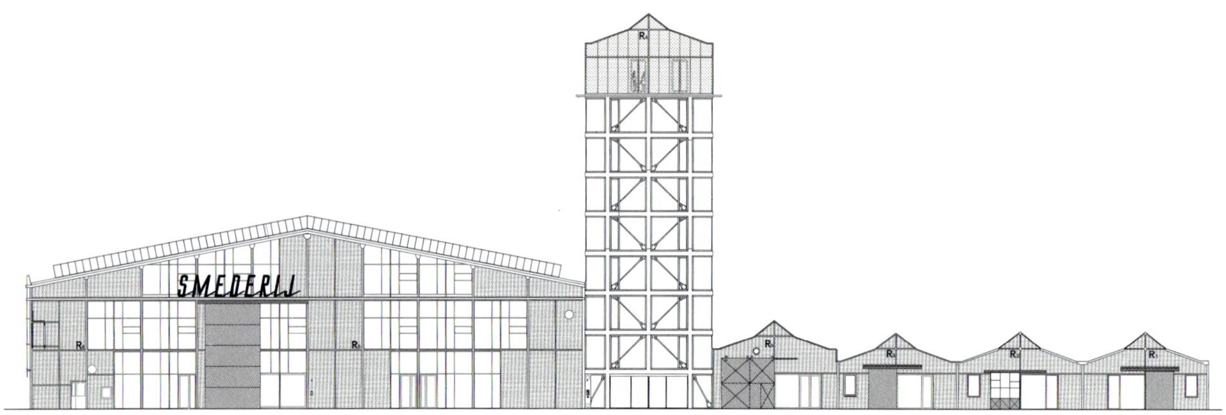

Elevation after transformation

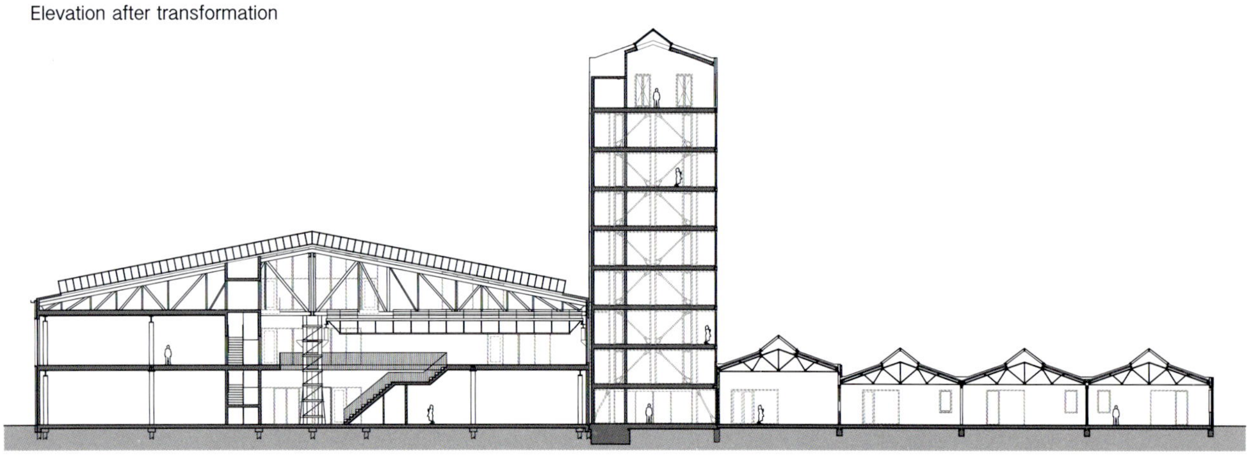

Longitudinal section

0 1 10m

The thorough refurbishment of a pre-existing steel grid, and infill that makes use of material harvested from elsewhere in the structure, have helped to retain the character of this former forge; this is further reinforced by the clear differentiation between old and new structural elements on the inside.

02|03
04

05- Transformed Smederij and newly added Double Tree by Hilton Hotel at the NDSM-wharf, Amsterdam

06- Impression of offices of tenant Greepeace in the transformed and renovated forge of the Smederij—the building's industrial character has been retained by maintaining the monumental steel structure

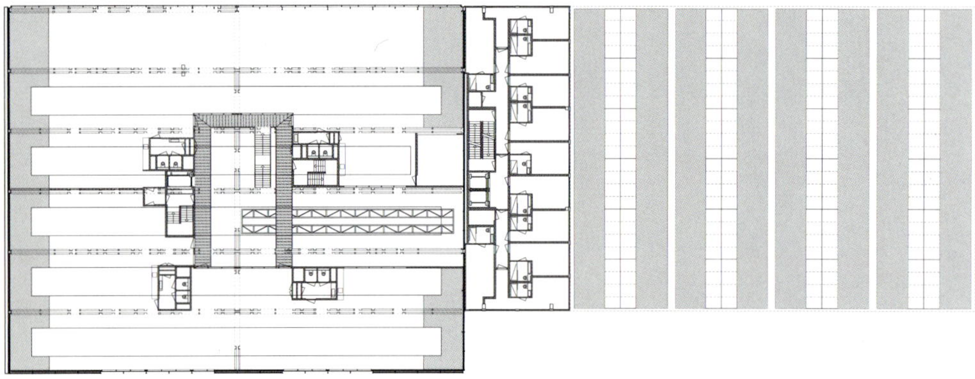

Second floor plan

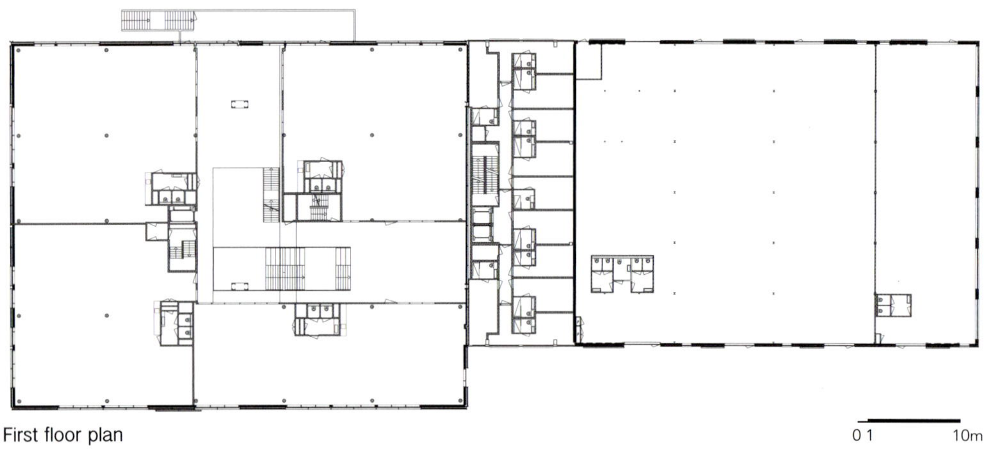

First floor plan

06
05

Index

Joliark P38
Web: www.joliark.se
Email: info@joliark.se

Kokaistudios P260
Web: www.kokaistudios.com
Email: info@kokaistudios.com

KOKO architects P252
Web: www.kokoarchitects.eu
Email: koko@koko.ee

KSS Architecture P82
Web: www.kssarchitects.com
Email: kssarchitects@kssarchitects.com

L'Atelier Architectes P110
Web: www.latelier-archi.fr
Email: communication@latelier-archi.fr

MAMOUT Architectes P222
Web: www.mamout.be
Email: info@mamout.be

Manuel Ocaña del Valle P60
Web: www.manuelocana.com
Email: manuelocana@manuelocana.com

office PROJECT P124
Email: zhanghao@officeproject.cn

Pietro Carlo Pellegrini Architetto P266
Web: www.pietrocarlopellegrini.it
Email: info@pietrocarlopellegrini.it

RoarcRenew P52
Web: www.roarc.cn
Email: robbenbai@roarc.cn

SAALS Ltd. P200
Web: www.saals.lv
Email: info@saals.lv

Saroki Architecture P116
Web: SarokiArchitecture.com
Email: info@sarokiarchitecture.com

Smith Vigeant Architectes Inc. P180
Web: www.smithvigeant.com
Email: Communication@smithvigeant.com

Studio Lotus P272
Web: www.studiolotus.in
Email: contact@studiolotus.in

Studio Macola P160
Web: www.studiomacola.it
Email: architetti@studiomacola.it

Studio Roosegaarde P76
Web: www.studioroosegaarde.net
Email: pr@studioroosegaarde.net

Tongji Architectural Design (Group) Co., Ltd P44
Web: www.tjad.cn
Email: mh@tjad.cn